SIR HOWARD VINCENT'S POLICE CODE
1889

WITH

AN ADDRESS TO CONSTABLES ON THEIR DUTIES BY
THE HONOURABLE SIR HENRY HAWKINS
One of Her Majesty's Judges

AND

A PREFACE BY
JAMES MONRO
The Commissioner of Police of the Metropolis

NEIL R A BELL and ADAM WOOD

FOREWORD BY
DEPUTY ASSISTANT COMMISSIONER NEIL BASU
Chairman of the Metropolitan and City Police Orphans Fund

Copyright © Neil R A Bell and Adam Wood

First published 2015 (Hardcover)
This edition 2019 (Softcover)

The right of Neil Bell and Adam Wood to be identified as the authors of this work has been asserted in accordance with the Copyright, Designs & Patents Act 1988.

All rights reserved. No part of this book may be reprinted or reproduced or utilised in any form or by any electronic, mechanical or other means, now known or hereafter invented, including photocopying and recording, or in any information storage or retrieval system, without the prior permission in writing of the publishers.

The contents of this book do not represent current United Kingdom law.

ISBN: 978-0-9931806-0-6 (Hardcover)
ISBN: 978-1-911273-66-0 (Softcover)

Published by Mango Books
www.MangoBooks.co.uk
18 Soho Square
London W1D 3QL

Dedicated to
the families of
officers who have
lost their lives
during service

FOREWORD

DEPUTY ASSISTANT COMMISSIONER NEIL BASU

Chairman,
Metropolitan and City Police Orphans Fund

Since their first inception, officers of the Metropolitan and City of London Police Forces have died in service, sometimes through acts of gallantry, sometimes through other causes. The Forces have a long and proud history of sacrifice for the people of our great city.

What is often hidden from the public gaze are the families deceased officers leave behind. It was to care for these children that the Metropolitan and City Police Orphanage was opened in 1870.

The first building quickly proved too small and in 1874 a site was acquired in Strawberry Hill, Surrey. At its height the Orphanage housed some 300 children.

The Orphanage was funded through Police Officers' subscriptions and public donations, never receiving a penny from Government funds. From then, until this day, the Orphanage and its fund were overseen by a Controlling Board of Management made up of serving Police Officers, of different ranks, who have given their time freely.

By the end of the First World War there were so many police orphans requiring care that it became impossible to home them all within the Orphanage. The Board began granting funding direct to the mothers of orphans so children could be kept at home. By the 1930s Police Widows' pensions had been introduced which meant that the need for residential care became much more limited as mothers kept their children at home. In 1937, when resident numbers fell to below one hundred, the then Board of Management decided to close the Orphanage, using proceeds from the sale of the site to form the new Metropolitan Police and City Police Orphans Fund. The income from those investments and continued police officer subscriptions and public donations enabled the board to pay Compassionate Allowance to all police orphans. This continues to this day.

The remarkable Sir Howard Vincent KCMG, CB, VD was Chairman of the Board of Management of the Orphanage in 1881 and 1882, at a time when he was Director of the Criminal Investigation Department of the Metropolitan Police.

A man of fair ranging talents, and a qualified Barrister, it was he who originally penned the book, re-published here, which for the first time brought criminal law and procedure within the easy understanding and grip of the ordinary Police Officer.

Sir Howard donated proceeds from the book to the Orphanage, which is testament to his support of and feeling towards the children cared for by them.

To see it reprinted, with once again profits being donated to the Orphans Fund, is both moving and welcome, and would, I am sure, receive the thorough approval of the great Sir Howard.

INTRODUCTION

When Miss Ethel Moffatt walked up the aisle of St Peter's Church in London's Eaton Square on the afternoon of 26th October 1882, she was wearing a dress of white satin trimmed with old Brussels lace, and a tulle veil fastened with diamond stars over a wreath of orange blossoms and jessamine. The bride, the daughter of the late George Moffatt MP, was accompanied by six bridesmaids whose dresses were of crimson plush and trimmed with brown marabout, and each wore a black velvet Rubens hat sporting a large crimson feather.

Waiting for her was the groom, Charles Edward Howard Vincent, the Metropolitan Police's Director of Criminal Investigations.

The large congregation, numbering several hundred, included all the senior officers and superintendents of the Metropolitan Police, along with as many members of the Criminal Investigation Department as duty would allow. Also present were officers from the Royal Welsh Fusiliers, the Royal Berks Militia and the Central London Rangers, all of which Howard Vincent had served with; the Duke of Teck and Home Secretary William Vernon Harcourt were also in attendance.

In the midst of the noblemen, Members of Parliament and high-ranking police officers, taking pride of place in the front seats of the north and south galleries were forty boys and forty girls from the Metropolitan and City Police Orphanage, along with all the officers and most of the servants of that institution.[1]

---

1 *The Nottingham Evening Post*, 27th October 1882;
   The Life of Sir Howard Vincent by S H Jeyes and F D How, 1912.

It is scarcely surprising that the Police Orphans should have played such a large part in the event. Howard Vincent had been Chairman of the Orphanage since 1881, and just three months before his wedding day had hosted the Prince and Princess of Wales at the opening of the Orphanage's newly-built Burdett Coutts Wing, which provided classrooms for boys, girls and infants. Addressing attendees including the Lord Mayor and Lady Mayoress, the Marquis and Marchioness of Bath and Baroness Burdett-Coutts, who had provided an interest free loan to fund the building of the wing now named in her honour, Howard Vincent stated that the institution provided for the maintenance and education of 150 boys and 100 girls, and that some 11,960 police officers subscribed to the Orphanage fund.[2]

Fundraising events were regularly staged around the capital, often featuring the Metropolitan Police Minstrels, a troupe of serving officers who performed popular songs while 'blacked up', and who would raise over £200,000 before being disbanded in 1933. The public donated freely at boxes positioned in police stations throughout the capital, and it was reported in 1896 that the Superintendent of G Division had been stopped in the street and given a cheque for £1,000 in aid of the fund.

Alongside these charity events were a constant stream of funds received through sales of *A Police Code and General Manual of the Criminal Law for the British Empire*, to give it its full 1889 title. The book was originally written by Howard Vincent in 1881 and subsequently updated several times. Editions from 1882 onwards featured an Address to Constables by the eminent judge Sir Henry Hawkins, and by 1889 a preface by the Commissioner of the Metropolitan Police had been added.

It was immediately successful, with the *Morning Post* stating "it would be difficult to accord too much praise to this clear and concise compendium. It should be in the hands of all justices, justices' clerks, and officers of police throughout the Kingdom", while the *Law Times* rather dryly commented that it had "tested Mr Vincent's information, and found it to be accurate."[3]

---

2   *The Illustrated London News*, 15th July 1882.
3   Reviews of *The Police Code* given in the 1889 edition.

The Morning Post's observation identified an important point; Howard Vincent had written the book as a guide rather than a set of rules, and it had been published independently rather than by the Metropolitan Police itself, with the result that copies were sold not only to the force which had most need for its contents, but also to judges, barristers and even the general public - with sometimes amusing results, as will be seen in the following pages.

Over 200 pages, Howard Vincent carefully described in simple terms the legality of more than 900 incidents which might occur in the daily life of a police officer, from baby farming and wandering lunatics to illegal burials and the identification of prisoners.

By 1889, the version we have used for this book, the *Police Code* was in its sixth edition; Howard Vincent had resigned from the Metropolitan Police to enter Parliament, and he and Ethel had had a daughter, Vera.

In using the 1889 version, we are able to examine how certain entries in the *Code* may have affected the investigation into the Whitechapel Murders and other crime of the 1888-1890 period, before the complete 1889 version is reproduced. As will be seen, it is a book which the reader can dip into at any page and gain an understanding of criminal law in the late Victorian era. Although the first edition of the *Code* bore a grey-brown cover, subsequent editions were bound in red cloth and we have endeavoured to make this book as faithful a reproduction of the 1889 edition as possible.

As well as providing information and entertainment, this book is also doing some good. By selling the original *Police Code*, Howard Vincent was able to provide funds to the Metropolitan and City Police Orphanage from profits, and although that institution has long ceased to exist, we are proud to say that we are restarting that tradition by donating an equal share of profits to its successor, the Metropolitan Police and City Orphans Fund, which means that by buying the book you are now holding in your hands, you too have made a contribution to that excellent charity, which continues to support the children of serving and former police officers.

NEIL R A BELL and ADAM WOOD, July 2015

We would like to thank Deputy Assistant Commissioner Neil Basu, Borough Commander Simon Ovens, Peter Smyth and Malcolm Cooper of the Metropolitan and City Police Orphans Fund, Paul Bickley, Curator of the Metropolitan Police's Crime Museum, Keith Skinner, Richard Jones, Lindsay Siviter and Debra Arif for their kind assistance during the preparation of this book.

THE METROPOLITAN AND CITY POLICE ORPHANAGE

It was a sad fact of life that the majority of working class men in the eighteenth and nineteenth centuries had little option but to seek employment in dangerous environments for their hard-earned wage.

But for a policemen, the risks were more unpredictable and, at times, more common. Apart from the obvious risk of assault by a determined escaping burglar or riotous crowd, a constable was expected to deal with all sorts of dangers during his working day, from stopping runaway horses and carts or rescuing those who somehow found themselves in the icy waters of the River Thames, to throwing themselves into the flames of a burning building to drag out those who had succumbed to the smoke and fumes. These acts, a small sample of the dangers which a constable was exposed to during his career, sometimes came at the heaviest of costs.

In fact, on 28th June 1830, just nine months after the formation of the Metropolitan Police, PC Joseph Grantham became their first officer killed on duty when he intervened in a fight between two drunken Irishmen. Grantham, whose wife had given birth to twins the previous day, was knocked to the floor and a kick to the temple from Michael Duggan ended his life. As an indication of the attitude to the 'New Police' at that time, at the inquest the jury cleared the defendants and returned a verdict of 'justifiable homicide', stating that Grantham had contributed to his own death by "over-exertion in the discharge of his duty".[1]

---

1 *The Official Encyclopedia of Scotland Yard* by Martin Fido and Keith Skinner, revised edition (2000). Gabriel Franks, employed by the Thames Police, was killed on 16th October 1798 during the Wapping Coal Riot.

A further 76 Metropolitan Police officers would lose their lives in the line of duty by 1869, when Lieutenant Colonel Edmund Henderson replaced the long-serving Richard Mayne as Commissioner.

The perils facing constables in their daily duty and, in addition, how these dangers had the potential to impact on his immediate family, were about to be addressed. The loss of the main provider put great stress upon the remaining family, and without support that family unit faced the reality of fracture and dispersal via workhouses and other parochial institutions.

There is an oft-quoted phrase used by many in relation to the police, chiefly in reference to self-preservation within the force itself. However, the phrase "they always look after their own" is never more apt than with regards a policeman's own family.

Commissioner Henderson was determined to create a fund to support those families left behind.

He released a memorandum throughout the force expressing the desire "that there should be established a Widows and Orphans Fund and an Orphanage of small size for the benefit who children who have lost both parents"; a Police Order released on 19th January 1870 outlined the proposed management structure, with one inspector, two sergeants and two constables to be elected to a Sub Committee in each division across the Metropolitan Police district.

The idea was universally welcomed, although the proprietors of the privately-owned Home for Destitute Orphans of Policemen were alarmed at the prospect of losing its revenue from police subscribers, on which it relied. On 16th September, the Secretary Miss Emily Blucke[2] wrote to Henderson, explaining how the Home, situated at 49 & 50 Hamilton Road, Brighton,[3] at that time cared for 28 children, of whom seventeen were orphans of officers who had served with the Metropolitan and City of London Police forces:

> *I feel it right to make it known how we are affected by the effort now being carried out... and compensation made on behalf of this Institution, whose interests have been greatly*

---

2   The letter was signed "E E Blucke"; christian name from 1871 census.
3   *Brighton Gazette*, 3rd November 1870.

hindered and crippled by this movement, that it be not said that the Orphanage "was founded at the expense of the original one.[4]

It was agreed unanimously by the managing General Court, in a meeting on 29th September, that Miss Blucke had no claim on the funds of the Metropolitan Police Orphanage.

What became of the Home for Destitute Orphans of Policemen, which had opened on 30th September 1867 with senior officers of police forces around the country in attendance, including Sir Richard Mayne of the Metropolitan Police and Colonel Sir James Fraser of the City of London Police,[5] is unknown. It appears to have been widely supported at the time of its founding, but perhaps the fact that the small home was run almost single-handedly by Miss Blucke with her sister Eliza,[6] daughters of a deceased army officer, made it unsuited to cope with the demands which the Metropolitan Police Orphanage was created to meet. It may be the case that Edmund Henderson learned of the Home from his predecessor Sir Richard Mayne, and the idea for the Orphanage grew from there.[7]

The Metropolitan Police Orphanage opened its doors in October 1870, with 20 children becoming the first residents. Admission was confined to children orphaned after 1st January 1870 and limited to two from each family, although this rule could be relaxed in cases of great distress. In addition, only children of officers who subscribed to the Fund were admitted, which no doubt saw the numbers of subscribers increase as a kind of 'insurance'.

Sometimes the death of a constable was not always as a direct result of exercising a particular duty. When R Division's Detective Sergeant George Purbook went missing on a summer's Wednesday in July 1887, it was clear something was not quite right. His body was found in the River Eden, Cumbria, four days later, with his hat, warrant and notebook found on a nearby bank. The evidence was clear that DS Purbook had decided to take his own life.

---

4   Minute dated 29th September 1870, *Metropolitan Police Orphanage: Minutes of Meetings of the General Court, 29th September 1870 to December 1877*.
5   *Sussex Advertiser*, 5th October 1867.
6   1871 census.
7   Emily Blucke died in London in 1878, aged 55 (Death Index).

The notebook was examined and the last entry, in the Detective Sergeant's handwriting, contained instructions to issue a telegram. He requested:

> Please telegraph to Superintendent McHugo,[8] Blackheath Road, London – GEORGE PURBOOK, Detective Sergeant, Metropolitan Police.

Purbook then continued with the main text of the telegram: "Oh my poor head! Ask Mr McHugo if he will recommend my children for the Orphanage".[9]

The Orphanage's original home was Fortescue House on London Road, Twickenham, and a second building opposite, Bath House, was taken on lease to accommodate 40 of the younger children. Yet this was not enough; within three years there were 115 orphans eligible for accommodation.

In 1874 Wellesley House on Hampton Road, Twickenham, was purchased. It had previously been used as a school, run by Thomas Scalé, with R D Blackmore, author of *Lorna Doone*, teaching Classics there for a time. Wellesley House provided accommodation for 200 children, later extended to house a further 60, and the Orphanage re-opened there on 25th September 1874. It would be its home for the next 63 years.[10]

A year after the Orphanage was founded the City of London Police were formally invited to join the Fund and its Commissioner, Colonel James Fraser, was appointed a Vice President, joining the Assistant Commissioners of the Metropolitan Police. City of London Police Superintendent Alfred Foster was appointed to the Board of Managers, and the name of the Fund was formally changed to The Metropolitan and City Police Orphanage.[11]

Colonel Fraser, acknowledging "the kindness of the Members" in agreeing to change the name,

---

8 Superintendent Christopher McHugo, R Division (Greenwich).
9 *Lloyds Weekly*, 17th July 1887.
10 met-cityorphans.com/history-and-archive/the-story-of-the-fund/the-orphanage.
11 Business Paper dated 2nd February 1871, held in *Metropolitan Police Orphanage: Minutes of Meetings of the General Court, 29th September 1870 to December 1877*.

spoke of the good feeling which exists between the Metropolitan and City Police Forces and the desirability of encouraging the same, and that he considered the step now taken a very important one to this end.[12]

* * *

Last year we directed attention to the admirable organisation known as the Metropolitan Police Minstrels. Now, when the stereotyped heading, "The Police and the Public", once more appears in our newspapers with unpleasant frequency, it is again pleasant to refer to those hard-working, self-denying inspectors and constables whose labours are so great a benefit to less fortunate members of the force. The Police Minstrels have one great object in view: the providing of funds for the Metropolitan and City Police Orphanage.[13]

Formed in 1872 by ten officers from A Division (Westminster), the Metropolitan Police Minstrels would prove to be the largest single source of fundraising for police charities throughout their 61 year existence. The troupe consisted of serving constables, sergeants and inspectors, and appeared in evening dress and blackened faces and hands. While undoubtedly frowned upon in the politically-correct world of today, their shows were typical of the period, with the group singing negro spirituals and popular ballads such as *Chiming Bells of Long Ago*, *My Own Guiding Star* and *The Anvil Chorus*. Extremely popular, venues were sold out whenever the Minstrels performed, and over the course of their history they would raise more than a quarter of a million pounds for police charities.

Long serving members included Inspector John Littlechild, Sergeant Marriner and Sergeant James Olive, who would go on to become Superintendent of the CID and eventually the first Deputy Commissioner. Each member was proficient at singing or playing an instrument, and performances were always reported as being of high standard.

---

12 Minute dated 2nd February 1871, held in *Metropolitan Police Orphanage: Minutes of Meetings of the General Court, 29th September 1870 to December 1877*.

13 *Pall Mall Gazette*, 11th May 1889,

John Littlechild, in particular, seemed suited to the stage, as reported by the *East London Observer* following a benefit concert for the Orphanage given by the Minstrels at the Bow and Bromley Institute on 28th October 1875:

> The effort on behalf of this deserving charity is always well supported, but on Thursday evening the spacious hall was crammed, every available seat being occupied, and many of the audience being obliged to stand throughout the performance, while we understand that many persons were refused admission for want to accommodation... The first part of the programme was commenced by an overture, played in excellent time, by the band, under the direction of Mr D Smith, the cornet solos of Mr H. Alexander being especially worthy of remark. Mr J B Smart sang Mother, Bear Me To The Window, *and* My Birthland Far Away *with fine effect. Mr C. Marriner received an encore in* We Meet Again, *whilst Mr J Finegan's fine bass voice was shown to full advantage in* Mother, Oh Sing Me To Rest. *The palm, however, for the vocal part of the entertainment must go to Mr J G Littlechild, who sang* Silver Threads Among The Gold *and a balled entitled* Only *in splendid style; in the latter he received two well-deserved encores.*[14]

The end for the Minstrels came in 1933, not because of changing attitudes to 'blacking up', but through internal pressure. Commissioner Sir William Horwood and his successor Lord Byng objected to the practice of sergeants selling tickets door-to-door, stating that it detracted from the dignity of the rank. When Lord Trenchard became Commissioner in 1932 he ordered that the door-to-door selling should cease.

Although still extremely popular, the Minstrels struggled to attract audiences and therefore funds, and disbanded the following year. To cover the loss of charitable income raised by the Minstrels, Trenchard set up the Commissioner's Fund.

Other fundraising events during the lifetime of the Orphanage included concerts by music hall artists, excursions, balls and fêtes, including the Annual Fêtes at Alexandra Palace and Crystal Palace, at which prizes were awarded.

---

14 *East London Observer*, 30th October 1876.

As well as financial donations, gifts for the children were made by numerous kind-hearted individuals and officers of the divisions, with items including a printing press, a Christmas tree, cards, toys, fruit and sweets being given freely.

Another source of income came from within. Serving police constables and sergeants were required to maintain a minimum subscription of one penny per week towards the Orphanage, with higher ranks providing more. In addition, officers could sign up for annual subscriptions, and a total of 15,156 Police officers subscribed to the Orphanage Fund in 1889. A look at the list of donations made in 1888 includes those made by familiar names including Assistant Commissioner Robert Anderson (£3 3s 0d), Superintendent Charles Cutbush (£1 1s 0d), Chief Inspector Donald Swanson, Inspector John Spratling and Inspector Frederick Abberline (all 10s 6d).[15]

In addition, boxes were placed in stations across the divisions for the public to donate, with a total of £87 0s 8d being given during 1889. Interestingly, £3 4s 9d of this was donated in H Division (Whitechapel), but none the previous year, when the Jack the Ripper murders gripped the East End.[16]

In total, some £13,962 6s 8d[17] was collected in 1889 through subscriptions, collections at fundraising events and public donations, with the cost of running the Orphanage and other costs amounting to £12,568 12s 8d.

By this time Howard Vincent, who had served as Chairman of the Orphanage in 1881 and 1882, had resigned as Director of the CID but remained on the General Court of Management, along with well-known officers including James Monro, Colonel Sir James Fraser, Robert Anderson, Melville Macnaghten, Colonel Henry Smith and Sir Charles Warren.

The ten-strong Board of Managers elected for 1889 included Superintendents Charles Cutbush and John Shore, with Major W

---

15 Names of Subscribers and Donors for 1889, found in *The Metropolitan and City Police Orphanage, Report for the Year 1889*.

16 Amount Collected in Boxes at the Stations in Police Divisions during the Year 1889, published in *The Metropolitan and City Police Orphanage, Report for the Year 1889*.

17 Equivalent of £750,000 today.

E Gilbert, Chief Constable of the Metropolitan Police, elected as Chairman.[18]

Arthur Kestin had replaced the long-serving Edwin Mills as Secretary, joining Headmaster Richard Gardner, Headmistress H E Evans and Minnie Smart, Mistress of the Preparatory School, in the day-to-day running of the Orphanage.[19] Mills had resigned in July 1886 to take a position in the Metropolitan Police Receiver's Office, having served as Secretary of the Orphanage for ten years.[20] Finding his replacement proved to be anything but straightforward, with the Board being less than impressed with an initial six candidates interviewed in October 1886.[21] They were reimbursed their travel costs and dismissed.

Sir James Fraser of the City of London Police moved a resolution to create a Special Committee to interview and select a Secretary from a new batch of candidates, and on 7th December 1886 this Committee, including the Met's Assistant Commissioner Alexander Carmichael Bruce, City of London Police Chief Superintendent Major Henry Smith and H Division's Superintendent Thomas Arnold interviewed seven new candidates including Major Edward Vanrenen, Francis Eardley-Wilmot and the splendidly-named William Lovely, a Fleet Paymaster in the Navy. Eardley-Wilmot gained eight votes but was easily surpassed by Arthur Kestin, a 38-year-old Managing Clerk to a firm of Indian Merchants, who impressed 24 members of the Committee enough to win their votes. None of the other candidates attracted a single vote.[22] Kestin would go on to be Secretary to the Orphanage for several years.

A look at the *Report for the Year 1889* provides a snapshot of the daily life of the orphans in that year, which began with 31 boys and 15 girls leaving the Orphanage on reaching the limit of 15-years-old, to be replaced by 26 boys and 9 girls. A total of 156 boys and 100

---

18 *The Metropolitan and City Police Orphanage, Report for the Year 1889.*
19 Ibid.
20 Minute dated 13th July 1886 in *General Court Minutes book, May 1880 to March 1894.*
21 Minute dated 5th October 1886 in *General Court Minutes book, May 1880 to March 1894*, which reveals that two candidates received no votes, one a single vote and the other interviewees sharing the remainder.
22 Minute dated 7th December 1886 in *General Court Minutes book, May 1880 to March 1894.*

girls between the ages of 7 and 15 were residing at the Orphanage during those twelve months; on top of these, 669 children at home under the care of their families were also provided for, making a total of 925 children.

The Preparatory School, consisting of children aged between seven and ten, saw seventeen youngsters taught the basics of subjects including reading, arithmetic, writing and grammar in readiness to move up to the older classes.

A typical day for the older boys would be half-hour lessons on Bible reading, history, arithmetic and geography, followed by a two-hour break for dinner, drill and recreation, with an afternoon consisting of lessons on science, bookkeeping and drawing, with the school day ending with a session of songs and prayer.

In addition to subjects such as arithmetic and reading, girls were schooled in more domestic pursuits including 'domestic economy', music and needlework. During the year, they had mended 2,805 pairs of girls' stockings, and made 177 undergarments, 75 aprons and 53 nightdresses in addition to smaller items such as pillowcases and pocket handkerchiefs. Nineteen girls aged 14 or 15 were employed at the Orphanage in addition to receiving an education.

All the children enjoyed a full, if not particularly varied diet. Mondays saw porridge and bread and milk for breakfast, cold roast beef or mutton, potatoes and bread, followed by rice pudding for dinner, and bread and butter with milk for tea.

Friday's menu consisted of cocoa, bread and butter for breakfast, fish and potatoes for dinner, and bread and butter or dripping for tea.

Their diet seemed to agree with the children; just 80 cases of illness across the 256 children were reported for the year by Dr J R Leeson, with the majority suffering minor skin diseases or throat afflictions. Mr Arthur Fox, dentist to the Orphanage, reported a total of 86 extractions and 104 fillings during 1889.

Those children leaving the Orphanage were given help finding a suitable position, and were supplied with a trunk containing the following items designed to prepare them for life in the outside world:

BOYS	GIRLS
2 suits	1 costume
1 overcoat	1 coat frock
3 day shirts	1 underskirt
2 pairs of pyjamas	2 pairs of knickers
4 pairs of socks	2 linings
2 vests	3 combinations
2 pairs of underpants	3 under bodices
6 handkerchiefs	4 pairs of stockings
6 collars	1 pair of corsets
2 neckties	2 vests
2 pairs of boots	2 nightdresses
1 pair of slippers	6 handkerchiefs
1 hat	1 jumper
1 cap	2 pairs of shoes
1 brush and comb	1 pair of slippers
1 toothbrush	1 hat
1 box	1 raincoat
	2 pairs of gloves
	6 towels
	1 brush and comb and sponge bag
	1 box
	1 umbrella[23]

Nearly all children found good positions on leaving the Orphanage, many boys joining the Metropolitan Police. By 1896, several others had emigrated to countries including Australia, New Zealand, South Africa, the United States and Canada, their passages paid by the Board of Managers. Between 1928 and 1936, 31 boys and one girl went to Australia, each met on arrival by the local police force and found accommodation and employment. In 1936, one former Orphan ran a 200 acre farm, and three others were serving as Constables in the Victoria Police Force.

As the years went by and the number of police casualties grew, the Orphanage struggled to fulfil its purpose. By 1878, there were 1,000 orphaned children, only 200 of who could be given accommodation. In 1883 it was decided to award a compassionate

---

23 Metropolitan and City Police Orphans Fund museum.

allowance of £2 12s 0d each year for those children for whom there was no accommodation, and between that year and 31st December 1969, £1,369,320 was paid to 5,243 widows in respect of 10,728 orphaned children.

The Police Pensions Act of 1921 gave a widow of a constable or sergeant a pension of £30 per annum, with an allowance of £10 for each child up to a maximum of £30. This probably hastened the closure of the Orphanage, as it provided a means for all but the very poor to keep their children at home. In 1933 only 277 out of 650 orphans were accommodated at the Orphanage, and the following year just 181.

With numbers dwindling, the Board approached the Trustees seeking the closure of the Orphanage; this happened on 31st July 1937. The very next day The Metropolitan and City Police Orphans Fund came into being, based on proceeds from the sale of Wellesley House. In the course of its 67 year existence, the Orphanage had accommodated, schooled and funded 2,807 boys and girls.

Wellesley House was taken over by Shaftesbury Homes and renamed Fortescue House School, with most of the boys in the Orphanage at that time staying on to continue their education. The school eventually closed in 1971, and most of the site was demolished.

The compassionate allowance was raised to £48 each year per child by 1942, and ten years later was increased to £52. An increase in the minimum rate of police subscriptions to five pence each week in 1963 allowed the annual allowance to be increased to £168 per child.[24]

This resulted in annual expenditure for £62,172 in 1970, £178,076 in 1980 and £448,357 in 1990. The expenditure in 2004 was in excess of £622,000.

Today, the Metropolitan and City Police Orphans Fund is based at Putney. It continues to rely on donations and subscriptions from police officers and kind-hearted members of the public.

To find out more about this excellent charity and to make a small donation, please visit www.met-citypoliceorphans.org.uk.

---

24 met-cityorphans.com/history-and-archive/the-story-of-the-fund/the-orphanage

SIR C E HOWARD VINCENT

Few high-profile people have experienced as varied a career as Sir Howard Vincent, and that he enjoyed fine military, legal and political success in addition to his important work reforming the Metropolitan Police's Criminal Investigation Department is a testament to his drive and purpose.

Charles Edward Howard Vincent was born on 31st May 1849, second son of Reverend Frederick Vincent, Rector of Slinford, Sussex. He was a sickly child and would suffer from coughing bouts, sometimes lasting three or four weeks at a time, throughout his life.

He was educated at Westminster School and then the Royal Military College at Sandhurst before being appointed ensign in the 23rd Royal Welsh Fusiliers in 1868,[1] and a year later had an early taste of crime when his gold watch, top coat and several items of jewellery were stolen by a deserter from the same regiment, a man named Joseph Cooke.[2]

Retiring in 1873 with the rank of lieutenant, Howard Vincent was then gazetted captain in the Royal Berkshire Militia, serving just two years before accepting the lieutenant-colonelcy of the Central London Rangers.

After serving a total of eight years in the military, he became a barrister of the Inner Temple in 1876 and the following year entered the Paris Faculté de Droit.[3] Not all went smoothly, as Howard Vincent recalled:

---

1 *The Tatler*, 30th March 1904.
2 *Bristol Mercury*, 12th June 1869.
3 *The Tatler*, 30th March 1904.

> *I joined the South Eastern Circuit, and the first time had sixteen briefs - all but two or three, of course, 'devils'. Baron Huddlestone was the senior judge, and very kind. He gave me at Maidstone an important defence, of which I am afraid I made a horrid muddle, for the Baron kept shaking his head during my address to the jury, and the unfortunate prisoner got convicted! I hope he was guilty.*[4]

At the outbreak of war between Russia and Turkey in 1877, he became War Correspondent for the *Daily Telegraph*, travelling through France, Germany, Austria and Russia, before his presence at the Kishineff headquarters of Grand Duke Nicholas was objected to by Russian authorities on account of his Turkophile interests and knowledge of Russian, a language he had learned while lodging with a Russian family during his travels.

As Howard Vincent was touring Europe, events were unfolding elsewhere which would have serious repercussions for the Metropolitan Police and, eventually, for Howard Vincent himself.

Following the conviction in April 1877 of a gang who had perpetrated the notorious Turf Frauds on the Comtesse de Goncourt, swindling the aristocratic Parisienne out of the equivalent of £450,000, the reason for the difficulty in their capturing became apparent when two of the fraudsters, Henry Benson and William Kurr, sought to have their sentences reduced by revealing that several officers of Scotland Yard's Detective Department had been in their pay.

After an investigation Det Inspector John Meiklejohn, Det Chief Inspector Nathaniel Druscovich and Det Chief Inspector William Palmer were arrested and charged with conspiring to defeat the ends of justice, along with a solicitor named Edward Froggatt. The quartet appeared at Bow Street police court on 19th July. The hearing lasted for two months, with the name of Chief Inspector George Clarke coming up several times in evidence, seemingly implicating him in the corruption scandal. By the beginning of September it was decided to include Clarke in the charges, and he was arrested on 8th September by his old friend Superintendent Adolphus Williamson.

---

4   *The Sheffield Daily Independent*, 8th April 1908.

What was termed the Trial of the Detectives opened a few days later on 24th October and continued for three weeks. On Tuesday, 20th November, the jury return guilty verdicts on Meiklejohn, Druscovitch, Palmer and Froggatt. George Clarke was found not guilty, but had become a political embarrassment and would be forced to take early retirement by the Home Secretary.

Each was sentenced to two years' imprisonment with hard labour.[5]

The Morning Post, never a newspaper to hold back its opinion, lamented the state of affairs at Scotland Yard and then cast an eye to the future:

> *We need not dwell upon a matter which is notorious, and which has proved beyond dispute that the Detective Service has broken down and is no longer to be relied upon. It is incumbent upon the Government to inquire into the means by which a similar scandal may be prevented in the future, and the Detective Service be so organised that it shall not be possible for those who are engaged in it to betray their trust. The question is one evidently of the greatest difficulty...*
>
> *In the inquiry which the Government has instituted into the means of placing the Detective Service of the Metropolitan Police upon a better footing it may be well that it should consider how this service is carried on in other countries. It might not be desirable to follow their example in its entirety, but much might be learnt from it. Let us look for a moment at the police system of Paris, concerning the details and management of which body a most lucid and valuable report has just been prepared by Mr Howard Vincent, of the English and French Bars.*[6]

In fact, when Home Secretary Richard Cross had appointed a committee to investigate the reorganisation of the Detective Department while the Trial of the Detectives was stilled underway, Vincent saw an opportunity for himself. Having knowledge of

---

5 See *The Trial of the Detectives* by George Dilnot (1928) for a transcript of the trial, and Chris Payne's *The Chieftain: Victorian True Crime through the Eyes of a Scotland Yard Detective* (2011) for an examination of the Turf Frauds and their aftermath.

6 *The Morning Post*, 15th December 1877.

police methods on the Continent, he had travelled to Paris and drafted an exhaustive report on the organisation of the Sûreté - the French detective system - with the assistance of the Prefect and his officers, eventually producing eighteen drafts before submitting his report to the committee together with testimonials from numerous legal acquaintances including Attorney-General Sir John Holker, Sir J Marle QC and Mr Overend QC, the latter two actually sitting on the Departmental Committee.

The Committee were impressed. Vincent was invited to the Home Office, where he met Under-Secretary Sir Henry Selwyn Ibbetson, and was appointed on a salary of £1,000 a year and would himself be responsible to the Home Office, but his officers were ruled by the Commissioner.[7] He was just 28-years-old.

The appointment was announced to Metropolitan Police officers in typically official fashion in Police Orders of 6th March 1878:

> *Department of Crime: Appointment. The Secretary of State for the Home Department has appointed Mr C E Howard Vincent to be Director of Criminal Investigations in the Metropolitan Police.*[8]

A further announcement, outlining the new incarnation of the Detective Department, appeared in Police Orders of Saturday, 6th April 1878:

> *Criminal Investigation Department: From Monday next, April 8th, the whole of the detective establishment will form one body under the Director of Criminal Investigation. With the exception of the undermentioned officers, promoted or appointed to responsible posts, the present staff will be placed on probation for three months.*[9]

Howard Vincent was the ideal man to take on the task of reorganising the old Detective Department. Basing the CID on the

---

7 *The Illustrated London News*, 13th October 1883; *Nottingham Evening Post*, 27th October 1882; *The Tatler*, 30th March 1904; and *The Life of Sir Howard Vincent* by S H Jeyes and F D How, 1912.
8 Police Order 6th March 1878.
9 Police Order 6th April 1878. The officers exempt from this probationary period were Adolphus 'Dolly' Williamson (appointed Chief Superintendent) and John Shore (appointed Chief Inspector).

Paris model, whereas the old Detective Department had consisted of 30 detectives of various ranks all based at Scotland Yard, the new structure meant a Central Office at Scotland Yard consisting of one Chief Superintendent, three Chief Inspectors, three First Class Inspectors and 17 Second Class Inspectors, with a clerical staff of four Sergeants and two Constables. Across the divisions, there would also be 14 local Detective Inspectors, one in each division, and a combined force of 159 Detective Sergeants.

His biography[10] records his office hours in those early years as nine in the morning to seven each evening, in addition to spending many hours working at home. The main reason was that the new Director had found a system in place for the Assistant Commissioners[11] which threatened to hinder the successful implementation of the new Department:

> *Instead of being placed in charge of specific departments, they were on duty in alternate months, and having very different views on things often upset one another's decisions. They were by no means favourable to the new order of things, which took all criminal matters completely out of their hands, and to prevent any relapse I never left my post for a single day for three years.*

As a result of this hands-on approach, Howard Vincent would later boast that he was able to recall the details of more than six hundred cases on which the CID had worked.

In addition to reforming the Detective Department, in 1881 he found time to compile *A Police Code and Manual of the Criminal Law*, believing that most of the errors committed by the police were due to ignorance of the law and deficient training in their duties.

Further changes saw an overhaul of the *Police Gazette*, founded in 1828 as *Hue and Cry*, a disorganised four-page document put together by the chief clerk at Bow Street. Under Howard Vincent's hand it became a valuable publication, featuring descriptions of wanted criminals and their portraits, as well as illustrations of

---

10 *The Life of Sir Howard Vincent* by S H Jeyes and F D How, 1912.
11 Those in office at this time were Douglas Labalmondière, Assistant Commissioner (Administrative) and Captain William Harris, Assistant Commissioner (Executive). Both had been in their roles for more than twenty years.

stolen property. The twice-weekly *Police Gazette* became a valuable means of gathering criminal intelligence, and was circulated around the Metropolitan Police divisions.

Also instituted by Howard Vincent were the Special Irish Branch, created to deal with the growing Fenian threat, and the Convict Supervision Office, with discharged criminals who had been recorded in the offices of the latter being offered help in the form of the Discharged Prisoners Aid Society, which sought to find employment for so-called 'ticket-of-leave' men.

During this time Howard Vincent was also Chairman of the Metropolitan and City of London Police Orphanage, working closely with Commissioner Sir Edmund Henderson and the Orphanage's Board.

Eventually, perhaps seeking a new challenge, Howard Vincent resigned from the CID in 1884, being replaced by his friend James Monro, and moved into politics. The following year he was awarded the CBE for his work in reforming the Detective Department.

Before entering Parliament, however, in 1884 he was appointed Colonel-Commander of the Queen's Westminster Volunteers, a position he would hold until 1904. The Volunteers were the forerunners of the Territorial Army, a movement close to Howard Vincent's heart; he had in fact lectured at a conference on the subject as early as 1878. He was appointed head of the City Imperial Volunteers at the outbreak of the Second Boer War and turned up to serve at the front, but was disappointed to be turned away when it was discovered during a medical examination that he had a heart defect - an ailment which would haunt him in later life.

At the general election of November 1885, Howard Vincent was returned as the Conservative MP for Sheffield (Central Division), holding on to the seat through five further elections and eventually dying in office. He was elected Chairman of Conservative Associations in 1895.[12]

He was knighted in 1896 and created KCMG in 1899 after acting as the British representative at an international conference at Rome which discussed the threat of anarchists, and was also a Knight of the Orders of the German Crown, and of the Crown of Italy.[13]

---

12 *Gloucestershire Echo*, 7th April 1908.
13 *Yorkshire Telegraph and Star*, 7th April 1908.

Four years before his death, Colonel Sir Howard Vincent gave an interview to *The Tatler* in which he looked back at his remarkable career. He remembered his days with the Metropolitan Police with fondess:

> *It is almost needless to say that I am very much interested in criminology, and my position as Director of Criminal Investigations gave exceptional opportunities of studying wrongdoers and their ways and provided me with an experience which has been of great help in connection with social science and kindred work which I have endeavoured to carry out. Of all my books the Police Code has been the most successful. It has now reached the twelfth edition and has attained a circulation of more than 40,000 copies. It still serves as a link between me and that splendid force with which I was connected nearly twenty years ago.*[14]

In fact, following Howard Vincent's death the future of the book he had first published in 1881 was thrown into almost immediate controversy.

Suffering from a heart affliction for three years, he had complained of feeling unwell for some weeks prior to his daughter Vera's marriage to Lieutenant Hutton Croft in April 1908, but had enjoyed that happy occasion before following doctor's orders and taking immediate rest. Planning to retreat to the family villa at Cannes with Lady Vincent intending to follow a week later, Howard Vincent rested at Mentone, southern France, booking into the Hotel d'Anglais. It was here that he passed away of sudden heart failure in the early hours of 7th April 1908. His body was transported to Cannes, as per his wishes, and interred at the family vault where his mother and father already lay.

The following day the local newspaper of his constituency, *The Sheffield Daily Independent*, ran a long obituary which included the following tribute:

> *Those who knew him had no necessity to seek the reasons of his popularity, as they had no reason to ask for the reasons of his success. In every respect he was a remarkable man, and at the same time a man who in his knowledge, his strength,*

---

14 *The Tatler*, 20th March 1904.

and his pride, had a kindly regard for all his fellows, and placed no one of them below his recognition...

Sir Howard never took up a thing half-heartedly. He had a genius for detail, an amazing gift of application, and enthusiasm which ran to the verge of exuberance.[15]

So came to an end the life of a remarkable man. Through his many endeavours, and the *Police Code* in particular, the legacy of Sir Charles Edward Howard Vincent would live on.

---

15 *The Sheffield Daily Independent*, 8th April 1908.

A POLICE CODE

On Friday, 8th July 1881, a small paragraph appeared at the bottom of page eight in *The Western Daily*, the newspaper of choice for England's south-western region. It was in relation to a new publication on legal reference, and read:

> Mr Howard Vincent, the Director of Criminal Investigations, has just published under the title of "A Police Code," a manual of the criminal law, designed expressly for the members of the police force, thought it appears to be well calculated to be of service to justices of the peace. It is founded in great part upon the general orders of the Metropolitan Police and the instruction books of the several constabulary forces.

This new book, *A Police Code and General Manual of the Criminal Law for The British Empire* to give it its full title, was envisioned by Howard Vincent to be a one-stop legal book for all people on all matters connected to two main topics: the day-to-day maintenance of order, and dealing with crime. Entirely funded by Howard Vincent himself, the main part of the book was an alphabetic listing of a constable's duty interspersed with numerous scenarios and advice on how the constable should deal with those situations. Each entry was lifted directly from the Police Orders,[1] meaning each serving constable should have already been familiar with the book's contents.

Not only was the *Police Code* a handy reference for a constable to refresh his memory, its availability to all meant that the public could now understand what action a constable could undertake and the legal reasoning behind it. It therefore became a valued

---

1   Police Orders are the daily instructions on various matters given to all constables of all ranks, and are cascaded from the Commissioner's Office at Scotland Yard to all stations.

source within the legal environment, and meant a constable now had to be extremely precise in the execution of his duty, chiefly out of fear of prosecution due to this widening of knowledge with regards what he could and could not do. The publication of *A Police Code* was a step toward what we today term 'transparency', a tool which enabled the public to question police accountability during times of dubious police action.

The *Code*, the abbreviated term by which it was to become known, was an instant global sensation. Howard Vincent noted this himself when he declared in the 1889 edition that "in a tour around the British Empire, and through America, I had the satisfaction of the larger edition in use as a text book by Chiefs of Police, and the abridged edition in the hands of many individual constables…" Indeed, he would later note that "the book is made use of by the American and continental authorities and by all English-speaking policemen."[2]

Therein lay one of the successes of Howard Vincent's book - its appeal to all police forces across the globe. To avoid confusion for overseas forces, Howard Vincent inserted asterisks to sections applicable only to the United Kingdom, but a quick flick through the *Code* reveals that these asterisks are very few, an indication that the British legal and policing system had been adopted in either identical or very similar format, not only across the British Empire, but even in far-flung places such as Japan, "where for two months the young recruits are instructed in *The Police Code*, and in the art of fencing, wrestling and boxing".[3]

By the time of the first Abridged Edition in 1882, Howard Vincent had persuaded the Honourable Sir Henry Hawkins[4] to pen an Address to Constables, in which Hawkins, a former barrister and QC who had successfully prosecuted Arthur Orton in the Tichborne Claimant case before becoming a Judge in 1876, reminded constables that their demeanour and behaviour was

---

2 *The Tatler*, 20th March 1904.
3 'Police Recruits in Japan', *Dundee Evening Telegraph*, 2nd January 1896.
4 Henry Hawkins (1817-1907) was called to the Bar in 1843 and appeared in several high profile cases. His career as a Judge saw him officiate in the cases of poisoners Dr Thomas Neil Cream and Dr George Lamson, as well as that of the Muswell Hill murderers, Albert Milsom and Henry Fowler. Hawkins retired in 1898, becoming Baron Brampton of Huntingdon.

almost as important as their upholding of the law. The Address by Hawkins, written in June 1882, would appear in all future editions of the *Code*, including the final version in 1931. In the years which followed, future editions of the *Code* saw various introductions and prefaces from the likes of Commissioner James Monro and his successor Edward Bradford, Assistant Commissioner Robert Anderson and Home Secretary Sir William Vernon Harcourt.

This all-encompassing reference book covered many offences for which an individual could be arrested. From the felony of bigamy to begging in the streets, all are included. One of the most frequent arrests constables made during the Victorian period - and any other for that matter - was for common burglary, also often referred to as breaking and entering.

Burglary was defined by the *Code* as the "breaking and entering, by night into, or out of, a dwelling house, with intent to commit a felony." An example of this can be seen during the early hours of 16th September 1887, when PC 240 H William Smith (on whose Berner Street beat Jack the Ripper victim Elisabeth Stride was to be found just over a year later) was patrolling near The Jews' Free School in Bell Lane, near Spitalfields Market. Here he noticed something suspicious. The *Code*'s guidance in connection with beat work, and more specifically building access points, was covered in the entry regarding 'Beats', with rule (g) clearly stating that constables were "to see that doors, window, gratings, cellar-flaps, fan-lights, and places through which a thief might enter, or obtain access, are not left open". Constable Smith was undoubtedly adhering to this guidance as he checked the school window to see if it was secure, before noticing the groove marks of a jemmy, a tell tale sign that something was amiss.

As Smith continued to examine the scene he heard a noise coming from inside. Not knowing what was to be expected on the other side of the glass pane, he immediately blew his whistle for assistance. Fellow Whitechapel Constable 226 H Thomas Barrett (who, ironically, was also to become embroiled in the investigation into the Whitechapel murders of 1888 when alleged victim Martha Tabram was found murdered on his beat in George Yard) came running to Smith's assistance. As the two constables debated a plan of action, three men, no doubt alerted by Constable Smith's whistle blasts, dropped down from a wall adjoining the school. The policemen pounced, and in the midst of their grappling restrained two burglars, with the third escaping into the dim gaslit streets. The constables marched their 'collars'[5] to Commercial Street Police Station, where the burglars were recorded as George Thompson, 22-years-old, and Alfred Lee, 18-years-old. A search revealed the incriminating evidence of a jemmy on Thompson's person, while Lee was found to be in the possession of a comb, an item later identified by the school's caretaker John Bennett as being stolen from the school's private room. The pair were held on remand while the hunt for the third man was stepped up.[6]

While the *Code* covered a wide range of circumstances and objects, none was more obscure than orange peel, which gets its own entry. Constables were expected to remove any pieces of orange peel found on the pavement, to avoid any accidents.[7] At the other end of the scale was the deadly serious, and perhaps nothing is more serious than an accusation of manslaughter against a police force set up to protect the public, typified in an event in 1887 known as the Mitchelstown Massacre.

Mitchelstown, a small agricultural town in the Munster province of Ireland, had been built around its 15th century castle which, by the late 1700s, had been pulled down and replaced with a mansion by the 2nd Earl of Kingston. Between 1879-1881 and again in 1886-1888 tenants who occupied land on the estate staged a series of rent strikes in protest of rent increases, imposed on them as a necessity to keep the estate financially afloat. Protests between 1879 and 1881 were successfully quelled by the then owner of the estate, who had borrowed £200,000 from the Disestablished Church against the estate mortgage to cover the maintenance costs.[8] The loan was, however, only a stop-gap solution and the matter arose yet again in 1886, by which time the estate had passed to the Dowager Countess of Kingston. Some tenants, with the blessing of their landlady, successfully sought a reduction in rent payment, but the majority were not so lucky and a series of protests arose throughout 1886

---

5 Police slang for an arrest.
6 *The Evening Standard,* 17th September 1887.
7 The fruit most often associated with pavement accidents, the banana, was not widely available in England until the turn of the twentieth century.
8 Testimony of Mr Henry Labouchere, *Te Aroha News,* 12th November 1887.

and 1887, culminating in an event which was to cost the lives of three men, with many more injured.

Tenants maintained the strike by constantly refusing to pay rent and barricaded themselves into their own homes once eviction notices were nailed upon their doors. The main instigators of the strike, local Members of Parliament William O'Brien and John Mendeville, were charged under William Gladstone's Protection of Person and Property Act of 1881 and summonsed to appear at Mitchelstown Magistrates Court. The men refused, stating that they did not recognise the jurisdiction of the magistrates involved. To coincide with the intended trial, a protest was organised on 9th September 1887 outside the court, in Mitchelstown's New Square. A series of speeches were arranged, and the protest was shadowed by the local constabulary, who were present both on the ground and observing from their barracks just across the square.

The Protection of Person and Property Act of 1881 decreed that any seditious speeches could lead to possible prosecution of the orator, so to gather evidence for a potential breaking of the law the constabulary attempted to place a note-taker in the midst of the crowd, right next to the platform. This drew an angry response from the protesters and they attacked the police with sticks and stones.

Seeing their colleagues under violent assault, the remaining constables on the ground drew their cutlasses and batons and waded into the crowd. The protesters rallied, repelling the constabulary out of the square and into the barracks. It was at this stage that some constables based inside the barracks, which was being pelted with stones and other missiles, opened fire out of fear of being overrun, an act which instantly left two men dead and scores of other protestors injured, with another man succumbing to his injuries in the aftermath. On hearing gun shots Magistrate Captain O'Neill Seagrave, who was in the vicinity because of the O'Brien and Mendeville hearing, made his way swiftly to New Square and upon viewing the scene before him read the Riot Act[9]

---

9 The Riot Act of 1714 enabled authorities to state that an assembly of twelve persons or more where events turn violent was illegal, and that the persons involved must disperse within the hour. Failure to comply with the Riot Act was deemed committing of a felony, resulting in the authorised use of strong force by the authorities.

and summoned military support to disperse the crowd.

An inquest into this awful event was arranged to be held in Mitchelstown itself in October 1887, during which the *Code* was to play an important part in the hearing. The issue concerned the firing of guns into the crowd by the police. Sergeant Kirwan claimed that his superior, Chief Inspector Brownrigg, ordered him to "go upstairs with six men and defend the barracks".[10] The *Code* stated that constables were permitted, as a very last resort, to open fire in defence of themselves, prisoners, the barracks, and arms held within those barracks; that firing was to be effective, namely only targeted at those perceived to be the ringleaders of the disturbance. Brownrigg claimed he did not give the order to defend the barracks, but witness statements seemed to contradict the Chief Inspector's recollection of events.

Ultimately, it was irrelevant who gave the order, for it was clear that the barracks were indeed under attack, and therefore Sergeant Kirwan's order to open fire was legally justified, if morally questionable. Those constables who opened fire were cautioned, and reminded of their responsibility "to preserve the utmost forbearance that humanity, combined with prudence, could dictate".[11]

On this occasion, the guidance given in the *Code* was followed. However, as Howard Vincent maintained, his book was just that - guidance - and he acknowledged that specific events must always be judged and acted upon depending on the scenario's individual merit. One suspects the caution issued to the constables who opened fire in Mitchelstown was to highlight the salient point that the individual constable is, ultimately, responsible for his own actions, and not the *Code*.

* * *

Drunkenness was, and still is, the main cause of petty crime, particularly with regard to the misdemeanour of assault. During the Victorian period alcohol was cheap, healthier to consume than water, and, as we know, highly addictive. This resulted in an 1889 annual return by H Division (Whitechapel) which revealed that some 2,300 people had been apprehended for drunkenness that

---

10 *Gloucester Citizen*, 4th October 1887.
11 Ibid.

year alone. The *Code* covers drink numerous times throughout its pages, and even gives guidance on drunkenness within specific vocations such as cabmen and postmen. Though occurring many years later the following bizarre yet comical exchange concerning public drunkenness comes from the inside pages of the *Nottingham Evening Post* of 3rd April 1923:

> *"Can a man who remains in full possession of his faculties, but loses the control of his legs, be said to be drunk?"* was the problem presented to Mr H G Rooth at Lambeth police court yesterday, when a Vauxhall labourer was charged with being drunk and incapable.
>
> A constable said the man's brain was clear but the legs had given way. "Some people get drunk in their heads and some in their legs" he said.
>
> Mr Rooth: The liquor, of course, goes into a man's stomach and not into his head or legs! I want to know whether a man whose brain is perfectly clear is drunk. Is there any definition in the Police Code?
>
> Inspector Kemp: I don't think there is.
>
> Accused: I am bad on my legs, and when I get a glass of ale I am worse.
>
> Mr Rooth (to the accused): I think you may be said to be overcome by drink. You will be fines 5s or one day.

It seems that many, including Magistrate Rooth, would turn to the *Code* for an explanation on almost any matter, including the medical conundrum on how the brain (or more importantly in this case, the legs) would be affected by alcohol.

At dinner parties Howard Vincent would often gleefully recall a tale of a constable patrolling the clubland of London's West End when he came across a drunken man supporting himself against a gas lamppost. The constable engaged the man in conversation with the intent of moving him along. As time progressed and the drunk did not move, the constable became increasingly frustrated at the drunk's obfuscation and general unwillingness to co-operate, and this frustration turned to tetchiness with the man propped up against the lamppost. Noting the policeman's irritation, the drunk began fumbling in his pocket and produced a small red-covered book, from which he began to quote, and, with all the vigour of a preacher delivering a sermon read the following passage to the perplexed constable: "Whatever duty you may be called upon to perform, *keep a curb on your temper*. An angry man is as unfit for duty as a drunken one". The passage was a direct quote from Sir Henry Hawkins' Address to Police Constables, found on page eleven of *A Police Code*, the very book the drunk was holding.

Howard Vincent's vision of a tome to be used by all was never more so beautifully illustrated.

Along with directions on how a constable should execute his duties, the *Code* also highlighted the common faults "most likely to be committed, and against which young constables should particularly guard..." These faults - around thirty in all - listed under Misconduct of Police, range from drunkenness to bringing discredit to the police force, and include taking off the armlet (the wearing of which being a sign a constable was on duty) in order to obtain drink from a publican, quarrelling with comrades and incurring debt. Along with these faults are listed the related disciplinary punishments. Again, these range from being charged before a Magistrate, with potential hard labour or imprisonment, to reprimand and a simple caution.

Along with guidance on execution of day-to-day duties and the perils of not adhering to the requirements of a constable, the *Code* would also be referred to by constables looking for direction on the more obscure.

Although a rare crime during the Victorian era, murder naturally caught the public's attention. It is a crime described in the *Code* as "unlawful homicide with malice aforethought, and its punishment is death". Given the seriousness of this most heinous of crimes, the reader will not be surprised to note that the entry on it within the *Code* is a lengthy one, although not the longest.

The *Code* gives instruction with regards management and investigation in a murder case, and we can cite the Jack the Ripper case of 1888 as a fine example. Howard Vincent's guidance on how to initially handle a murder investigation can be found within two entries entitled 'Dead Bodies' and 'Murder', and we can see how this advice manifests into action upon the discovery of many of the Ripper's victims.

When he came across the body of Mary Ann Nichols, just off the Whitechapel Road on the last day of August 1888, J Division Constable John Neil was initially unsure whether a murder had taken place.[12] He therefore followed the *Code*'s 'Dead Bodies' protocol, which stated that "When a dead body is found, and there is no doubt that life is extinct, it should never be touched until the arrival of a constable, who should forthwith carefully note its appearance, and all surrounding it".

PC Neil duly noted the position of the woman's body, its location outside a gated stable yard and the fact that her left hand rested against the gate. Constable Neil also noted her clothing, including the fact her bonnet had fallen and was located just off her head.

When he inspected the body directly, however, Neil spotted something which promoted suspicion above that of someone who had died of exposure. The experienced constable noticed blood oozing and gathering upon the pavement around her neck and, following directions in the *Code*'s 'Dead Bodies' entry,[13] he saw that her eyes were indeed "dim and glassy". The evidence suggested the woman was dead, and on closure inspection Constable Neil found that her throat had been savagely cut, meaning that Neil moved swiftly from the dead bodies procedure to that of murder.

The *Code*, in reference to murder, decreed that "when a dead body is found, whereof the cause of death was evidently due to foul means, the constable whose attention is first called thereto should on no account move it or anything surrounding it". It also stated that a superior officer, preferably an Inspector, should be sent for, as well as a surgeon.

By this stage Constable Neil had signalled his adjacent beat officer, Constable John Thain, by means of his bullseye lamp, and sent his J Division colleague to fetch the nearest surgeon, Dr Ralph Rees Llewellyn. The next aiding policeman to arrive on the scene, H Division's Jonas Mizen, was sent to Neil's own police station in Bethnal Green to bring back a superior officer and handcart ambulance.[14]

---

12 Mary Ann Nichols was actually first discovered by two passing carmen, who reported their find to the nearest constable. PC Neil, unaware of this, acted as he should have as first on the scene.

13 Section 2, sub-section (c) to be precise, which was guidance for constables on signs of death.

Also contained within the 'Murder' entry is guidance for inspectors and surgeons on what to do upon arrival at the scene. Again taking a murder from the Whitechapel series of 1888, that of Catherine Eddowes, we see that the first inspector and surgeon upon the scene, City of London Police Inspector Edward Collard and Divisional Surgeon Dr F G Brown, both adhere to this guidance, specifically the six points of observation of the body and the scene, namely that they should pay attention...

a) For any footmarks about the body, which should be modelled or covered over before fresh imprints are made by the Surgeon or the police.
b) Of the position of the body.
c) Of the condition of its clothing.
d) Of the position of the wound, and judging by the body and clothing, in what way, and from which quarter, and with what instrument, and under what circumstances it was probably inflicted.
e) Whether the murderer has left his weapon or any trace of his identity in the vicinity of the body.
f) Whether there is in the pockets, or about the person of the deceased, any paper or article disclosing his identity, if unknown, or the name of his probable murderer, or any circumstances pointing in any particular direction.

Inspector Collard's testimony given at the inquest into Eddowes' murder shows that the above guidance was followed dutifully by the City of London officer, despite it being laid down by the former Head of the CID of London's other police force, the Metropolitan Police.

The following exchange between Inspector Collard, Coroner Langham and City of London Police Solicitor Crawford shows how the former worked within *A Police Code*'s observation of murdered body guidelines:

Collard - The body was not touched until the arrival shortly afterwards of Dr Brown. The medical gentleman examined the body, and in my presence Sergeant Jones picked up

---

14 Mizen had been notified of the incident in Buck's Row by two passing carmen, the initial finders of Nichols' body.

from the footway by the left side of the deceased three small black buttons, such as are generally used for boots, a small metal button, a common metal thimble, and a small penny mustard tin containing two pawn-tickets. They were handed to me. The doctors remained until the arrival of the ambulance, and saw the body placed in the conveyance. It was then taken to the mortuary, and stripped by Mr Davis, the mortuary keeper, in presence of the two doctors and myself. I have a list of articles of clothing more or less stained with blood and cut.

Coroner - Was there any money about her? - No; no money whatever was found. A piece of cloth was found in Goulston-street, corresponding with the apron worn by the deceased. When I got to the square I took immediate steps to have the neighbourhood searched for the person who committed the murder. Mr M'Williams, chief of the Detective Department, on arriving shortly afterwards sent men to search in all directions in Spitalfields, both in streets and lodging-houses. Several men were stopped and searched in the streets, without any good result. I have had a house-to-house inquiry made in the vicinity of Mitre-square as to any noises or whether persons were seen in the place; but I have not been able to find any beyond the witnesses who saw a man and woman talking together.

Crawford (City of London Police Solicitor) - Was there any sign of a struggle having taken place? - None whatever. I made a careful inspection of the ground all round. There was no trace whatever of any struggle. There was nothing in the appearance of the woman, or of the clothes, to lead to the idea that there had been any struggle. From the fact that the blood was in a liquid state I conjectured that the murder had not been long previously committed. In my opinion the body had not been there more than a quarter of an hour. I endeavoured to trace footsteps, but could find no trace whatever. The backs of the empty houses adjoining were searched, but nothing was found.[15]

---

15 Inquest report into the murder of Catherine Eddowes, *Daily Telegraph*, 5th October 1888.

***

Although he had left the Metropolitan Police in 1884, the welfare of those children orphaned by the loss of their fathers who served as officers remained close to Howard Vincent's heart, and he continued to make donations for many years.

Now, near the end of his life, an ailing Howard Vincent sought to secure the Fund's financial future. According to his solicitor, arrangements had already been made regarding future profits, with the former Director of Criminal Investigations bequeathing the copyright of the *Code* to "the Commissioner of the Police of the Metropolis", and expressing a desire that his copyright successors would continue to have "fresh Editions [sic] of it published from time to time" and "apply the profits to the Metropolitan & City Police Orphanage".[16]

Although the *Code* had been revised numerous times during Howard Vincent's lifetime in order to incorporate revisions of law, the actual main guidance content had remained untouched in the three years following his death in 1908. By 1911 it was apparent that a new edition was required and with it came new publishers, Messrs Butterworth & Co. of Bell Yard, Temple, who took over from Cassell & Co. An agreement between Butterworth & Co. and the Metropolitan Police was entered into, with Assistant Commissioner Major Sir Frederick Wodehouse[17] taking on the responsibility of compiling the new edition. Butterworths promised to pay the Orphanage "a scale of royalties graduated to the sale of the book", with Clause 3 laying out that percentage as between 10% for the first 4,000 copies and 20% for every 1,000 sold after that.[18]

New amendments to law resulted in new editions of the *Code* in 1912 (15th edition) and in 1924 (16th edition), the final amendment for some years. Matters came to a head in 1931 upon the publication of the 17th edition, when the holder of the Metropolitan Police purse strings, Receiver Sir John Moylan,

---

16 MEPO 2/7153. Letter to Metropolitan Police Commissioner Sir Edward Henry from Sir Howard Vincent's solicitors, Bray & Warren, 19th June 1908.

17 Major Sir Edwin Frederick Wodehouse (1851-1934) served as Assistant Commissioner in the City of London Police Force before transferring to the Metropolitan Police.

18 MEPO 7/7153. G.R. 24/OP/402 (L929-1935).

noted that despite selling around 13,000 copies that year, only £400 was received by the Orphanage whereas the publishers, Messrs Butterworth & Co, recovered over twice that amount.[19] This flew in the face of Howard Vincent's insistence that the Orphanage Fund should be the chief beneficiary, or receive at least an equal share. At the same time, one simple, yet seemingly sinister fact was not lost on the Metropolitan Police: Butterworth & Co. also published a rival book to the *Code*, C C H Moriarty's *Police Law*.

Cecil Charles Hudson Moriarty hailed from imperial Irish stock, born in Tralee in 1877 to Reverend Thomas Alexander Moriarty. He graduated with a Law Doctorate from Trinity College, Dublin, in 1898 and joined the Royal Irish Constabulary the following year. Shortly afterwards a 22-year-old Moriarty represented the Irish Rugby Union team in their Home Nations Championship game against Wales in front of 40,000 people in Cardiff. The Welsh won narrowly, three-nil, in what seems to have been a dull affair, and the debutant Monkstown No. 8 must have made little impression on the selectors, as Moriarty was never selected to play for Ireland again.[20]

Four months after Moriarty gained his one and only cap for Ireland, Belfast man Sir Charles Haughton Rafter was appointed Chief Constable of the Birmingham City Police Force. Rafter joined the police as a Gentleman Cadet in the Royal Irish Constabulary, and was one of the first to patrol Dublin's Phoenix Park after the infamous 1882 murders of Lord Frederick Cavendish and Under Secretary Thomas Henry Burke. He went on to serve this Midlands city with great dignity for over thirty-five years.

In 1918, during a Chief Constables Association meeting Rafter raised his concerns regarding a constable's execution of an arrest, stating that he "did not know of any book published for the use of English police forces which gives full and adequate instruction on this subject".[21] Fundamentally Rafter was correct, as Howard Vincent's *Police Code* merely covered four points of arrest execution and did not provide a detailed list of powers of law to support the reasoning behind the arrest, as it was expected of the constable to be comprehensively aware of the precise law he was upholding.

---

19 MEPO 7/7153. G.R. 24/OP/402 (L929-1935).
20 ESPN Ireland Players & Officials: Cecil Moriarty.

By this time, Moriarty had risen through the ranks of the Royal Irish Constabulary and had successfully applied for the newly-created Assistant Chief Constable vacancy in the Birmingham City Police Force, a post which put him as assistant to Rafter.

Borne out of the strike action undertaken by members of the National Union of Police and Prison Officers (NUPPO) throughout 1918 and 1919, the Police Act of 1919 banned the membership of police officers of any trade union. However, the Act also improved employment conditions for the police, and enforced a standardisation across England and Wales. It was the introduction of this Act which, unbeknownst to the Metropolitan Police force, would lead to a drawn-out funeral procession for *A Police Code* and, ultimately, the slow strangulation of donations to the Metropolitan and City Police Orphanage and Fund.

Moriarty noted that standardisation brought a necessity for professionalism and, equally as important, a transparency within all police constabularies. He therefore formed a concept for a single publication which would be both a training aid for new recruits and a thorough reference book for the more established constable.[22] Initially Moriarty part-trialled his idea in two police publications, *The Police Journal* and *Police Review*, before sitting down and writing his book fully, which was to be titled *Police Law: An Arrangement of Law and Regulations for the Use of Police Officers*.

This new guidance book was extremely detailed. Broken down into thirty-nine chapters with three appendices, a table of statutes, cases and an index as well as notes on emergency legislation, it was set out in a similar manner to Howard Vincent's *Police Code*. However, unlike the *Code*, *Police Law* consisted of six sections containing the relevant procedures, regulation and legislation pertaining to those sections, which were:

1) Legal Principles, Procedure and Evidence
2) Offences against persons
3) Offences in connection with property
4) Offences effecting the community in general

---

21 C C H Moriarty: *Police Law* (Butterworth & Co.), 1929.
22 Professor Carl Chinn MBE: *Birmingham Irish: Making our Mark* (Birmingham City Council), 2003.

5) Traffic law
6) Other statutory offences and regulations

Another difference was that instead of just scenarios and offences listed in alphabetical order, the relative laws were also cited as an aid for the constable who would be able to pinpoint the exact legality upon which he was making the arrest.

Butterworth & Co. published the first edition of Moriarty's *Police Law* in 1929, pitting it against another of its own publications, Howard Vincent's *Police Code*. It is clear, when reading through the MEPO files on the *Code*, that the Metropolitan Police felt that the publisher favoured the more modern *Police Law*, an understandable conclusion when one analyses the evidence. Whilst *Police Law* was a larger publication, it was far more detailed than the *Code*, reducing the need for supplementary publications, some of which were published by rival publishing houses or the government's own stationers. *Police Law* returned a larger profit, primarily due to the attraction of an all-encompassing and precisely detailed book, which was more expensive to purchase than the *Code*.

The agreement between Moriarty and Butterworths was also straightforward; there was no charitable payment to be made to the Widows and Orphans Fund. Taking all these facts into consideration, one can understand why Butterworths favoured Moriarty's modern book to Howard Vincent's more dated work; it was sound business sense to do so. The difficulty Butterworth & Co. had was that the largest police force in the Empire, the Metropolitan Police, remained fiercely loyal to the *Police Code*. Throughout the 1930s the Metropolitan force felt Howard Vincent's work was still sufficient for the task and would not turn to Moriarty's *Police Law*, not to mention the Met's dedication in maintaining a steady succession of donations to the Widows and Orphans Fund.

The fact remained, however, that following the introduction of Moriarty's work, sales of the *Code* declined until, upon the outbreak of the Second World War, and after fifty years of continuous use, the Metropolitan Police did the unthinkable and stopped using Howard Vincent's *Police Code*.

The end was messy, drawn out and confusing. Just two years after Moriarty's work first appeared in 1931, the Metropolitan Police noticed that Butterworth & Co. made an approximated profit on the *Code* of around £800, whereas the Widows and Orphanage Fund, which was meant to be the principle beneficiary, received £400. The Metropolitan Police instructed their solicitors to who investigate the original contract with Butterworths.

A major problem centred on Clause 6 of the original 1911 agreement, which read: "It is agreed that the said Messrs Butterworth & Co shall have the right of publishing all future editions of the work on terms to be hereinafter agreed upon",[23] suggesting that Butterworth & Co. could argue that they were the copyright holders. Confusion reigned within the office of Ellis & Ellis, solicitors for the Metropolitan Police, as they were unsure upon the proper definition of that particular Clause, and as a result, who actually owned the copyright to the *Code*.

The 1911 Copyright Act, Section 3, stipulated that copyright ownership lay with the author and his estate for fifty years after the author's date of death. However, upon his death in 1908 (therefore prior to the 1911 Copyright Act) Howard Vincent passed copyright on to the Commissionership of the Metropolitan Police. Metropolitan Police solicitor G R Ellis Danvers argued, in an internal 1935 legal report on the matter, that any assignment made after the death of the original author, Howard Vincent, legally should be declared null and void twenty five years after said death,[24] meaning that the contract between the Commissionership and Butterworth & Co. was actually invalid as from 1933.[25]

The fact that the matter was still being internally investigated by the Metropolitan Police in 1935, some four years after the subject was first raised, gives an indication that they were not wholly sure of the legal footing they were standing upon. To avoid a legal minefield suggestions were made to either trigger Clause 10 of the 1911 publishing agreement, which laid out procedures

---

23 MEPO 7/7153. Memorandum of Agreement between Sir Edwin Frederick Wodehouse, Acting Commissioner of New Scotland Yard, and Messrs. Butterworth & Co., of 11 & 12 Bell Yard, London.

24 MEPO 7/7153. G.R. 24/OP/402 (L929-1935).

25 The 1889 edition of the *Police Code*, which we have used in this book, was therefore initially under the copyright of Howard Vincent for fifty years after his death (ie to 1958), although the 1911 Copyright Act stated that as copyright had been assigned to another party (in this case the Commissioner of the Metropolitan Police), the copyright was valid for 25 years, not 50, therefore expiring in 1933.

for settlement by arbitration, or alternatively to enter into fresh negotiations on a completely new contract.

The Metropolitan Police initially did neither and dallied on making a decision. They were unsure if triggering Clause 10, with its associated legal action, was worth the cost. While the dispute with Butterworth & Co. lingered, sales of Moriarty's *Police Law* had been increasing annually, whereas sales of *A Police Code* had being running in the opposite direction. In the late summer of 1935 Secretary of the Metropolitan Police Office Sir Hamilton Howgrave-Graham instructed the force's solicitors, Ellis & Ellis, that they would "have to stand out for better terms when the question of a new edition arises, and then reconsider the position according to the outcome of negotiations".[26]

Those fresh negotiations between the Metropolitan Police and Butterworth & Co. were delayed yet another four years before commencing in the late summer of 1939. However, the announcement on 3rd September of hostilities with Germany scuppered plans for a revised edition and, in fact, sounded the final death knell for *A Police Code* itself.

Just over a fortnight after this declaration of War, Scotland Yard received a letter from the Publishing Director of Butterworth & Co., which read:

> Dear Sir
>
> VINCENT'S POLICE CODE
>
> *With reference to the recent interview between yourself and my representative, when the possibility of a new edition of the above book was discussed, I presume that now we are at war, this matter will be shelved for the duration of hostilities. If and when peace comes again, we can meet mutually to agree about the course to be taken.*
>
> *Yours faithfully*
> *BUTTERWORTH & CO (Publishers) LTD*[27]

---

26 MEPO 7/7153. Letter from Metropolitan Police Secretary Sir Hamilton Howgrave-Graham to Metropolitan Police Solicitor Mr G.R. Ellis-Danvers of Ellis & Ellis, 17th August 1935.

27 MEPO 7/7153. 24/DP/402. Letter from Butterworth & Co. to Scotland Yard, 14th September 1939.

This letter ended all possibility of any future discussion of Howard Vincent's *Police Code*, with the blame placed squarely on the unpredictability of War. Once hostilities ended, it was clear to all that *Moriarty's Police Law* was far more suited for the modern police world, and the 1931 edition of *A Police Code* was the last. *Moriarty's* followed the *Code's* longevity, and would be published for over fifty years before ceasing in 1981.

The trail of these police guidance books ends with the ultimate guide for all policemen and women of today, the *Police and Criminal Evidence Act*, better known as PACE, which was introduced in 1984 as a result of the Scarman report into the 1981 Brixton riots in Greater London. However, one must not forget that these publications all evolved from Sir Charles Edward Howard Vincent's germ of an idea to provide guidance on police conduct and execution of duty, for all citizens.

A Police Code and General Manual of the Criminal Law for The British Empire was of its time, and captures the Victorian and Edwardian period not just in relation to the Metropolitan Police, but also of the public and day-to-day life during those eras.

It provides an excellent insight into policing of the time, and takes one back to a world where the contrast of fortunes in human life was never more profound. It existed in the period of extreme hardship and also extreme wealth, where the poor and rich mingled, where the honest hard-working populace and victims of misfortune mixed with chance takers and criminals; and, perhaps, shows that life was not really much different from today.

It is worth remembering, perhaps with a chill as one thumbs through the following pages, that *A Police Code* was used by policemen investigating such infamous crimes as the horrific baby farming atrocities committed by Amelia Dyer, the Lambeth poisonings of Dr Thomas Neil Cream, and probably the most notorious murderer of them all, the uncatchable serial killer known only as Jack the Ripper. And while we recall the heinous acts inflicted upon one human being by another, it is also worth remembering the men who had to deal with those crimes in an attempt to bring the perpetrators to justice, as well as protect a populace from the evil that others do, sometimes paying the highest price.

It is now time to take a step back in time.

Colonel Sir Charles Edward Howard Vincent

Cover of the first edition of *A Police Code*
Courtesy Metropolitan Police Crime Museum

Lieutenant-Colonel Sir Edmund Yeamans Walcott Henderson,
Commissioner of the Metropolitan Police in 1870

Minute recording the appointment of C E Howard Vincent
to Chairman of the Metropolitan and City Police Orphanage

GROUP OF CHILDREN

OF THE

𝔐etropolitan and 𝔈ity 𝔓olice 𝔒rphanage.

BYRNE & C°.  HILL STREET,
PHOTOGRAPHERS. RICHMOND.

© Metropolitan and City Police Orphans Fund

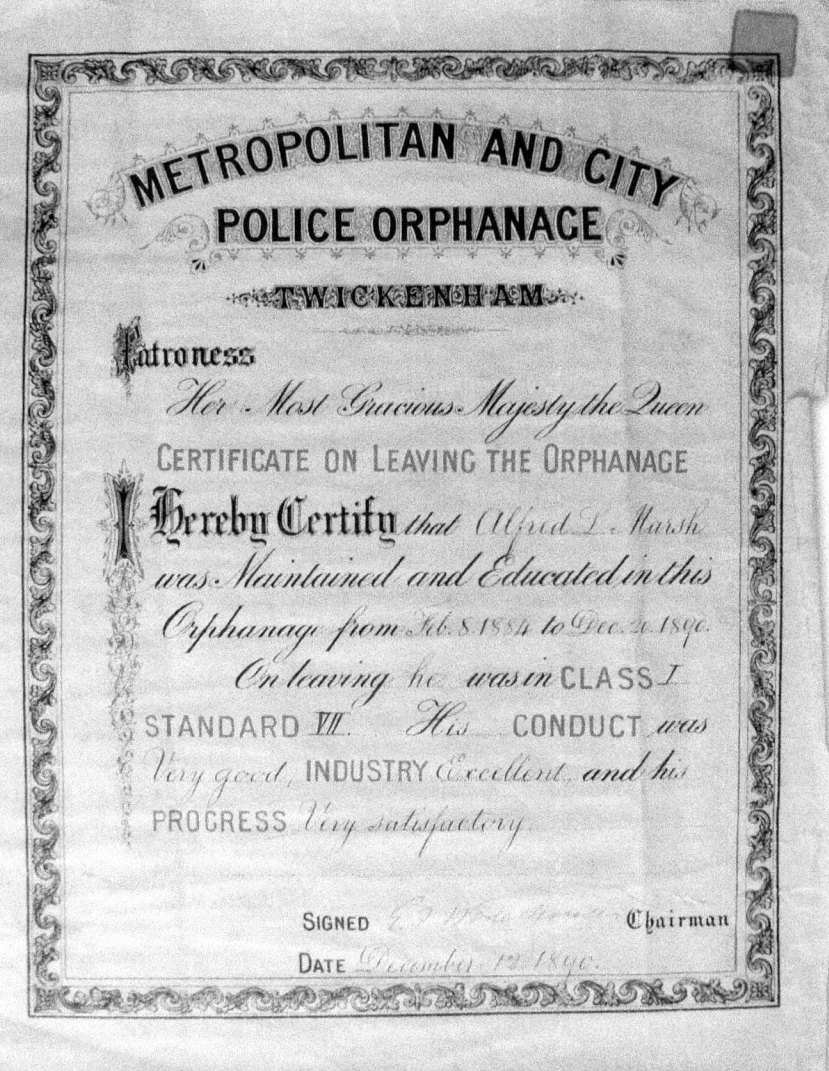

Arthur Kestin, Secretary of the Metropolitan and City Police Orphanage in 1889

James Monro, Commissioner of the Metropolitan Police, who wrote a Preface for the 1889 edition of *A Police Code*

The Hon. Sir Henry Hawkins, later Lord Brampton,
who prepared the Address to Constables for the *Police Code*

A POLICE CODE,

AND

General Manual of the Criminal Law

FOR THE BRITISH EMPIRE.

BY

C. E. HOWARD VINCENT, ESQ., C.B., M.P.,

Deputy-Lieutenant for London, a Justice of the Peace for Middlesex and
Berkshire, a Member of the London County Council,
And formerly
Director of Criminal Investigations, Metropolitan Police.

PRECEDED BY

AN ADDRESS TO CONSTABLES ON THEIR DUTIES,

BY

THE HONOURABLE SIR HENRY HAWKINS,

One of Her Majesty's Judges.

AND

A PREFACE BY

JAMES MONRO, ESQ., C.B.,

The Commissioner of Police of the Metropolis.

———◆◆◆———

1889.

PREFACE
BY
JAMES MONRO, ESQ., C.B.,
Commissioner of Police of the Metropolis.

AMONGST the subjects which claim the attention of any one interested in the well-being and efficiency of our Police Force, there is none of greater importance than the education and legal training of the officers and men who compose it. Important, however, as this subject is, the acquisition of such legal knowledge as is necessary is by no means an easy matter for police. Our criminal law and procedure is still in an uncodified state, and a young policeman wishing to ascertain his legal duties in connection with the multifarious cases constantly coming under his notice has no inconsiderable difficulties to contend with. Any publication, therefore, which simplifies these difficulties — which acts, so to speak, as an interpreter of the numerous statutes dealing with matters of police action, and which aids the members of our Police Force in acquiring a knowledge of the law — must be welcomed as a gain to the public and to the police. The abridged Code of Mr. Howard Vincent, the first Director of Criminal Investigations, Metropolitan Police, was originally designed by its author as a practical help to police officers in their legal education. It has now been before the public and in use amongst police forces for several years; and the fact that a sixth edition of the work is now called for testifies more forcibly than any words of mine can do to the need which this publication was meant to supply, and to the successful way in which by the Code such need has been met.

J. MONRO,
Commissioner of Police of the Metropolis.

March, 1889.

AN ADDRESS

TO

POLICE CONSTABLES ON THEIR DUTIES,

BY

THE HONOURABLE SIR HENRY HAWKINS,

One of Her Majesty's Judges.

———◆———

IN the few words I purpose addressing to you, it is not my intention to define every duty of a Police Constable, but rather to point out some matters which all who desire to become good officers ought constantly to bear in mind, for by strict attention to them every man may assuredly raise himself to a high position in the force, and by neglect of them he is equally sure always to occupy a low one.

First of all, let me impress upon you the necessity of absolute obedience to all who are placed in authority over you, and rigid observance of every regulation made for your general conduct. Such obedience and observance I regard as essential to the existence of a Police Force. Obey every order given to you by your superior officer without for a moment questioning the propriety of it. You are not responsible for the order, but for obedience. In yielding obedience let the humblest member of the force feel that by good conduct and cheerful submission he may himself rise to be placed in authority to give those orders he is now called on to obey. As to the Regulations, a single moment's reflection will teach you that when so many men of different classes and habits are enrolled in one service, some rules applicable to all are necessary for the purpose of ensuring uniformity in discipline, action, conduct, and appearance, therefore it is that there are regulations exacting sobriety, punctuality, cleanliness, and many other matters to which I need not refer.

The slightest disobedience in one begets a bad example to others, and if this bad example is followed by a few, it is calculated to disorganise and bring discredit upon the whole body.

Let me now say something to each of you as to the mode in which your obligations to the public ought to be performed. Depend upon it, to become a good and efficient officer you must, *when on duty, allow nothing but your duty to occupy your thoughts.* You must studiously avoid all gossiping. You must not lounge about as though your sole object was to amuse yourself and kill the hours during which the public has a right to your best services, and during which constant vigilance and attention to what is passing around you is expected from you. It is this gossiping lounging habit which sometimes gives rise to the observation that a policeman is never to be found when he is most wanted. Moreover, a man who gives way to such a habit never observes with so much accuracy that which occurs before his eyes, as he who makes it his endeavour to fix his attention upon all that is passing about him. This is a habit not difficult to acquire if you are in earnest, and when once acquired you will find the cultivation of it a source of pleasure, and the hours of duty will be much less irksome. I may add, too, that the man who takes no pains to acquire this habit, for want of attention, generally makes a very bad and inaccurate witness.

I wish you to feel the importance of a steady constant *endeavour by your vigilance to prevent crime* as much as possible, and not by your negligence tempt persons to commit it; as you do if you fail in attention to your duty. To my mind the constable who keeps his beat free from crime deserves much more credit than he does who only counts up the number of convictions he has obtained for offences committed within it. It is true the latter makes more show than the former, but the former is the better officer. The great object of the law is to *prevent* crime; and when many crimes are committed in any particular district one is apt to suspect that there has been something defective in the amount of vigilance exercised over it.

Whatever duty you may be called on to perform, *keep a curb on your temper*. An angry man is as unfit for duty as a drunken one, and is incapable of calmly exercising that discretion which a constable is so often called on to exercise. *Be civil and listen respectfully* to everybody who addresses you; and if occasionally you are remonstrated with for the course you are taking, do not hastily jump to the conclusion, as some constables do, that the person who so remonstrates wishes to obstruct you in the execution of your duty.

Beware of being over-zealous or meddlesome. These are dangerous faults. Let your anxiety be to do your duty, but no more. A meddlesome constable who interferes unnecessarily upon every trifling occasion stirs up ill-feeling against the force, and does more harm than good. An over-zealous man, who is always thinking of himself, and desiring to call attention to his own activity, is very likely to fall into a habit of exaggeration, which is a fatal fault, as I shall presently show you.

Much power is vested in a police constable, and many opportunities are given him to be hard and oppressive, especially to those in his custody. Pray avoid harshness and oppression; be firm but not brutal, make only discreet use of your powers. If one person wishes to give another into your custody for felony you are not absolutely *bound* to arrest. You ought to exercise your discretion, having regard to the nature of the crime, the surrounding circumstances, and the condition and character of the accuser and the accused.

Be very careful to distinguish between cases of illness and drunkenness. Many very serious errors have been committed for want of care in this respect.

Much discussion has on various occasions arisen touching the conduct of the police in listening to, and repeating statements of, accused persons. I will try, therefore, to point out what I think is the proper course for a constable to take with regard to such statements.

When a crime has been committed, and you are engaged in endeavouring to discover the author of it, there is no objection to your making inquiries of, or putting questions to, *any person* from whom you think you can obtain useful information. It is your duty to discover the criminal if you can, and to do this you must make such inquiries, and if in the course of them you should chance to interrogate and to receive answers from a man who turns out to be the criminal himself, and who inculpates himself by these answers, they are nevertheless admissible in evidence, and may be used against him.

When, however, a constable has a warrant to arrest, or *is about to arrest a person* on his own authority, or has a person in custody for a crime, it is wrong to question such person touching the crime of which he is accused. Neither judge, magistrate, or juryman, can interrogate an accused person, and require him to answer questions tending to criminate himself. Much less, then, ought a constable to do so, whose duty as regards that person is simply to arrest and detain him in safe custody. On arresting a man a constable ought simply to read his warrant, or tell the accused the nature of the charge upon which he is arrested, leaving it to the person so arrested to say anything or nothing as he pleases. For a constable to press any accused person to say anything with reference to the crime of which he is accused is very wrong. It is well also, that it should be generally known that if a statement made by an accused person is made under or in consequence of any promise or threat, even though it amounts to an absolute confession, it cannot be used against the person making it. There is, however, no objection to a constable listening to any mere voluntary statement which a prisoner desires to make, and repeating such statement in evidence; nor is there any objection to his repeating in evidence any conversation he may have heard between the prisoner and any other person. But he ought not, by anything he says or does, to invite or encourage an accused person to make any statement, without first cautioning him that he is not bound to say anything tending to criminate himself, and that anything he says may be used against him. Perhaps the best maxim for a constable to bear in mind with respect to an accused person is, "Keep your eyes and your ears open, and your mouth shut." By silent watchfulness you will hear all you ought to hear. Never act unfairly to a prisoner by *coaxing* him by word or conduct to divulge anything. If you do, you will assuredly be severely handled at the trial, and it is not unlikely your evidence will be disbelieved.

In detailing any conversation with an accused person, be sure to state the whole conversation from the commencement to the end in the very words used; and in narrating facts, state every fact whether you think it material or not, for you are not the judge of its materiality. Tell, in short, everything; as well that which is in favour of an accused, as that which is against him, for your desire and anxiety must be to *be fair*, and assist the innocent, and not convict any man by unfair means, such as by suppressing something which may tell in his favour, even though you feel certain of his guilt. Unfairness is sure to bring discredit upon those who are guilty of it. If an accused in a conversation with you states any circumstances which you have the means of inquiring into, you ought, whether those circumstances are in his favour or against him, to make such inquiry, and the witnesses who can prove or disprove the truth of the statement ought to be taken before the magistrate when the accused is examined; and if an accused person desires to call witnesses, the police should assist him to the best of their power.

I cannot too strongly recommend every constable, however good he may fancy his memory to be, to write down *word for word* every syllable of every conversation in which an accused has taken a part, and of every statement made to him by an accused person, and to have that written memorandum with him at the trial.

The last but most important duty I would enjoin upon you is, on every occasion " SPEAK THE TRUTH, THE WHOLE TRUTH, AND NOTHING BUT THE TRUTH." Let no considerations, no anxiety to appear of importance in a case, no desire to procure a conviction or an acquittal, no temptation of any sort, induce you ever to swerve one hair's-breadth from the truth—the bare, plain, simple truth. Never exaggerate, or in repeating a conversation or statement add a tone or colour to it. Exaggeration is often even more dangerous than direct falsehood, for it is an addition of a false colour to truth; it is something more than the truth, and it is most dangerous, because it is difficult to detect and separate that which is exaggeration from that which is strictly true; and a man who exaggerates is very apt to be led on to say that which he knows to be false. On the other hand, suppress no part of a conversation or statement, nor any tone or action which accompanies it, for everything you suppress is short of the whole truth. Remember always what reliance is of necessity placed in courts of justice upon the testimony of policemen, and bear constantly in mind that in many cases the fate of an accused man, which means his life or his liberty, depends upon that testimony, and seriously reflect how fearful a thing it is for a man to be convicted and put to death, or condemned to penal servitude or imprisonment, upon false testimony. Remember, also, when you are giving evidence, that you are not the person appointed to determine the guilt or the innocence of a person on his trial, nor have you any right to express an opinion upon the subject. Your duty is a very simple and easy one, namely, to tell the Court all you know. The responsibility of the verdict, whether it be guilty or not guilty, rests entirely with the jury or the magistrate (if the case is tried in a police court), and they have a right to expect from you everything within your knowledge to enable them to form a just conclusion. It is right I should tell you that wilfully to tell a falsehood, or pervert the truth in a court of justice is **PERJURY**; and you all know perjury is a crime punishable with seven years' penal servitude, and your own common sense will tell you that when perjury is committed by an officer of justice he deserves and ought to receive a very severe sentence. Resolve, then, on every occasion to tell the plain, unbiassed, unvarnished truth in all things, even though it may for a moment expose you to censure or mortification, or defeat the object or expectations of those by whom you are called as a witness. Depend upon it, such censure or mortification will be as nothing compared to the character you will earn for yourself as a truthful, reliable man, whose word can always be implicitly depended upon, and the very mortification you endure will be a useful warning to you to avoid in the future the error you have candidly confessed.

I could write a great deal more on the subjects I have touched, but then my address to you would be too long for this useful work, which is intended for your guide, and wherein you will find your duties upon various occasions more fully defined. I have only endeavoured in a few friendly sentences to point out to you a line of conduct, the steady adoption of which will enable every man in the Police Service to feel that he is on the high-road to all that he can desire, having regard to the important and very responsible calling he has selected for himself.

H. HAWKINS.

June 5, 1882.

POLICE CODE.

———:o:———

Abandoning Children.—Every one who unlawfully abandons any child under the age of two years, whereby the life of such child is endangered, commits a misdemeanor. (24 & 25 Vict., c. 100, s. 27.)

***Abduction.**—1. *Of Girls under Eighteen.*—To take out of the possession of a parent or lawful guardian, against his or her will, any unmarried girl under eighteen years of age, is a misdemeanor. (CRIMINAL LAW AMENDMENT ACT, 1885.)

2. *Abduction of a Woman.*—If, with intent to marry or carnally know any woman, or cause her to be married or carnally known, by any person, a woman, of any age, is *by force* taken away, or detained, against her will, it is felony.

Abortion.—1. Abortion is the unlawful taking or administration of poison, or other noxious thing, or the unlawful use of any instrument, or other means whatsoever, with intent to procure miscarriage. It is a felony, and if death ensues, it becomes murder. To supply, or procure, any drug or instrument for a like purpose, is a misdemeanor. (24 & 25 Vict., c. 100, ss. 58 & 59.)

2. In cases of supposed abortion, immediate possession should be taken of all bottles of medicine used by the injured woman, and all instruments in her possession.

***Absconding from Duty.**—A constable absconding from his duty, or quitting it without giving one calendar month's notice, is liable to a penalty of £5, and to one month's imprisonment with hard labour, if he fails to

* Paragraphs thus marked are applicable to the United Kingdom alone.

B

deliver over the clothing and appointments supplied to him by the public service. (POLICE ACTS.†)

Abusive Language.—1. The use of threatening, abusive language, with corresponding behaviour, justifies arrest without warrant, in extreme cases, if spoken in a constable's presence and a breach of the peace appears imminent. (POLICE ACTS.)

2. Otherwise, the name and address of the offender should be obtained, with a view to his being summoned; and a constable, before resorting to apprehension, should advise him to desist.

Access to Premises.—Police must constantly observe in what manner felonious access to premises is most likely to be attempted, and pay particular attention to those points in going their rounds.

Accessories to Crime.—1. There are two classes of accessories to crime—those who are accessories *before* the fact, and those who are accessories *after* the fact.

2. *An accessory before the fact* is one who, directly or indirectly, so counsels, procures, commands, or instigates another, that a crime is committed. He may be indicted, convicted, and punished, precisely as if he had alone and independently committed the unlawful act.

3. *An accessory after the fact* is one (except married women screening their husbands) who, knowing a felony to have been committed, receives, comforts, or assists the felon, in such manner as to enable him to escape from punishment.

Accidents.—1. In all cases of accident or illness in

† The Police Acts referred to are:—
(a) The Metropolitan Police Act (2 & 3 Vict., c. 47).
(b) The City Police Act (2 & 3 Vict., c. 94).
(c) The Town Police Clauses Acts (10 & 11 Vict., c. 89; & 52 & 53 Vict., c. 14), incorporated in most local Acts, and the provisions of which, as regards the regulation of the streets, fires, hackney-carriages, and public bathing, are made applicable to every urban district (boroughs and local government districts), by the Public Health Act, 1875 (38 & 39 Vict., c. 55, s. 171).
(d) The Constabulary Acts (2 & 3 Vict., c. 93; 3 & 4 Vict., c. 88; 19 & 20 Vict., c. 69; 22 & 23 Vict., c. 32), which frequently, as in this case, contain similar provisions.

the streets or in public places, the police should render all assistance in their power, by—

(*a*) Taking care that the crowd does not press on the sufferer, so as to exclude air.

(*b*) Applying, so far as may be possible, in the absence of a medical man, the maxims laid down in AID TO THE INJURED, p. 21.

(*c*) Sending for the nearest surgeon.

(*d*) Sending to the station for an ambulance or stretcher, to take the sufferer there or to the nearest hospital.

2. The names and addresses of the sufferer, and the person causing the accident, and as far as possible of the persons witnessing it, should be obtained; and the name and number of the constable present at the occurrence, or immediately afterwards, furnished if desired.

3. The points to which the police should attend in cases of accidents may be set down in the following order:—

(1.) The welfare of the sufferer.

(2.) The name and address of the person causing the accident.

(3.) The regulation of the traffic.

(4.) Watchfulness that advantage is not taken of the confusion to pick the pockets of bystanders.

(5.) To see that the sufferer does not lose any property.

Accidental Death.—Death or bodily harm, accidentally caused by an act which is not unlawful, is not a criminal offence, unless accompanied by an *omission* (*see* CULPABLE NEGLIGENCE, p. 58) to perform a legal duty.

Accomplices.—There is no difference between accomplices and accessories before the fact. They are both principals, and punishable as such.

Acquittal.—When once a person has been acquitted by a jury of any indictable offence, he cannot, under any circumstances, be again tried for it, whatever additional evidence is subsequently obtained. This is not the case with prisoners discharged by magistrates, who can be re-apprehended if any new facts are brought to light.

Actions against Police.—1. It is necessary for every police officer to bear in mind, that, although protected by the law in all acts authorised by law, if he oversteps the legal boundary of his duty in the slightest degree, he is then answerable to the law, either criminally, for the exercise of undue violence in performing an act, even although lawful in itself; or civilly, when damages may be recovered against him.

2. All actions against police for an act done in the exercise of their calling must be commenced within six calendar months of the cause arising, and one calendar month's notice of action must be given. (24 Geo. II., c. 14, s. 8; 5 & 6 Vict., c. 97, s. 4.)

Activity.—Activity in the performance of duty should be the first care of every constable, but it must be at all times tempered by judgment and due caution.

Acts of Parliament.—Acts of Parliament or of the Legislature form the statute law of the land. The duties of the police are, for the most part, defined by statute.

Adulteration of Food.—Any person mixing, or ordering, or permitting any other person to mix, with a view to sale, any ingredient or material, with any article of food, so as to render it injurious to health, is liable to a penalty. (38 & 39 Vict., c. 63.)

Advertising Reward for the Return of Stolen Property.—Whoever publicly advertises a reward for the return of any property whatsoever, which has been stolen or lost, and implies that no questions will be asked, or that a reward will be given or paid without any inquiry being made after the person producing it, commits an offence, and is liable, with the printer and publisher, to a penalty of £50. (24 & 25 Vict., c. 96, s. 102; and 33 & 34 Vict., c. 65, s. 3.)

Affidavits.—An affidavit is a written statement upon oath, which may be administered by a Justice, or one of the numerous solicitors nominated for the purpose.

Affirmations.—Persons—Quakers and others—objecting from conscientious motives, to be sworn in criminal proceedings, are permitted to make, instead, a solemn affirmation. (24 & 25 Vict., c. 66, s. 1.)

Agents.—Misappropriation by agents, and factors, is a misdemeanor. (24 & 25 Vict., c. 96, s. 75.)

Aid to the Injured.—The following simple rules may be borne in mind in giving first aid to the injured (*see* ACCIDENTS, p. 18) :—

(1.) Give air, and prevent people crowding in.
(2.) Loosen the collar.
(3.) Raise the head.
(4.) Reassure the sufferer, speaking quietly, and not annoying by idle questions.
(5.) If there is extensive bleeding, tie a handkerchief as tightly as possible three inches above the wound, and another over the wound itself. If the blood is black, and running freely (not spurting), from a wound in the leg, the limb should be raised, and a handkerchief be tied tightly below the bleeding point.
(6.) Move the sufferer as carefully as possible.
(7.) Prevent any broken limb from hanging down.
(8.) If animation is suspended, as in the case of persons rescued from hanging and drowning, endeavour to restore breathing. (*See* TREATMENT OF PERSONS RESCUED FROM DROWNING, HANGING, AND SUFFOCATION, p. 181.)

Aiding Prisoners to Escape.—1. It is a felony to aid any prisoner to escape, or endeavour to escape, from any prison, or to convey, or cause to be conveyed, into any prison any disguise, or any letter, or any thing, with intent to facilitate the escape of any prisoner. (*See* PRISONS, p. 140.) (28 & 29 Vict., c. 126, s. 37.)

2. If an officer, having a prisoner in his lawful custody, knowingly, and with intent to save him from trial or execution, permits him to regain his liberty otherwise than in due course of law, he is guilty of misdemeanor if the prisoner was in custody for and guilty of misdemeanor, and if for felony and guilty thereof, he becomes an accessory after the fact to the felony. (*See* ESCAPE OF PRISONERS, p. 74.)

Alarm of Fire.—Upon an alarm of fire, a constable should immediately arouse the inmates of the building, and of the houses immediately adjoining, have the nearest electric call bell rung, or send notice to the nearest Fire Brigade station, fire escape standing, as well as to the turncock, and to the police station. It is the duty of every constable to know exactly whence to obtain such assistance with the least delay from every part of his beat. Until the arrival of the engines he should take every possible step to get all persons out of the premises on fire. (*See* FIRES, p. 85.)

Animals.—1. Unlawfully and maliciously to kill, maim (*i.e.*, permanently injure), wound, or steal any cattle (*i.e.*, horses, oxen, &c.), is a felony.

2. Similar offences as regards birds, and other animals not being cattle, are punishable by imprisonment with hard labour, or a fine, over and above the amount of injury done. (24 & 25 Vict., c. 96.)

Annoyance.—A person who annoys another by behaviour such as constantly following him, whereby a breach of the peace may occur, may be summoned, or in gross cases given into custody. (*See* ABUSIVE LANGUAGE, p. 18.) (2 & 3 Vict., c. 47, s. 54.)

Antecedents of Prisoners.—It is most important in the interests of justice that the correct antecedents of prisoners should be brought to the knowledge of the Court, before sentence is passed, and especially in the case of burglars, and persons guilty of robbery with violence, as also first offenders. (*See* REMANDS, p. 158.)

Applications.—1. All applications made by police on any subject should be transmitted through the Superintendent of the Division.

2. Other situations should not be applied for by police officers without the written consent of the Chief Officer of Police.

Appointments.—1. When an appointment is fixed for a police officer to meet any person at a particular time, on duty, it is most desirable that it should be kept punctually.

2. When police resign or are dismissed, all articles of appointment must be returned to store, failing which, any Justice may issue a search warrant, and the defaulter is liable to one month's imprisonment.

Apprehension.—1. An apprehension is the taking of another person into custody, to answer according to law for some specified offence.

2. An apprehension is effected either by warrant or on the responsibility of the person carrying it out.

3. Every individual, who either sees a felony committed or knows one has been actually committed, may

arrest the offender and hand him over to a constable, and the latter is justified in arresting a person, against whom a charge of felony is preferred, *upon reliable grounds by a responsible individual.*

4. A constable in whose presence a misdemeanor is committed may also arrest the offender without warrant, if the circumstances render such a course necessary and the delinquent is not known. But mere information of the commission of a misdemeanor, except escape from custody or attempted felonies of a serious character, should not under ordinary conditions be followed by arrest, unless a warrant has been obtained.

5. Application for a warrant is also advisable in all cases where there is any doubt as to the guilty party, or if he has gone beyond the jurisdiction, or if there is any suspicion that the object of the person aggrieved is rather to recover the stolen property than to enforce the law.

6. The following is a list of the principal crimes—to arrest for which no warrant is required :—†

Abduction, Abortion, Accessories to Crime, Accusation of Crime to obtain Money, Aggravated Assaults, Attempted Murder or other Attempted Felonies, Bestiality, Bigamy, Burglary, Coining, Corrosive Fluid Throwing, Counterfeit Coin Uttering, Damaging Bridges, Demanding Money with menaces, Embezzlement, Escape from Custody, Extortion, Forgery, Gunpowder or Dynamite Placing to endanger life or property, Horsestealing, Housebreaking, Larceny by any means, trick or otherwise, Manslaughter, Murder, Rape, Receiving Stolen Goods, Rescue from Custody, Robbery, Sacrilege, Sodomy, Stealing, Threatening-Letter Writing. (*See* ARREST, p. 24; SUSPECTED PERSONS, p. 175; WARRANTS, p. 185.)

Apprentices.—Every one commits a misdemeanor, who, being liable, either as a master or a mistress, to provide for any apprentice or servant necessary food, clothing, or lodging, wilfully neglects to provide the same, or causes any bodily harm to such apprentice or servant, so that his or her health has been, or is likely to be, permanently injured. (24 & 25 Vict., c. 100, s. 26.)

† Whenever the Criminal Code Bill for England becomes law, the distinction between felonies and misdemeanors will probably be abolished, and every offence for which a person may be indicted, termed an "indictable offence."

Areas.—1. Many serious offences against property are committed in towns by entries effected through areas.

2. Police should notice area-gates left open, and be on the watch for suspicious persons termed "area sneaks," going down them, under pretence of buying broken food, old bottles, or selling cheap articles to the servants.

Argument.—There is nothing a police officer should more studiously avoid than argument. Suggestions should be courteously received and freely invited, for they will often prove of value, and however ridiculous it does no harm to hear them.

Armlets.—1. The armlet is the badge worn in most British forces on the coat-wrist of a sergeant or constable, showing that he is nominally on duty. He can never be strictly off duty, for his whole time belongs to the public.

2. The removal of the armlet during the hours prescribed for duty, either to procure drink, or for any purpose, is one of the most serious offences against police discipline. (*See* MISCONDUCT OF POLICE, p. 115.)

Arrest.—1. A lawful arrest on a criminal charge may be made anywhere, and at any hour of the day or night, and a person may be followed anywhere when flying from justice; but doors should not be broken open until a summons to surrender has been disregarded.

2. Unnecessary violence should be studiously avoided, as much because it will probably entail legal consequences as provoke resistance. Care should be taken to make the arrest quietly, without attracting attention or inflicting any needless exposure on the prisoner.

3. The usual way of effecting an arrest is to touch the shoulder of the accused lightly, and, if in plain clothes, saying, "I am a police-officer, and arrest you for ⸻;" or, "I arrest you on this warrant for ⸻," reading it over to the prisoner as early as practicable.

4. The answer of the accused should be carefully listened to, and written down as soon as possible; and although no question must be asked as to the offence, anything the prisoner says voluntarily must be noted. (*See* Sir H. Hawkins' Advice, p. 12; APPREHENSION, p. 22; CONFESSIONS, p. 48.)

Arson.—Every one commits a felony who unlawfully and maliciously sets fire to any building, mine, or ship, or who, by any explosive substance, damages any building, or who attempts the same, or sets fire to growing crops, or to woods, gorse, or heath. (24 & 25 Vict., c. 97.)

Assaults.—1. Assaults are of various kinds, viz., among others:—
(*a*) Common Assaults.
(*b*) Aggravated Assaults.
(*c*) Assaults causing actual Bodily Harm.
(*d*) Indecent Assaults.
(*e*) Assaults on Police.

2. *A Common Assault* is the beating, or it may be only the striking, or touching, of a person. Police should never apprehend in such cases, unless they see the offence committed, but leave the party injured to summon the aggressor. (24 & 25 Vict., c. 100.)

3. *Aggravated Assault.* If there is corroborative evidence of wounds or injuries received, a constable may, in such case, take into custody a person charged by another with having committed such offence, even without his having witnessed it; at the same time, husbands and wives should not, as a rule, be interfered with. (*See* HUSBAND AND WIFE, p. 97.)

4. *Assaults on the Police* in the execution of their duty are punishable by a fine, or imprisonment. (34 & 35 Vict., c. 112, s. 12.)

Assaults on the police frequently arise from unnecessary interference, impetuosity, or loss of temper on the part of a young officer. Before such a charge is taken the circumstances should be strictly inquired into.

Assistance to Police.—1. A police constable may if necessary call upon any person to assist him in the execution of the law; and if unable to arrest a prisoner alone, he should say to a bystander, "In the Queen's name" (in America, "In the name of the Law"), "I call upon you ——" (naming him if possible) "to assist me, a police officer, in the execution of my duty, to convey this person to the police station"

2. To refuse, without physical impossibility or lawful excuse, is an indictable misdemeanor, and punishable by fine and imprisonment.

Assuming the Character of a Constable.—Any person who puts on the dress, or takes the name, designation or character of a constable, for the purpose of doing any act, which such person would not be entitled to do of his own authority, or for any other unlawful purpose, is liable to punishment. (POLICE ACTS.)

Attempted Crime.—Every attempt to commit an offence, whether felony or misdemeanor, is itself a misdemeanor, unless otherwise provided for, as in the case of attempted murder, which is a felony.

Attention.—When a police sergeant or constable is addressed by his Superintendent, Inspector, or other superior officer, he should invariably stand at attention, as also in the witness-box, or when giving evidence before a Board of Inquiry. The same rule should be followed when a constable is addressed by a Judge or Magistrate, or an officer of the army or navy in uniform.

Attic Larcenies.—1. Many of the most serious burglaries and housebreakings in towns are committed by means of what are known as attic larcenies, that is, by the attic being entered through an adjacent empty house.

2. When the police arrive, they should commence by ascertaining whether the thieves have left the house through which the entry was effected, for accidental circumstances may have hindered them. The door of the empty house should not be left unwatched until every room has been explored.

***Baby Farming.**—Not more than one child under the age of one year, or twins, can be maintained for hire apart from his or her parents for more than twenty-four hours, except in a house registered for the purpose. (INFANT LIFE PROTECTION ACT, 1872.)

***Backing Warrants.**—1. The warrant of a Metropolitan Police Magistrate runs over the whole of the United Kingdom. (2 & 3 Vict., c. 71, s. 17.)

2. With this exception, and that of the Lord Mayor and Aldermen of the City of London (p. 186), warrants of arrests granted by Justices, are only in force within the jurisdiction in which they were issued, and in case of fresh pursuit seven miles beyond, unless they are endorsed (APPENDIX F.) for execution within the new district.

3. The handwriting and seal of any Justice of the Peace, on any warrant, may be proved by a solemn declaration, taken before a Justice of the Peace, or a Commissioner to administer oaths, in the form provided, given in APPENDIX H. (*See* WARRANTS, p. 185; SUMMARY JURISDICTION ACT, 1879, s. 41.)

Bail.—1. Bail is the guarantee, under pecuniary liability, to appear, or to produce an accused person, to be tried according to law, at an appointed time and place. It is of two kinds:—
  (*a*) That admitted by a police officer.
  (*b*) That allowed by a Judge or Magistrate.
2. *Admission to Bail by a Police Officer*—
The Inspector, or other officer in charge of a British police station, may, under the provisions of the Summary Jurisdiction Act, 1879, s. 38, admit to bail, with or without sureties, persons charged with any petty misdemeanor for which they are liable to be summarily convicted by a Magistrate—such as drunkenness, assault, disorderly conduct, carelessly doing any hurt or damage, &c.; or who are in custody without warrant for any trifling offence, even light felonies, and cannot be taken before a Magistrate within twenty-four hours, provided that they are well known and not likely to escape. (For Form of Recognisance *see* APPENDIX F.)

Bailees.—A bailee is a person to whom goods are entrusted for a specific purpose. Application thereof to some other purpose, to defraud the principal, is larceny or theft. (24 & 25 Vict., c. 96, s. 3.)

Bank Notes, Forgery of.—It is a felony—
  (*a*) To purchase, or receive from any person, any bank note, knowing it to be forged.
  (*b*) To make, use, utter, or knowingly have in custody or possession, any bank note paper, resembling that used by any bank, or any instrument, for making such paper.
  (*c*) To engrave upon any material, anything purporting to be a bank note either British or foreign, or any part thereof. (24 & 25 Vict., c. 98.)

***Bank Notes, Lost or Stolen.**—1. When English bank notes are either lost or stolen, they should be stopped without delay at the Bank of England, and similarly at the principal office of the bank of issue in the case of other bank notes. To do this, the amount, date, and number are necessary.

2. When a stopped note is paid into the Bank of England, notice is sent to the person stopping it, of the source from which it came to the bank, when inquiry can be made to trace through whose hands it passed. For this purpose mention should be made of all marks or endorsement, but the note itself cannot be sent for inspection, except to a branch of the Bank of England.

***Bankrupts.**—If a person leaves England or attempts to leave England, with any property of £20 or upwards, in contemplation of bankruptcy, he commits a felony; if with property of less value a misdemeanor. (32 & 33 Vict., c. 62, s. 12.)

Bastardy.—The father of a child not born in wedlock is none the less bound to maintain it. He may be summoned by the mother, or the guardians of the parish to whom the child has become chargeable, and an affiliation order may be made on him. If the payments are not regularly made a warrant of arrest may be issued, and the amount due, together with costs, be recovered by distress, subject to imprisonment. (35 & 36 Vict., c. 65.)

Battery.—Battery, in the legal sense, includes every touching, or laying hold of another, in an angry, revengeful, rude, insolent, or hostile manner. (*See* ASSAULT, p. 25.)

Bawdy Houses.—A common bawdy house is a house or room, or set of rooms in any house, kept for the purpose of prostitution. To keep such in England, to the annoyance of any two inhabitants who will prosecute, is a common nuisance, and therefore a misdemeanor. Proceedings may also be taken by any person under the Summary Jurisdiction Acts by application to a Magistrate. (*See* BROTHELS, p. 32; DISORDERLY HOUSES, p. 66.)

Beats.—1. The portion of ground to be protected by each constable is termed his beat.

2. The method of working beats must be frequently changed, and police be careful not to allow evil-disposed persons to ascertain the system of working, and the consequent hour of absence from a given spot. The beats

should be walked over, at about two and a-half miles an hour. In towns, constables on day duty should keep near the curbstone, and by night next the houses.

3. Apart from a close observance of all persons passing, lest any should be recognised as having been advertised for apprehension in the *Police Gazette*, or *Police Informations*, or come within the category of suspected persons, and be stopped and questioned (p. 175), the following rules may be advantageously borne in mind, by constables on beat:—

(*a*) Not to loiter or gossip, but to work the beat continuously and regularly.

(*b*) To move smartly, and not slouch or look slovenly.

(*c*) To answer all questions with civility and good temper.

(*d*) To act quietly and discreetly, not interfering unnecessarily, but when need arises showing firmness and discretion.

(*e*) Not to leave the beat except in cases of fire, accident, or other emergency, returning as soon as possible.

(*f*) To mark places likely to be attempted by thieves; and if the marks are disturbed, to ascertain the cause.

(*g*) To see that doors, windows, gratings, cellar-flaps, fan-lights, and places through which a thief might enter, or obtain access, are not left open.

Beggars. — Every person wandering abroad, or placing himself, or herself, in any public place, to beg alms, or causing or procuring any child to do so, may be apprehended as an idle or disorderly person. (5 Geo. 4, c. 83.) Beggars dressed as soldiers or sailors, or exposing wounds, or deformities, to public view, in order to attract sympathy, should be especially noticed. (*See* ROGUES AND VAGABONDS, p. 162.)

Bells.—Every person who wilfully and wantonly disturbs any inhabitant, by pulling or ringing any door bell, or knocking at any door without lawful excuse, may be apprehended by any constable, witnessing such act, without warrant, but preferably his name and address should be obtained for summons. (POLICE ACTS.)

Bestiality.—Bestiality is the crime of men defiling themselves with beasts, and is punishable in England by a minimum sentence of ten years' penal servitude. (24 & 25 Vict., c. 100, s. 61.) It is desirable that such charges should be supported by at least two witnesses.

*Betting.—Betting Houses.—1. A common betting house is a place (including a temporary stand) kept or used for the purpose of betting between persons resorting thereto, or for the receipt by the owner, or other person, of any money or valuable thing, on any event or contingency, of or relating to any race, fight, game, sport, or exercise. (16 & 17 Vict., c. 119, s. 1.)

2. Any magistrate, upon complaint made before him on oath that there is reason to suspect any place to be used as a betting-house, may give authority by special warrant to any police officer to enter, and to arrest, search, and bring before a Justice of the Peace, all such persons found therein, and to seize all lists, cards, or other documents relating to racing or betting, found in such house or premises.

3. *Betting in Public Places, the Streets, or on Highways.*—Every person playing or betting, by way of wagering or gaming, in any open and public place to which the public are permitted to have access, with any table or instrument of gaming, or any coin, cards, or other article, may be apprehended as a rogue and a vagabond. (36 & 37 Vict., c. 38, s. 3.)

Roulette tables, three-card, and other fraudulent tricks at races and elsewhere come under this category.

4. In the Metropolitan and City Police Districts any three or more persons assembled together in any part of a street for the purpose of betting may be apprehended without warrant for obstructing the street. (30 & 31 Vict., c. 134, s. 23.)

Bicycles.—Regulations as to bicycles and tricycles are made by the local authorities. In most districts they are obliged, between sunset and sunrise, to carry a light; and the name and address of any rider not carrying such light should be obtained with a view to his being summoned.

Bigamy.—The felony of bigamy is committed by one who being legally married goes through a lawful form of marriage with any other person, during the life of his or her wife or husband.† (24 & 25 Vict., c. 100.)

Bill in Criminal Cases.—The bill in a criminal case is the indictment preferred to a grand jury.

*****Billiards and Bagatelle.**—1. Every person keeping any public billiard table, or bagatelle board, or instrument used in any game of like kind, for public use, without being duly licensed so to do, and not holding a victualler's license, is liable to a penalty.

2. All police officers may enter any house, room, or place, where any public table or board is kept for playing at billiards, bagatelle, or any game of a like kind, when and so often as is necessary, but it should not be done without the authority of a Superintendent or Inspector. (8 & 9 Vict., c. 109, s. 11.)

*****Birds.**—1. Any person not the owner or occupier of any land, or person authorised by him, who between the first day of March and the first day of August in any year knowingly and wilfully shoots or attempts to shoot, any wild bird, or uses any lime, trap, net, or other instrument for the purpose of taking any wild bird, or exposes or offers for sale, or has in his possession, after the 15th of March, any wild bird recently killed or taken, is liable to a penalty of £1 in respect of any of the following birds, viz.:—Cuckoos, goldfinches, gulls, kingfishers, larks, nighthawks, nightingales, owls, petrels, plovers, sandpipers, snipe, teal, widgeon, wild ducks, woodcocks, woodpeckers, &c.

2. Any person may require an offender to give his Christian name, surname, and place of abode, and in case of refusal, or giving an untrue name or place of abode, he is liable to a further penalty. (43 & 44 Vict., c. 35.)

Bird Stealing.—Every person who steals or wilfully kills with intent to steal any bird, or has on his premises or in his possession any bird or the plumage thereof, knowing that the same has been stolen, is liable to imprisonment with hard labour, or to a fine besides the value of the bird. (24 & 25 Vict., c. 96, ss. 21 & 22.)

† In cases of bigamy, as in others of a like, so to say, domestic nature, a warrant should be invariably applied for before police proceed to an arrest, except on the strongest evidence of facts.

Bonds.—A bond is a written acknowledgment of a debt under seal. Forgery of a bond, or uttering a bond knowing it to be forged or altered, is punishable by penal servitude. (24 & 25 Vict., c. 98, s. 20.)

Bonfires.—Persons making bonfires in the streets or on highways within view of a constable, may be apprehended, and are liable to a penalty. (POLICE ACTS.)

Borrowing Money.—1. Police officers, who borrow or attempt to borrow money from a subordinate, or from a licensed victualler, or any person licensed by the Police authorities, render themselves liable to immediate dismissal.

2. Constables should not lend money to a superior in rank.

Breach of the Peace.—A breach of the peace is any violation of that quiet, peace, and security, which is guaranteed by the laws, for the personal comfort of every individual. Any person may act as a peace officer, and it is the duty of a police officer to arrest any one committing a breach of the peace in his presence.

Bribery of Police.—1. The bribery of police would generally be attempted to turn them from their duty in a criminal proceeding. In such cases the offence is either in the nature of a Conspiracy to defeat the ends of Justice (*see* p. 49), or the misdemeanor of Dissuading a Witness from Testifying (*see* p. 66). The bribery must be entirely spontaneous, and in no way invited.

2. The giving to or taking of any bribe by any public officer or servant for an official act is a misdemeanor. (*See* OFFICIAL SECRETS, p. 123.)

Bridges.—1. Every one is guilty of a misdemeanor, who, being bound by law to repair a bridge, fails to do so.

2. Every one commits felony, who pulls, or throws down, or in any way destroys, any bridge, or any viaduct or aqueduct over or under which any highway, railway, or canal passes. (*See* RAILWAYS, p. 156.) (24 & 25 Vict., c. 97, s. 33.)

***Brothels.**—Proceedings may be taken by any person under the Summary Jurisdiction Acts against any person keeping, managing, or assisting in the management of any premises used for habitual prostitution, or against the landlord, lessor, or agent. (CRIMINAL LAW AMENDMENT ACT, 1885.)

Burden of Proof.—The burden of proving that any person has been guilty of a crime, or wrongful act, is on the person who asserts it. It is, therefore, in criminal proceedings, for the prosecution to prove the prisoner guilty, and until this has been done he is presumed to be innocent.

Burglary.—1. Burglary is the breaking and entering by night into, or out of, a dwelling-house, with intent to commit a felony.

2. To constitute the offence of burglary, there must be five essential conditions.

(a) "*The night time,*" that is between nine in the evening and six in the morning.

(b) "*A dwelling-house,*" that is a permanent building in which some person habitually sleeps.

(c) "*A breaking,*" that is by either breaking or taking out the glass of a window, or, in any way opening it, picking a lock, opening it with a key, lifting the latch of a door, or unloosing any fastening, either to get in or get out, or obtaining an entrance by any threat or artifice used for that purpose, or by collusion with any person in the house.

(d) "*An entry,*" that is the introduction of any part of the body into the house, therefore putting a hand in at a window to draw out goods.

(e) "*A felonious intent,*" that is a design to commit robbery, murder, rape, or some other felony, whether actually perpetrated or not.

3. Burglary will be best detected by the alacrity of the constables on beat duty, who, besides watching for marks disturbed, for doors, shutters, and windows forced, for lights at unusual hours, in their ordinary duty, should let no suspicious-looking person (*see* SUSPECTED PERSONS, p. 175) pass them, at an unreasonable time, without calling upon them civilly to explain their business and show in the interests of the public that the contents of a bag or bundle he or she may be carrying is not other than lawful.

4. When a burglary has been committed, every effort must be made to ascertain who the delinquent is. His description should be circulated at once in the force and

the adjacent districts, and transmitted to the *Police Gazette*.

5. No time should be lost in obtaining as accurate a description as possible of the stolen property, and particularly of any having special marks of identity—peculiar shape, inscriptions, crests; sketches being obtained, if possible.

The lists should be circulated as widely as possible.

If printed on bills, care should be taken that they are in proper legal form (*see* REWARD BILLS, p. 160), and that sufficient are sent to every force—less than 1,000 are almost useless in the Metropolitan Police District.

6. In cases of burglary, almost more than in any other crime, it is important to act with the utmost promptitude and dispatch, and the fact of a burglary having occurred should be notified, in serious cases, far and near, without the loss of a moment.

7. Police approaching a house in which burglars are supposed to be, should first make sure that the retreat of the thieves is cut off, for there are not wanting instances of a too eager search giving them the opportunity to escape.

Burial.—Every one commits a misdemeanor who prevents the burial of any dead body, or who without authority disinters a dead body; or who, being legally bound to bury a dead body, and having the means, neglects to do so; or who buries or otherwise disposes of a dead body, on which an inquest ought to be held, without giving notice to a Coroner. (*See* DEAD BODIES, p. 59.)

Cabs.—1. The police are frequently appealed to, in disputes between the public and fly, car, or cab-drivers. In such cases, they should give any reasonable help, and advise the complainant to address himself to the nearest police court or station.

2. Police observing any cab-horse unfit for use, or any cab in a dirty or broken condition, should take the number, note the appearance of the horse, and report the same, on going off duty, with a view to the institution of proper inquiry. If the driver of a hackney carriage, or driver or conductor of an omnibus, is to blame in any matter, the number of the carriage or omnibus should be taken, and police must do this on the requisition of any individual. The badge-number will identify the offender.

3. The numbers of public carriages, whose drivers commit any of the following offences, should be taken, with a view to their being summoned:—

(*a*) Plying for hire at unauthorised places.

(*b*) Standing across the end of a street longer than is necessary for taking up or setting down.

(*c*) *Leaving a carriage unattended*, especially outside public-houses, a frequent source of accident.

(*d*) Causing obstruction by loitering, or other wilful misbehaviour.

(*e*) Refusing to give way to any other carriage.

(*f*) Forcibly or clandestinely taking a fare away from another.

4. At the same time, it is not desirable that the law on the above heads should be harshly exercised, nor until a caution has been given, except in the case of persistent offenders, whose wilful disregard of the conditions of their license is manifest; but no instance should be passed over of—

(*a*) Wanton or furious driving.

(*b*) Causing hurt or damage to persons or property in any highway, by careless or wilful misbehaviour.

(*c*) Being drunk. (If so drunk that danger is likely to accrue to the public, a cabman should be taken into custody. His horse and cab should be led by another constable to the station, and a telegram or message sent to the proprietor to fetch them.)

(*d*) Using insulting or abusive language, or being guilty of insulting gesture or misbehaviour. (6 & 7 Vict., c. 86 ; 10 & 11 Vict., c. 89 ; 16 & 17 Vict., c. 33.)

Cab Ranks.—Police, on cab-rank duty, should especially study *Printed Informations* and the *Police Gazette*, having many opportunities of rendering valuable service.

Candidates.—1. A person wishing to join the Metropolitan Police Force must address his request to the Commissioner of Police of the Metropolis, London. A printed form will then be sent to him, stating what certificates of character are requisite, and explaining the conditions of the service.

2. The minimum standard of height varies from five feet seven inches to five feet ten inches, and no candidate must be over thirty-five years of age, or have more than

two children depending upon him for support. With the rarest exceptions, every candidate must await his turn to be called up and pass through the regular course.

3. Persons desirous of joining a constabulary force should communicate with the Chief or Head Constable.

Cardsharping.—(*See* BETTING, p. 30.) (36 & 37 Vict., c. 38.)

Carriages.—1. All Royal carriages conveying Royal personages or the Queen's representative should be allowed to pass without interruption at all times, and every facility should be given by the police to enable them to do so without falling into the rank, if one has been formed.

2. Any carriage with company going to a ball, party, theatre, &c., should be allowed to pass empty carriages waiting, or going to take up their company, and drawing up to the entrance, set down immediately, and drive away. Any carriage waiting to take up company at the same time, should wait until the carriage which has just set down company has drawn off.

3. Whenever means are provided, by covered awning, &c., for several carriages to set down or take up company at the same time, the police should arrange that as many carriages draw up together in front of the doors, &c., as the space admits of; and for this purpose the foremost carriage should be required to go on to the furthest door, or point in the line in which they are to move away. In carrying this into effect, great discretion should be used by the police employed, that danger or annoyance may not be caused, and no carriage should be required to move forward at a moment when the owner is about to enter or leave it.

4. When there are streets crossing or coming together at a point, carriages should be admitted by a few at a time alternately from the several streets, to pass across, or fall into a line, if one has been formed. This arrangement should be carried out especially when great numbers of carriages are going to one place, and on all public occasions.

5. Carriages formed in line should not be allowed to obstruct the crossings of streets or the entrances to private houses, where other carriages are going to set down or take up company.

6. The police on duty regulating carriages at evening parties, theatres, &c., should not interfere unnecessarily, and when they do, it should be done quietly and civilly, and not in a tone or manner calculated to give offence or provoke resistance.

7. The police should not lay hold of the bridles of horses unless absolutely necessary to prevent danger at the moment, or unless the coachman, after warning, persists in disregarding the necessary regulations. Under no circumstances should reins be unbuckled.

8. A coachman should not be taken off his box, and charged with an offence except in the presence of a Sergeant or Inspector, and the person to whom the carriage belongs must be informed as early as possible. (*See* REGULATING TRAFFIC, p. 158.)

Carriage Larcenies.—In crowded thoroughfares, rugs and other articles are frequently stolen from open carriages, or broughams, which are waiting for their owners. Police should be on the watch for this class of offence.

***Cattle Plague.**—1. The owner or person in charge of any animal affected with cattle plague, pleuropneumonia, foot and mouth disease, sheep pox, sheep scab, glanders, or farcy, is bound to give notice to the police (by whom the information must be immediately conveyed to the local authority), subject to a penalty of £20, and in the case of cattle plague, to the Agricultural Department.

2. A constable, if he has no doubt that an animal is infected, is justified in detaining it, and obtaining the name and address of the person in charge thereof and of the owner, but in general he should content himself with the latter course.

3. Any place where cattle plague exists may be declared by the Inspector of the local authority to be an "infected place."

4. No animal can be moved out of an "infected place" alive, or any portion of it if dead, without a license, or any dung, hay, straw, litter, or thing used in or about such animal.

5. In "infected districts" a constable may stop and detain any animal, including a horse, illegally moved, and apprehend the person in charge without warrant. (41 & 42 Vict., c. 74.)

Cattle Stealing, Maiming, Killing, &c.—(*See* ANIMALS, p. 22.)

Cattle Straying.—Cattle found straying should be taken to the greenyard or pound, and a description of them circulated. The owners may be summoned. (*See* GREENYARDS, p. 90.) (27 & 28 Vict., c. 101, s. 25.)

Causing Death.—(*See* KILLING, p. 107.)

Cautions.—When any offence is prevalent in a particular locality, or there is need for any special care on the part of householders, bankers, or any trade, a cautionary notice, in concise and moderate language, may be most advantageously issued under the authority of the chief officer of police to put people on their guard.

Cautioning a Prisoner.—1. Before a prisoner in custody is *asked* any question, however necessary, even for the preservation of the life of an injured person, or the furtherance of the ends of justice in relation to any crime—and especially murder—with which he is charged, or about to be charged, he should be distinctly cautioned that his answer may be given in evidence against him. The law is very strict on this head, and does not permit persons charged with offences to be interrogated as to their guilt. (*See* DETERMINATION TO ARREST, p. 65.)

2. But on the other hand, it is the duty of a police officer to listen to all a prisoner says, and faithfully to give evidence of the same.

(*See* p. 12; *see* CONFESSIONS, p. 48, and PRISONERS, p. 138.)

Cells.—1. Cells should be kept very clean and well ventilated, carbolic acid being freely used to prevent infection. The door must always be carefully double-locked and bolted upon a prisoner, and the inspection wicket fastened after each visit. Every prisoner should be visited at least every hour, and drunken persons every half-hour, or oftener in cases of illness, the keys being kept in the Inspector's office.

2. No person should be ever allowed to visit occupied cells from motives of curiosity.

3. Great care must be taken to prevent prisoners communicating with each other, and, in serious cases, an empty cell should if possible separate accomplices.

Challenging to Fight.—Every one commits a misdemeanor who challenges any other person to fight a duel, or who endeavours, by words or by writings, to provoke any other person to send a challenge to fight or to commit a breach of the peace.

Character, Evidence of.—In criminal proceedings, the fact that an accused person has a good character is important, but the fact that he has a bad character unimportant, unless it is itself a fact in issue, or unless evidence has been given that the prisoner has a good character.

Charges.—1. When prisoners are brought to police stations and charged with any offence, the statements of persons charging, of witnesses, and of police, must be made to the Inspector on duty, in the presence and hearing of the prisoners.

2. No statement relative to the charge should be made except in the hearing and presence of the prisoner.

3. Good order should be strictly preserved, whilst the witnesses are giving evidence, and their statements, as well as any made by the person charged, should be patiently and attentively heard.

4. Persons who come to a police station as witnesses or spectators, when a charge is being made, should not be taken into custody and charged with being concerned in the offence. Such a practice may prevent persons from appearing who can give important evidence, and has the appearance of a desire by the police to suppress evidence in the case, especially where the charge is for an assault on the police themselves, or for obstructing them in the performance of their duty. If persons against whom a charge ought to be made, and who have not been previously arrested, come to the station as witnesses, their names and addresses should be asked, and their personal recognisance taken to appear before the Magistrate.

Charge of Stations.—1. Inspectors and Sergeants in charge of stations should always bear in mind that on them rests, not only the credit of the police service, but also the responsibility for the legality of all police action within their control.

2. They should treat all persons having business at

the station with becoming respect and civility, and with a manifest desire to oblige.

Chattel.—A chattel is any article, either movable or immovable, belonging to a person.

Cheating at Play.—Every one is guilty of obtaining money by false pretences, with intent to cheat or defraud, who wins from any other person, any sum of money or valuable thing, by any fraud or unlawful device, or its practice, in playing at any game. (8 & 9 Vict., c. 109, s. 17.)

Children Found.—Children lost by their parents, and found by the police, should be taken to the station and their friends be informed, if they can say who they are and whence they came; if not, their description should be circulated, and after a reasonable time has elapsed to allow of their being owned, they should be sent to the workhouse.

Children Found Dead.—Congenital or birth marks should be particularly sought for in the case of children found dead, and inquiry made among accoucheurs and midwives. (*See* INFANTICIDE, p. 101.)

Children's Offences.—No act of a child, under seven years of age, is a crime, nor yet under fourteen years of age, unless it can be shown or reasonably inferred, that the person knew the particular act to be wrong.

Children, Offences against.—1. *Child stealing* is a felony. Unlawfully to decoy, or entice away, or detain any child under fourteen years of age constitutes the offence. (24 & 25 Vict., c. 100.)

2. To receive or harbour any such child, knowing it to have been so dealt with, intending to deprive any parent or guardian, or other person having the lawful care or charge of such child, of the possession of it, or with intent to steal any article about or on the person of such child, entails the same punishment.

3. *Child abandonment.* (*See* ABANDONING CHILDREN, p. 17.)

4. *Neglecting to Provide Food for Children.*—Every one commits a misdemeanor who, being the parent, master, or mistress of any child of tender years unable

to provide food for itself, and, being able to do so, refuses or neglects to provide sufficient food, clothes, bedding, and other necessaries for such child, so as to injure its health.

5. *Parents Neglecting to Provide Necessaries for Children.*—A parent who wilfully neglects to provide adequate food, clothing, medical aid, or lodging for his child under fourteen years of age, being in his custody, and whereby the health of such child is, or is likely to be, seriously injured, commits a misdemeanor. (31 & 32 Vict., c. 122, s. 37.)

6. *Defilement of Children.*—Every one is guilty of felony, who unlawfully and carnally knows and abuses any girl under the age of thirteen years, even with her consent. (*See* INDECENT ASSAULT, p. 99.) (38 & 39 Vict., c. 94, s. 3.)

7. Every one commits a misdemeanor, who unlawfully and carnally knows and abuses any girl, even with her consent, under sixteen years of age. (CRIMINAL LAW AMENDMENT ACT, 1885.)

8. *Dangerous Performances by Children.*—Any person causing any child under fourteen to take part in any public exhibition or performance, whereby its life is endangered, is liable to a penalty, as well as the parent or guardian aiding and abetting the same. (42 & 43 Vict., c. 34.)

9. *Prevention of Cruelty to Children.*—Any person over sixteen years of age who wilfully treats or neglects any boy under fourteen years of age, or any girl under sixteen, in a manner likely to cause unnecessary suffering, or to be injurious to health, or causes such child to be in any street for the purpose of begging or receiving alms under any pretence, or to be in any street or public-house for the purpose of performing for profit, or offering any thing for sale between 10 p.m. and 5 a.m., or causes any child under ten to be at any time in such place, is guilty of a misdemeanor, and liable to a fine of £50, or to imprisonment, with or without hard labour, for three months, or to both. The local authority may extend or restrict the above hours, either generally or temporarily, or with regard to specific places.

A constable may take into custody without warrant any person whose name and address are unknown and cannot be ascertained, who, within his view, commits any such offence. The same or any other constable may take the child in respect of whom the offence was committed to a place of safety, and it may be there detained until it can be brought before a Court of Summary Jurisdiction. (52 & 53 Vict., c. 44.)

Child Murder.—(*See* INFANTICIDE, p. 101.)

Chimneys on Fire.—When a constable observes from without that a chimney is on fire, he should acquaint the occupiers of the house, and if it appears necessary send to the Fire Brigade station, remaining near at hand until it is extinguished, in case it assumes a dangerous character.

Choking.—It is a felony to attempt by any means whatsoever to choke or strangle any other person, or to attempt any means calculated to produce that result, and to render such other person insensible, or incapable of resistance. (24 & 25 Vict., c. 100, s. 21.)

Circumstantial Evidence.—1. Circumstantial evidence is that which may be inferred from particular actions, or from the circumstances, which either usually or necessarily attend a given condition of fact.

2. Direct testimony is in all cases preferable; but in the absence thereof, circumstantial evidence may be accepted, until the contrary is proved.

3. In criminal cases, and especially in murder, where the act can rarely be proved directly, circumstantial evidence has often been found to produce a strong assurance of the prisoner's guilt.

Civility.—1. All persons should be treated with the utmost civility, forbearance, and good temper by the police.

2. Whenever a question is put to police by any person, they should not answer it in a short or abrupt manner, but with the greatest possible attention; avoiding, however, entering into unnecessary conversation with any one.

3. A civil question will frequently elicit a courteous answer and valuable information.

4. Above all, ladies, foreigners, and strangers, should be treated with civility, and every person calling at a police station upon any business whatever.

5. Occasional mistakes and errors of judgment may

be unavoidable on the part of the police, but civility will do much to prevent any resentment being felt.

Clubs.—A club is an association to which individuals subscribe for purposes of mutual entertainment and convenience. A club-house, being available to subscribers alone, is as a private house belonging to them collectively, and represented by their committee.

***Cock and Dog Fighting.**—1. Every person keeping, using, or acting, in the management of any place for the purpose of fighting or baiting any bull, bear, badger, dog, " *cock*," or other kind of animal, whether of domestic or wild nature, or who permits or suffers any place to be so used, may be apprehended without warrant. (12 & 13 Vict., c. 92, s. 3.)

2. Similarly, any person may be apprehended, and punished, who in any manner encourages, aids, or assists at such fighting or baiting. (*See* CRUELTY TO ANIMALS, p. 56.)

Coercion.—Coercion is the compulsion, or forcing, of one person by another to do some act against his own or her will.

Coining.—1. Every one commits a felony and is liable to penal servitude—

(*a*) Who makes any counterfeit gold or silver current coin.

(*b*) Who gilds or silvers any counterfeit current coin, or any material of fit size and figure to be coined, with intent to make counterfeit coin.

(*c*) Who alters any current coin, with intent to make it resemble, or pass for one of higher value.

(*d*) Who, without lawful authority and excuse, buys, sells, or puts off, any counterfeit gold or silver current coin.

(*e*) Who makes, mends, buys, sells, or has in custody or possession any instrument, engine, or machine intended to be used for counterfeiting any current coin.

2. *Clipping Coin.*—Every one commits felony, who impairs, diminishes, or lightens any current gold or silver, with intent, that when so dealt with, it may still pass as current coin.

3. *Coining Copper or Foreign Money.*—Every one commits a felony—

(*a*) Who counterfeits the Queen's current copper coin.

(*b*) Who, without lawful authority and excuse (the proof whereof lies upon him), knowingly makes or mends, or has in custody or possession any instrument, tool, or engine, adapted and intended for counterfeiting the Queen's current copper coin.

(*c*) Who makes counterfeit gold or silver coin, of any foreign prince or state, or brings, or receives the same into the United Kingdom. (24 & 25 Vict., c. 99.)

Colonies, Surrender of Criminals to or from.— The Fugitive Offenders' Act, 1881, came into retrospective operation on New Year's Day, 1882.

1. A person accused of any felony, serious misdemeanor, or crime, may be surrendered to or from the United Kingdom and any British possession.

2. If a fugitive criminal from one part of the Queen's dominions is, or is suspected of being, in, or on his way to, another part, any Magistrate in such latter part may be applied to to issue a provisional warrant for his arrest, under such circumstances as would in his opinion justify the issue of a warrant, if the offence of which the fugitive is accused had been committed within his jurisdiction.

3. The procedure of the police of the United Kingdom in obtaining the arrest of a fugitive offender to a British possession should be as follows:—

(*a*) Obtain a warrant upon sworn information and depositions.

(*b*) Send to the Secretary of State for the Home Department the original documents and certified copies of the warrant, the information, and the depositions, and verify the signature of the Magistrate (unless he be the Lord Mayor of London, or a Metropolitan Police Magistrate) by the statutory declaration of some person who either saw the Magistrate sign or is familiar with his signature. (Appendix H.)

(*c*) Annex to the covering letter to the Home Office a description (p. 61) of the accused, if possible a photograph, and all details serving to identify him, or to contribute to his discovery.

(*d*) Ask the Secretary of State in the letter to authenticate both the original documents and the copies with his official seal, to return the authenticated originals, and to forward the authenticated copies, together with the description, etc., to the Secretary of State for the Colonies for transmission to the Governor of the British possession in question, telegraphing in the meantime for the provisional arrest of the fugitive.

4. The same procedure will obtain in any British possession for the arrest of a fugitive to the United Kingdom, *mutatis mutandis*—that is, substituting for the Secretary of State for the Home Department the officer of the Colonial Government responsible for the administration of Justice, and substituting His Excellency the Governor for the Secretary of State for the Colonies.

5. The whole of the expenses fall upon the prosecutor under present regulations, and an indemnity in the form given in Appendix D should be signed by him, stamped, and forwarded with the papers.

Common Lodging-Houses.—1. A common lodging-house is one in which persons of the poorer classes are received for short periods, and, though promiscuously brought together, are allowed to inhabit one common room. Hotels, inns, public-houses, or lodgings let to the upper and middle classes, are not common lodging-houses.

*2. Keepers of common lodging-houses have to register their names and addresses with the local authority, to give the appointed officers free access to any part of the house at all times, to cleanse it throughout to their satisfaction, to limewash the walls and ceilings twice a year, and to give immediate notice when any person in their houses is ill of fever or any infectious disease, subject to a penalty, recoverable by summons. (14 & 15 Vict., c. 28, s. 11.)

3. No person can keep a common lodging-house, or receive a lodger therein, unless his name has been registered, except a member of his family for four weeks after his death.

4. By "The Prevention of Crimes Act, 1871," every person who keeps any lodging-house, and knowingly lodges, or knowingly harbours thieves, or reputed thieves, or knowingly permits or knowingly suffers them to meet or assemble therein, or knowingly allows the deposit of goods therein—having reasonable cause for believing them to be stolen—is guilty of an offence against that Act, and may be dealt with accordingly.

Common Nuisance.—1. A common nuisance is an act not warranted by law, or an omission to discharge a legal duty, which act or omission obstructs, or causes inconvenience or damage to the public, in the exercise of rights common to all persons.

2. Every one who commits any common nuisance is guilty of a misdemeanor.

Communications to Police.—1. It is absolutely necessary, as much for the security of individuals as for the maintenance of the honour of the public service, that all communications from one police force to another, or from private individuals to police authorities, should be regarded as most strictly confidential.

2. Except in the rarest cases they should not be shown to private persons, nor even the name of a person conveying information be disclosed; and, above all, should never be communicated, directly or indirectly, to the public press.

3. The rule holds with equal, if not greater, strictness to anonymous denunciations; for the handwriting may be recognised, and the individual, possibly seeking to do a public service, may be exposed to extreme annoyance.

4. When an individual has to be informed of the contents of a letter from another police force, or of a report made by another officer, or of directions by a superior, the gist should be read out, but under ordinary circumstances the papers should not be shown.

*****Compassionate Allowances.**—1. The Secretary of State may grant a pension to the widow, or a compassionate allowance to the children of a Metropolitan police officer killed in the execution of his duty, or who has died from the effects of injuries so received.

2. The Court of General or Quarter Sessions for any county, and the Watch Committee, subject to the approbation of the Council, for any borough, may, upon the recommendation of the Chief or Head Constable, grant a gratuity out of the superannuation fund of their county, or borough, to the widow of any constable who has died in the service, provided the sum so granted does not exceed the amount of one year's pay of such constable, and that he has contributed to the superannuation fund for a period of not less than three years.

Competency of Witnesses.—All persons are competent to testify in all cases, except—

(*a*) Those who, in the opinion of the Judge, are prevented by extreme youth, from disease affecting the mind, or from any other analogous cause, from recollecting the matter on which testimony is to be given, from understanding the questions put, or giving rational answers to them, or from not knowing the nature of an oath, and that the truth must be spoken.

(*b*) The wife or husband of an accused person, save when the infliction of bodily injury, or violence, by one against the other, or of cruelty to children, is the subject of the charge.

(*c*) Any person jointly indicted with a prisoner, unless such person has pleaded guilty, or the wife or husband of such person.

(*d*) A juror, as to what passed between the jurymen, in the discharge of their duty.

Complaints.—1. The statement of any person wishing to make a complaint against police of the same force should be taken down at once in writing, without referring the person complaining to the station of the division to which the constable complained of, belongs.

2. Complaints against the action of another police force should not be received, but the complainant referred to the chief officer of that force.

Complaints by Police.—1. Complaints by police against each other should be made in writing, and be fully inquired into, and duly submitted.

2. Police having any complaint to make against any order given them by an Inspector or Sergeant, *should first obey it*, providing it is not to commit some illegal act, and then report to the Superintendent, who will lay the matter before his superiors through the usual channel. This is the proper manner to prefer all complaints and applications of any sort.

*****Compounding Felonies and Misdemeanors.**— 1. The compounding of felonies and misdemeanors was very common in England prior to the Prosecution of Offences Act, 1879, and people often had recourse to the police for assistance, and when their efforts had resulted in the arrest of the delinquent, they declined to appear and prosecute.

2. In all such cases now, the prisoner should be charged by the police, and a remand obtained, the Magistrate being made acquainted with the facts. (*See* p. 154.)

3. Every one commits a misdemeanor who, in respect of any valuable consideration, enters into an agreement not to prosecute any person for felony, or to show favour to any person in any such prosecution.

Concealment of Birth.—1. If any woman is delivered of a child, and endeavours to conceal the birth thereof, by any secret disposition of the dead body of the said child, whether such child died before, at, or after its birth, she commits a misdemeanor. (24 & 25 Vict., c. 100, s. 60.)

2. A woman found to have concealed the birth of a child soon after delivery, must not be charged until a medical man certifies that it may be done with perfect safety. If she has no friends to receive her, she should be taken with care to the workhouse, and arrangements made for the police to be informed when she is well enough to be moved.

* **Conditions of Police Service.**—1. No person can be appointed to or retained in any police office, who holds any other office or employment for hire or gain (2 & 3 Vict., c. 93, s. 10), or who has any interest in the sale of any beer, wine, or spirituous liquors.

2. Every police officer must give his whole time to the service.

3. Every police officer is bound to report to his Superintendent any Inspector, Sergeant, or constable whom he knows to be obtaining any other employment off duty, for the service demands the whole available energies of every individual.

Conduct Money.—Conduct money is the sum which must be tendered to a witness for his travelling expenses, when a subpœna is served to attend and give evidence. (*See* SUBPŒNAS, p. 174.)

Confessions.—1. A confession is an admission made at any time, by a person charged with a crime, and suggesting the inference that he committed that crime.

2. A confession must be entirely voluntary. This will not be the case if it appears to the Judge to have been caused by any inducement, threat, or promise,

proceeding from a person in authority, and having reference to the charge against the accused person, whether addressed to him directly or brought to his knowledge indirectly; or if, in the opinion of the Judge, such inducement, threat, or promise, gave the accused person reasonable grounds for supposing that by making a confession he would gain some advantage, or avoid some evil, in reference to the proceedings against him.

3. Persons in authority include the prosecutor, Magistrate, *and police officers, or their representatives.*

Consent.—1. Consent is the permission to do a certain act, freely given, without force, fraud, or threats, by a rational and sober person, so situated as to be able to form an independent opinion upon the matter to which he consents.

2. Every person has a right to consent to the infliction of any bodily injury, in the nature of a surgical operation, upon himself, or any child or imbecile under his care.

3. No one has a right to consent to the infliction upon himself of death, or an injury likely to cause death (except in the nature of a surgical operation), or to the infliction upon himself of bodily harm amounting to a maim, for any purpose injurious to the public—*e.g.*, castration—or to the infliction of bodily harm in such manner as to amount to a breach of the peace, or in a prize fight or other exhibition calculated to collect together disorderly persons.

*4. The consent of any girl under sixteen to be carnally known by any man, is not recognised by the law.

Conspiracy.—1. Conspiracy is the agreement of *two or more persons* to commit a crime, or to do a lawful act by unlawful means.

2. Conspiracy is a misdemeanor, punishable by fine and imprisonment, with hard labour, except in the case of persons conspiring and agreeing together to murder any person, or soliciting, encouraging, persuading, or endeavouring to persuade, or proposing to any person to murder any other person, either a British subject or not, and in the United Kingdom or elsewhere, when it entails penal servitude. (24 & 25 Vict., c. 100, s. 4.)

3. *Conspiracy to Defeat Justice.*—Every one is guilty of misdemeanor who conspires with any other person to accuse any person falsely of any crime, or to do anything

to obstruct, prevent, pervert, or defeat the course of justice. (*See* OBSTRUCTION OF JUSTICE, p. 122.) (14 & 15 Vict., c. 100, s. 29.)

Conspirators.—When two or more persons conspire together to commit any offence, or actionable wrong, everything said, done, or written, by any one of them, in the execution or furtherance of their common purpose, is deemed to be so said, done, or written by every one, and is a relevant fact as against each of them.

*****Constabulary Forces.**—1. Borough Constabulary Forces were established under the provisions of the Municipal Corporation Act (5 & 6 Wm. IV., c. 76), and the administration thereof by the Mayor and a Watch Committee appointed by the Council was authorised. The same statute laid down the general powers of the Watch Committee in the appointment, suspension, punishment, and dismissal of constables. These are here defined, as far as possible, under the several heads.

2. The establishment of a Constabulary Force in counties was authorised by 2 & 3 Vict., c. 93, confirmed by 3 & 4 Vict., c. 88, but made compulsory in 1856 by 19 & 20 Vict., c. 69; all which statutes, regulating the entire administration of county constabulary, are construed as one Act. (20 Vict., c. 2.)

3. The police of both county and borough forces are constables, the latter in all the boroughs within the county, the former throughout the county in which the borough is situated, as well as seven miles beyond. The public service demands that the utmost cordiality and co-operation shall prevail between county and borough police forces.

Constables' Duties.—1. A constable must readily and strictly obey the orders of his superiors in rank in the police.

2. He must be very civil and respectful in his demeanor and conduct to the public, giving the best answers he can to the numerous questions which may be put to him, and showing at all times a readiness to do all in his power to oblige, consistently with the rules of the service.

3. He must report to his Inspector or Sergeant, the first time he sees either of them, the particulars of any accident or occurrence, which has come under his notice.

4. He must speak the truth at all times and under all circumstances, and when called upon to give evidence, state all he knows respecting the case, without fear or reservation, and without any desire to influence the result, either for or against the prisoner.

5. To enable him to speak quite confidently, and to prevent the possibility of his evidence being shaken, he should provide himself with a pocket-book and pencil, in which he can take down at the time, dates, and other particulars, respecting accidents or occurrences, and to which he can always refer, and submit, if required, to his superior officer. (*See* EVIDENCE, p. 74.)

6. Untruthfulness is the gravest disqualification for the police service.

7. When called upon by a person to take another person into custody, he must be guided in a great measure by the circumstances of the case, and the nature of the charge or offence; but if he has any doubt as to how he ought to act, the safest course is to ask all the persons concerned to go with him to the station, where the Inspector will hear and determine whether the charge is to be entered or not, and the responsibility is then taken off the constable.

8. If a constable is called upon to act, he must do so with energy, promptness, and determination; for if he wavers or doubts, the thief may escape, or the opportunity to render assistance may be lost.

9. The duties and powers of constables are defined under the different heads of this code. It would therefore be superfluous to say more than repeat that a constable may follow a criminal wherever he goes; if he takes refuge in any house, he may break into it, if absolutely necessary, first stating who he is, and his business. He is also justified in forcing an entry, when parties are fighting furiously, or when a felony is about to be committed inside, as when there is a violent cry of "Murder," and calls for assistance.

Contraband Goods.—Contraband goods are those whereof the importation into, or exportation from, the Kingdom is prohibited, save on the payment of Customs' duty. They are specified by law or special treaties with foreign states, and comprise wine, spirits, tobacco, besides a variety of raw and manufactured goods.

Convicts.—1. A convict is a person found guilty of a crime, and sentenced to penal servitude.

*2. During every such sentence a certain number of marks have to be earned by good conduct and industry. This can be done in about three-fourths of the total period of punishment in the case of men, two-thirds in the case of women. Every day, so many marks are awarded towards the total, and for misconduct and offences against prison discipline marks are forfeited, thus prolonging the period of actual detention.

3. Convicts who give information advancing the interests of justice, and especially with reference to receivers of stolen goods, and contemplated crime, are occasionally permitted by the Secretary of State to earn double marks; and so, while the period of release still depends on their behaviour, they can materially shorten their term of penal servitude.

4. A convict desiring to give information to the police, has only to signify his wish to the Governor, who communicates with the Chief Officer of the police force interested, and, under proper authority, two officers should be sent to take his statement, which must be treated as absolutely confidential.

*Convicts on License. — When convicts have earned the total required number of marks, they are released on license, and allowed their liberty so long as they conform to the subjoined conditions :—

Firstly.—That they report themselves where directed within forty-eight hours after liberation.

Secondly.—That they (women excepted), report themselves every month at the nearest Police Station to their place of abode, between the hours of Nine in the morning and Nine in the evening, on the day of the month named in the notice.

Thirdly.—That they reside—that is, sleep—at the address notified to the Police, in order that they may be at once found if required for any legal purpose.

Fourthly.—That they get their living by honest means, and regular employment.

Fifthly.—That if they change their address, or leave any Police District at all, they give notice of their removal at the Police Station at which they are reporting, and also at the nearest Police Station within forty-eight hours of arriving in any other Police District, in any part of the United Kingdom.

Sixthly.—That Convicts at liberty produce their Licenses when called upon to do so by a Police Officer.

*Convict Supervision Office.—1. At the Convict Office of the Metropolitan Police are kept criminally classified albums, of photographs and marks, of all convicts discharged on license, and persons under police supervision, in England. The antecedents of those residing in the Metropolitan Police District are further recorded in supervision registers, together with such particulars as to their conduct while on license, or under police supervision, as can be obtained in the periodical visits which are ordered.

2. The albums, registers, and records of the Convict Supervision Office, are open from 10 a.m. to 5 p.m., to the police of all forces and the warders of H.M.'s prisons, either in uniform, or on production of their authority.

3. At the Convict Supervision Office is also kept the property of all prisoners who have been convicted in the Metropolitan Police District, during the period of their punishment. (*See* PRISONERS' PROPERTY, p. 141.)

Co-operation.—1. Co-operation between all forces, between every individual composing each force, between all ranks, between the public and the police, is absolutely essential for the achievement of complete success. It is perfectly immaterial by what force, by what division, by what officer, or by what legal means, an offender is brought to justice, so long as the end is gained.

2. All the assistance it is possible for the Metropolitan Police to give, may be invariably relied on by every county, city, or borough constabulary force to the utmost extent of their numerical strength, the exigency of internal duties, and legal power.

Coroners.—1. Immediate information of the finding of a dead body should be communicated to the Coroner, who will then decide whether or not an inquest is to be held thereon, fix the day, time, and place, and give the necessary directions for the convening of the jury.

2. Under ordinary circumstances, a body should not be moved from a place in which it is found, except on the Coroner's order (*see* MURDER, p. 117); but, of course, this does not apply to bodies found in places open to public view. (*See* DEAD BODIES, p. 59.)

Correspondence.—1. In order that correspondence on police business may be properly conducted, it should invariably pass through the same channel; for confusion is absolutely inevitable if police officers of different ranks correspond with other forces and private individuals on public matters.

2. In the Metropolitan Police, correspondence on general subjects, complaints against police, requests for police aid, applications to join the force, on the public carriage service, concerning common lodging-houses, &c., are dealt with by the Commissioner or Assistant-Commissioners, and all reports on such matters and the general discipline of the service, the disposition of the men, the regulation of the traffic, bastardy, desertion, and non-payment of rates are submitted to one or the other; whilst all communications relating to the operation of the criminal law, and all reports bearing on crime, and the measures to be taken, or which have been taken with regard to it, are addressed to the Assistant-Commissioner, Criminal Investigation Department, and dealt with in his office.

3. All letters received by any police officer, on police duty, should be at once submitted to the Superintendent.

4. In constabulary districts the Superintendent of the Division concerned is usually addressed to avoid loss of time. His station is given in the Police Almanac.

5. Police are, however, perfectly free, and invited to communicate by letter, or otherwise, with any other member of the same force, for the purpose of obtaining, or giving, information, on any subject connected with the discovery of crime, but the letters should be entirely private and unofficial.

Corrosive Fluid Throwing. — 1. Every one is guilty of felony, and liable to penal servitude, who unlawfully sends or delivers or causes to be taken or received by any person, any explosive substance, or other dangerous or noxious thing, or puts, or lays at any place, or casts or throws at, or upon, or otherwise applies, to any person any corrosive fluid, or destructive, or explosive substance. (24 & 25 Vict., c. 100, s. 29.)

2. In these cases, olive-oil should be immediately applied to the burn, and its surface covered by cotton wool, while search is made for the bottle containing the fluid thrown, which may be of very material service in bringing home the crime to the miscreant who perpetrated it.

Counterfeit Coin.—1. Every one commits a misdemeanor who utters (that is, sends or puts into circulation) counterfeit current "gold or silver" coin, knowing it to be counterfeit.

2. *Uttering Base Copper or Foreign Coin.*—Every one commits a misdemeanor—

(*a*) Who, without lawful authority or excuse, to be proved by him, exports or puts on board any vessel for the purpose of being exported from the country any counterfeit current coin whatever, knowing the same to be counterfeit.

(*b*) Who utters any counterfeit current copper coin, knowing the same to be counterfeit.

(*c*) Who has in his possession three or more pieces of such counterfeit coin, knowing the same to be false, and with intent to utter any of them.

(*d*) Who, with intent to defraud, utters as gold or silver coin, any coin which is not such coin, or any medal or piece of metal, or mixed metal, resembling in size, figure, and colour, the current coin, as which it is uttered, but being of less value.

(*e*) Who defaces any current coin whatever by stamping thereon any names or words.

(*f*) Who utters any counterfeit gold or silver coin of any foreign prince, state, or country, knowing it to be counterfeit.

(*g*) Who has in his custody or possession more than five pieces of counterfeit gold or silver coin, or any counterfeit copper coin of any foreign prince, state, or country, without lawful authority or excuse, to be proved by such person.

3. A person arrested for uttering counterfeit coin should be searched as soon as possible, and great care taken that he throws nothing away. (*See* COINING, p. 43.) (24 & 25 Vict., c. 99.)

County Councils.—By the Local Government Act, 1888 (s. 9), while the Justices of the Peace remain the Conservators of the Peace, to whom the Chief Constable and all other constables owe the obligation of obedience to lawful orders in that behalf, the general administration of the County Police was removed from Quarter Sessions, and vested in a standing joint committee of the Quarter Sessions and County Council.

Cross-Examination.—1. Cross-examination is the examination of a witness for the opposite side, with a view to shake and discredit his evidence in the opinion of the jury.

2. Cross-examination of police is almost invariably hostile, and directed to create an impression among the jury unfavourable to the officer, by insinuations that he is unduly striving for the conviction of the prisoner, that he hopes thereby to gain promotion or reward, by endeavouring to prove that his present evidence differs from that given before the Magistrate, or on some previous occasion, and more than all by provoking the officer to some hasty and unguarded answer in an ebullition of temper. If any witness, and more especially a constable, loses his temper under cross-examination, the success of the opposite side is all but secured.

3. However disagreeable, irritating, and even insulting the questions, they should be answered coolly, briefly ("Yes," or "No," whenever possible), good-temperedly, truthfully, and respectfully. The advocate is but acting upon his instructions, and performing his duty. The questions he puts, convey no personal feeling whatever, and a hasty, disrespectful reply is what he seeks, but should never obtain, from the police.

4. If a question is put, the answer to which might involve a breach of confidence, such as giving the name of an informant, or bring suspicion upon innocent persons, or be otherwise disadvantageous to the public service, the witness should reply, "I decline to answer;" or ask the Judge if he is compelled to answer that question. If two questions be so blended as to appear one, and yet require two answers—the one "No!" and the other "Yes!"—the witness should appeal to the Judge to have the question amended.

The sympathy of the court is invariably with a truthful, candid, good-tempered, respectful witness.

* **Cruelty to Animals.**—1. A constable witnessing the perpetration of any gross act of cruelty, upon any animal whatsoever (including birds) may, without warrant, apprehend the offender and take him before a Magistrate.

2. The law also enables a constable to apprehend, without warrant, upon the complaint and information of

any other person, who declares his or her name and place of abode. (12 & 13 Vict., c. 92.)

If this course is necessary, owing to the grossness of the case, or the uncertain residence of the delinquent or his master, the animal should be conveyed to the greenyard or other place of safety.

3. But it is more desirable, when the offender is known and not likely to abscond, that he should be summoned, rather than summarily arrested.

In any case the constable should carefully observe, and note in writing, the exact nature of the cruelty, the condition of the animal, and the character of its wounds, their situation, and especially if old, discharging, and in contact with the harness, and examine the same for adhering particles of matter and dried blood. If lameness is the source of complaint, it should be *particularly* ascertained whether or not there is suffering or inflammation in the injured part, as lameness is not always an indication of pain. If weakness or infirmity, take care to have a witness to give evidence of the bodily condition, age, and incapacity of the animal, and the labour exacted from it. If over-loading, it is indispensable to show painful distress of the animal—*e.g.*, trembling, falling, unusual perspiration, or exhaustion—or to show violence on the part of the driver. If mutilation or any other torture, observe minutely and take down in writing the precise character of the same in detail. If for starving animals, overstocking cows, exposing shorn sheep to cold atmosphere, or other acts difficult for a private person to prove, a veterinary surgeon should be called to examine the animals at the time of the offence, or as soon afterwards as possible, and he should be produced as a witness at the hearing.

It is important for the exact words of the accused when stopped to be remembered, as they frequently amount to an admission of guilt.

In every case (if possible) obtain the name and address of a respectable witness, willing to give supporting evidence.†

---

† The Secretary of the Royal Society for the Prevention of Cruelty to Animals, 105, Jermyn Street, London, will gladly assist the Police by every means in his power, and the Council will be grateful, too, for the friendly bearing of the Police towards the officers of the Society located in different parts of the country.

Culpable Negligence.—Every one upon whom the law imposes any duty, or who has, by contract of service, or by any act, taken upon himself any duty tending to the preservation of life, and who neglects to perform that duty, by want of attention and caution, and thereby causes the death (or bodily injury) of any person, is guilty of culpable negligence.

Damage to Machinery, Rivers, Vessels, and Buoys.—Every one commits felony who does any of the following acts, unlawfully and maliciously, viz.—

(*a*) Damages any agricultural or manufacturing machine, or engine, with intent to render it useless.

(*b*) Hinders the working of a mine, by damaging any mining operation or machinery.

(*c*) Does any mischief to a river or canal, with intent to obstruct navigation.

(*d*) Does any act to destroy the fish in a fish-pond.

(*e*) Puts lime or other noxious material in a salmon river, with intent to destroy any fish then being, or afterwards to be put, therein.

(*f*) Cuts through or destroys the dam or floodgate of any mill-pond, reservoir, or pool.

(*g*) Damages any ship or vessel, with intent to render it useless. (24 & 25 Vict., c. 97.)

Damage to Property.—Every one commits a misdemeanor who does any of the following acts, unlawfully and maliciously—

(*a*) Being a tenant for a term, pulls down, demolishes, or severs from the freehold, any fixture.

(*b*) Destroys or damages any tree, shrub, or underwood, to the value of one shilling.

(*c*) Destroys or damages any production growing in a garden, or hot-house.

(*d*) Destroys or damages any cultivated root or plant, not being in a garden, used for food of man or beast, or for medicine, or in any manufacture.

(*e*). In any way destroys any fence, wall, stile, gate, or any part thereof.

(*f*) In any way impedes the working of the electric telegraph.

(*g*) Destroys or damages any article in a museum, or monument in a church or cemetery, or statue exposed to public view.

(*h*) Kills, maims, or wounds, either cattle, or any dog,

bird, or domestic animal:—the former, felony punishable by penal servitude; the latter, a misdemeanor.

(*i*) Obstructs, by any unlawful act or wilful omission, any railway engine or carriage.

(*j*) Who unlawfully and maliciously commits any damage, injury, or spoil to, or upon, any real or personal property whatsoever, either of a public or private nature. (24 & 25 Vict., c. 97.)

Dead Bodies.—1. When a dead body is found, and there is no doubt that life is extinct, it should never be touched until the arrival of a constable, who should forthwith carefully note its appearance, and all surrounding it. If he suspects that death was caused by violence, he should not move the body, or allow any part of the clothing, or any article about it, to be touched, or moved, by any person, until the arrival of a Sergeant or Inspector, who should be sent for by a messenger. (*See* MURDER, p. 117.)

2. The most obvious signs of death are—

(*a*) A cessation of breathing—no movement of the chest—no moist breath to dim a looking-glass placed before the mouth.

(*b*) A cessation of the heart's action—no impulse against the side, or pulse beating in arteries.

(*c*) The eyelids half closed, the eyes dim and glassy, and the pupils dilated.

(*d*) The jaws clenched.

(*e*) The tongue appearing between the teeth.

(*f*) A frothy mucus about the nose and mouth.

(*g*) The fingers half closed.

(*h*) The surface of the body pale and cold.

(*i*) The body rigid.

3. If the death is probably owing to natural causes, or to suicide, the body should be taken to the mortuary, or other convenient place near at hand, and immediate notice be sent to the Coroner (p. 53); the body and clothes being first searched for any marks or papers which may establish its identity, and any property taken possession of. To fail to give notice to the Coroner prior to putrefaction, is a misdemeanor. The death must also be registered.

4. If the body is not identified, it should be photographed prior to burial or post-mortem examination, and dressed as nearly as possible as it was in life.

Death by Misadventure.—Death by misadventure arises where a man doing a lawful act, without any intention of hurt, unfortunately kills himself or another.

Deer Stealing.—Every one commits an offence, who unlawfully and wilfully courses, hunts, snares, or carries away, kills, wounds, or attempts to kill, and wound any deer kept in any enclosed or unenclosed land. (24 & 25 Vict., c. 96.)

Defilement of Children.—(*See* p. 41.)

*****Defilement of Women and Girls.**—Every one commits a misdemeanor, who, *by intimidation, false pretences, or false representations, or other fraudulent means,* procures any woman to have illicit carnal connection, or who has unlawful intercourse with a woman he knows to be an idiot or imbecile. (24 & 25 Vict., c. 100, s. 49.)

Demanding Property with Menaces.—Every one is guilty of felony, who with menaces or force demands, either for himself or for any other person, any valuable thing with intent to steal the same, whether the thing demanded is received or not, or whether there is or is not power to carry out the threat. (24 & 25 Vict., c. 96, s. 45.)

Demeanour.—1. The utility of a constable mainly depends on his own individual bearing and conduct. The exercise of his authority as representing the law on every petty occasion, will only provoke opposition and resentment.

2. A polite forbearing demeanour will, on the other hand, if accompanied by intelligence and zeal, enlist the sympathies and respect of the public, and greatly assist him in the discharge of his duties in such manner as will entitle him to the confidence of his superiors, and secure him ultimate honour and advantage.

Depositions.—1. The deposition of a witness is his evidence before a Magistrate taken down in writing. It is read over to each witness and signed by him.

2. Police should be very careful that it contains an absolutely accurate statement of their evidence; for if there is any omission or error, it will be made the ground of cross-examination at the trial, and tend to cast a doubt upon the officer's truthfulness.

3. If by accident anything is omitted, it must not be

added at the trial, save under very unusual circumstances, and in such cases it will be best to say to the Judge, after the examination in chief, and without its being elicited, by any question or cross-examination, " I inadvertently omitted, my lord, to state before the magistrate, a certain fact, of which I have a note, made at the time of my ascertaining it; am I at liberty to do so now?" If the Judge consents, the evidence can be given.

4. Important as it is that the evidence given at a trial should correspond with that given before the committing Magistrate, the police must never lose sight of the far greater importance of their testimony being absolutely true, and if a mistake has been made it should be candidly admitted.

5. Copies of depositions, when required, can be obtained by either prosecutor or prisoner from the Magistrate's clerk on payment of the usual fee.

Description.—1. The description of individuals suspected of offences whose apprehension is sought, or who are missing, or have been found dead, should be fully given, particular mention being made of any peculiarities of dress and appearance. The following form may be advantageously used:—

(Designation of Police Force.)

Photograph.

DESCRIPTION
OF

Name*_____

Alias_____

* If a married woman, give also maiden name.

Born at_____

Age_____

Profession or Calling _____

Wanted for _____
* * _____
Height _____
Build _____
Hair _____
Eyebrows _____
Forehead _____
Eyes _____
Nose _____
Mouth _____
Chin _____
Face _____
Complexion _____
Beard _____
Moustache _____
Marks about the Face, Hands, or Person _____
Peculiarities of Manner, Gait, or Speech _____
Dress _____
Where likely to be found, known, or heard of _____

NOTE.
(*Place*),
   day of   18

* * State if a warrant has been issued.

2. Descriptions of property stolen should be equally minute, and especial prominence given to any word, inscription, engraving, or shape, by which it may be identified.

 ***Deserters.**—1. Soldiers, sailors, or marines, who have deserted, may be arrested at any time without warrant, except in a dwelling-house, and conveyed before a Magistrate.

 2. Rewards are given for the apprehension of deserters.

 ***Desertion.**—Any person who procures or persuades a soldier to desert, or assists him in so doing, or, knowing any soldier to be a deserter, conceals him, or aids or assists him to conceal himself, is liable to imprisonment with hard labour.

Deserting Families.—If a person runs away, and leaves his wife, and his or her child or children, chargeable to any parish, he may be apprehended on warrant issued at the instance of the parish. (*See* ROGUES AND VAGABONDS, p. 162.)

Destitute Persons.—1. Destitute persons coming under the observation of the police, should be taken, or directed, to the workhouse of the parish wherein they are found, except in special and urgent cases, when they should be taken to the nearest Union.

2. Police should not remove sick or destitute persons from any house or dwelling. If applied to, they should refer the proprietor to the Relieving Officer of the district, who will take the necessary steps.

Detached Constables.—Detached constables in rural districts, are generally men selected for steadiness of conduct. They should never forget that on their own bearing depends the credit of the entire force to which they belong, and in proportion as they honour it, will they be watchful of their action and behaviour.

Detection of Crime.—1. The certainty of the detection of criminals is a point to be aimed at by all ranks of police, and it can only be attained by cordial co-operation, an absence of craving for individual credit, free interchange of information, great activity, and the constant adoption of fresh and unexpected measures.

2. Every constable on his beat or fixed point has many opportunities for bringing offenders to justice. If this is done by honourable and legitimate means, it is the surest road to future success. Every meritorious action is certain to meet with recognition; and in no case will a constable be deprived of the merit of initial discovery, even if the subsequent following out of the case necessitates the employment of other officers.

3. In every instance it must be borne in mind, not only that the culprit has to be discovered, but that his delinquency must be brought home to him by legal evidence.

4. Precipitancy is therefore as much to be discouraged as any act repugnant to law and public feeling.

Detectives.—1. The unravelment of crime must necessarily depend in a very great measure upon the energy, the ability, the judgment, the zeal, and the integrity of the detective force.

2. The work is more varied and interesting than the ordinary street duty; the officer is brought into contact with a greater variety of persons, and he is more prominently before his superiors and the public. It is of the utmost importance that the duties should only be undertaken by men who have a voluntary inclination for them, and who have given proof of skill while on beat duty, for without genuine perseverance and zeal, they cannot be performed.

3. Detective officers should be especially guarded against the arrogation of individual credit; and if they have any information which may secure the arrest of a criminal, they should communicate it to the officer who is placed in a position to work it out, instead of reserving it for themselves.

4. They should be watchful against taking cases away from each other, and especially from a uniform constable.

5. But, above all, they should remember that it is far better to let ten guilty persons escape than that one innocent person should be apprehended.

6. Every one is liable to make mistakes, and an error should be freely acknowledged the instant it is discovered; for sooner or later, the truth is certain to come out, and it may then be too late to repair it.

7. Detectives must necessarily have informants, and be obliged to meet them when and where they can. But it is very desirable that the public-house should be avoided as much as possible. Tap-room information is rarely worth much. Occasionally, perhaps, refreshment must be given to an informant, but when possible it is best to give money.

8. A detective should keep his own counsel, hear everything others have to say, but draw his own conclusions; follow out every channel which may possibly lead to the discovery of the truth, and be slow to adopt positive theories; and above all, not communicate mere suspicions to any one.

9. It is highly undesirable for detectives to proclaim their official character to strangers, by walking with police in uniform, by walking in step with each other, and in a drilled style, or by wearing very striking clothing,

or police regulation boots, or by openly recognising constables in uniform, or saluting superior officers.

Determination to Arrest.—When once the mind of an officer is made up to arrest a delinquent he must not be asked any question, without a strict caution that the answer may be used against him; but as was said in effect by the late Lord Chief Justice Cockburn, at the Central Criminal Court, on July 16th, 1870, "if you ask a man questions with an honest intention to elicit the truth, and to ascertain whether there are grounds for apprehending him, it is quite a different thing to asking questions with a foregone intention to arrest."†

Director of Criminal Investigations.—1. The author of this Police Code was appointed Director of Criminal Investigations in March, 1878, and resigned in order to enter Parliament in June, 1884.

2. The criminal administration and correspondence of the Metropolitan Police was under his direction, and the whole detective establishment under his absolute control.

3. All letters and reports bearing on criminal matters in the Metropolis should now be addressed to the successor to his duties, viz., the Assistant Commissioner, Criminal Investigation Department, Metropolitan Police Office, London, S.W. (*See* p. 198.)

Discharging Firearms.—Every person wantonly discharging any firearm in or near any thoroughfare, to the damage or danger of any person, within view of a constable, may be apprehended, and is liable to a fine. (POLICE ACTS.)

Discipline.—1. Discipline is the obedience and respect to lawful authority which distinguishes an organised body from a rabble.

2. While the public interest demands that discipline shall be rigidly maintained, and neither disrespect nor disobedience tolerated, it should not be enforced by an habitually harsh and dictatory manner.

Dismissal.—1. Any police officer may be dismissed, forfeiting all claim to pension or gratuity, without any reason being assigned; but, in the Metropolitan Force, one is usually given and published in orders.

† This dictum is strongly affirmed by Sir Henry Hawkins. (*See* p. 13.)

2. A constable dismissed from one police force can never obtain admission to any other.

Disobedience of Orders.—1. No disobedience of an order can be allowed in any force, and every officer must recollect that it is his *duty first to obey*, and then, if necessary, to complain.

2. The officer giving an order is responsible for its consequences, unless the method of carrying it out has been improper, negligent, and contrary to the instructions received.

***Disorderly Houses.**—1. Disorderly houses are common bawdy houses, brothels, gaming houses, betting houses, and disorderly houses of entertainment.

* 2. A disorderly place of entertainment is one kept for public dancing or music without being properly licensed.

3. Complaint can be preferred against any disorderly house by two inhabitants, who make an information upon oath, and enter into a recognisance to prosecute; or action may be taken, in the case of a brothel, against the landlord or his agent, by summary process. (*See* BROTHELS, p. 32.) (25 Geo. II., c. 36, s. 5.)

***Disputed Ownership of Property.**—1. If the ownership of property in the custody of the Metropolitan Police is disputed, proceedings should be taken, under 2 & 3 Vict., c. 71, ss. 29 & 40.

2. In other districts, where no special statutory provisions exist, the best course will be for proceedings to be taken in the County Court, to show cause why the property in question should not be delivered over.

3. If the circumstances of a case do not admit of solution by these means, then the property may be given up to the party appearing best entitled thereto, upon his giving an indemnity. (*See* PRISONER'S PROPERTY, p. 141; and INDEMNITY, p. 100.)

Dissuading Witnesses from Testifying.—Every one commits a misdemeanor who, in order to obstruct the due course of justice, dissuades, hinders, or prevents any person lawfully bound to appear and give evidence as a witness, from so appearing and giving evidence, or endeavours to do so.

Distraint of Goods.—1. Police are bound to assist duly authorised officers of the law in the execution of warrants of distraint of goods or premises or otherwise issued to them, but such assistance should, as far as possible, be limited to the prevention only of a breach of the peace, and not extended to the absolute execution.

2. On no account should police leave their beats to enter the premises to be distrained, but should refer the bailiff to the nearest station.

Divine Service.—1. Police should, as far as possible, be encouraged to attend divine service.†

2. Every one commits a misdemeanor, and is liable, upon conviction, to a fine, who wilfully and maliciously or contemptuously disquiets or disturbs any persons lawfully assembled for religious worship, or in any way disturbs, molests, or misuses any preacher, teacher, or person officiating, or any person in the congregation.

3. Every one commits a misdemeanor, who is guilty of riotous, violent, or indecent behaviour in any authorised place of worship, either during divine service or at any other time, or in any churchyard or burial ground, or who, by any unlawful means, disquiets or misuses any duly authorised clergyman, ministering or celebrating any divine service or sacrament. (23 & 24 Vict., c. 32, s. 2.)

Divisions.—1. The division is the unit of police organisation.

2. All business relating to a division should pass through the superintendent in charge, and although divisional feeling, or *esprit de corps,* is by no means to be discouraged, police should at all times recollect that the boundaries of divisions are by no means the boundaries of their duty, and that although they are more immediately responsible for all that occurs within their own defined sphere of action, they are bound to give all possible assistance to the police of neighbouring divisions, whether of the same or of an adjacent force.

Divorce Proceedings.—With divorce proceedings, police have nothing whatsoever to do, and on no account should any inquiries be made or information be furnished, on any matter, the object of which is evidently, or probably, to obtain evidence in support of proceedings for divorce, or judicial separation, or any subject connected therewith.

† The Christian Policeman's Association has in recent years done much good, and its monthly organ, *On and Off Duty,* is a valuable and interesting publication.

Documentary Evidence.—Documentary evidence is that founded upon documents produced for the inspection of the Court. It is not admissible in criminal cases, save in the instance of DYING DECLARATIONS. (*See* p. 71.)

*****Dog Carriages.**—Every person using any dog for the purpose of drawing, or helping to draw, any cart, carriage, truck, or barrow, is liable to a fine. (17 & 18 Vict., c. 60, s. 2.)

Dog Fighting.—(*See* p. 43.)

Dogs Found.—1. Any dog found by a constable straying on a highway, not under the control of any person, and which there is reason to suppose is savage or dangerous, may be seized by any police officer or constable, and detained until the owner has claimed the same, and paid all expenses incurred. (34 & 35 Vict., c. 56.)

2. Dogs found by the police undoubtedly suffering from rabies should be killed with the truncheon † or some other weapon as speedily and painlessly as possible, the officer taking great care to avoid being bitten, or to allow any of the saliva to touch him or his clothes. If he receives a wound, however slight, from a mad dog, he should proceed at once to the nearest surgeon and have the bite cauterised, submitting the expense thereby incurred. (*See* MAD DOGS, p. 111.)

*****Dog Licences.**—Every person keeping a dog is bound to take out an annual 7s. 6d. licence, for each one, from the Excise, to be obtained at every Money Order Office, subject to a penalty. All licences expire on the 31st of December, and must be renewed before the end of January.

Dog Stealing.—1. A person who steals any dog is liable to imprisonment with hard labour.

2. A person who unlawfully has in his possession or on his premises any stolen dog, or the skin of any stolen dog, knowing such dog to have been stolen, or such skin to be the skin of a stolen dog, is guilty of an offence.

---

† The truncheon should be carefully cleaned after such use. Police need not, however, assume that every half-starved, hunted dog, unable to get a drop of water, is suffering from hydrophobia. While the public safety demands that every precaution should be taken, care is necessary that precaution is not converted into wanton cruelty.

3. He who corruptly takes any money or reward, directly or indirectly, under pretence or upon account of aiding any person to recover any stolen dog, or any dog in the possession of any person not its owner, is liable to imprisonment with hard labour. (24 & 25 Vict., c. 96.)

Doors and Windows Open.—1. When police on night duty find doors or windows left open in such a place and in such manner as to afford ingress to a thief, the attention of the inmates should be immediately called thereto; or if this appears difficult or inexpedient, the constable should either close the open door or window himself, or give the house such additional attention as he can, reporting the fact on going off duty.

2. The occupier should be acquainted next day by an Inspector or Sergeant with the occurrence.

Dress of Police.—There is nothing which redounds more to the credit of a force than the smart appearance of its members, and their having all their appointments clean and properly put on.

Drill.—The candidates on the preparatory class are usually instructed in elementary drill, as well as constables and Sergeants prior to promotion. This is absolutely necessary, as, without some practice in drill, bodies of men cannot possibly move with that discipline and regularity which enables them to cope with a mob superior in numbers.

Drinking.—1. Drinking when indulged in by the police wholly unfits them for their calling, deprives them of all chance of promotion and advancement, and is certain to lead them to punishment and speedy dismissal.

2. Police who accept drink from persons whom they meet, from publicans or their barmen, or from persons to whom they are sent on some matter of duty, are unworthy of the service. (*See* p. 154, sub-section *f*.)

3. Above all, police should avoid drinking with witnesses, or persons they purpose arresting, or who have been just discharged from custody. If a constable requires refreshment, whether on beat, special, or Court duty, he should obtain the permission of his Sergeant or Inspector to purchase it.

4. Police who are drunk on or coming off duty, are invariably reported, and most severely punished.

*Drivers Asleep, or not Holding the Reins.—Any person having the care of any cart or carriage, and riding on the shafts or any part thereof, without having and holding the reins, or who is at such distance therefrom as not to have complete control of the horse drawing it, is liable to a fine, recoverable by summons. (POLICE ACTS.)

Drovers.—Police should also be very watchful to see that no cruelty is practised upon animals by drovers.

Drugging.—1. Every one is guilty of felony, who unlawfully administers to any person any chloroform, laudanum, or other stupefying or overpowering matter, or attempts to do so. (24 & 25 Vict., c. 100, s. 22.)

2. In these cases, as in vitriol-throwing, the bottle which held the drug should be searched for without delay.

Drunkenness.—Drunkenness is no excuse for any offence, of omission or commission, unless involuntarily brought about by the unlawful administration of some drug.

Drunken Persons.—1. Every person found drunk in any highway or other public place, whether a building or not, or on any licensed premises, is liable to a penalty. (35 & 36 Vict., c. 94, s. 12.)

*2. Every person who, in any highway, or other public place, whether a building or not, is guilty while drunk of riotous or disorderly behaviour, or who is drunk while in charge, on any highway or other public place, of any carriage, horse, cattle, or steam engine, or who is drunk when in possession of any loaded fire-arms, may be apprehended, and is liable to a penalty of 40s., or imprisonment, with or without hard labour.

3. A drunken person should in no case be interfered with by the police, unless he is disorderly, and likely to do himself or others some injury, or so incapable as to be likely to sustain injury, in which case he should be taken to the station as quietly as possible with a few words of gentle persuasion.

4. But on no account should a constable leave his beat to conduct a drunken person to his home or elsewhere; and even if a man appears inclined to become disorderly, he should be cautioned and advised to keep quiet, before the law is enforced.

5. Police should be watchful for prostitutes and

others accosting drunken persons, and ensnaring them into a secluded place for purposes of robbery.

6. Persons are frequently found insensible in the streets, in reality suffering from apoplexy or other natural causes, the symptoms of which give them much the appearance of persons under the influence of drink, and such will be especially the case if their breath does not smell of alcohol. The police should be especially careful not to assume that a person is drunk, save on sufficient and incontestable grounds, for illness, or the excitement of being taken into custody, may at first contribute to such conclusion. (*See* PERSONS FOUND INSENSIBLE, p. 128.)

7. In all such cases, the first thing to do, is to try and arouse the drunkard by gently shaking him; if that fails, the neckcloth and collar should be loosened, and the head raised a little, by which means breathing is made easier.

8. A message in towns should be sent to the station for the stretcher and some further assistance. (*See* STRETCHERS, p. 173.)

9. The police should be very careful in conveying a person apparently drunk or insensible to the stations.

10. When being conveyed on the stretcher, or placed in the cell, the head should be kept slightly raised by a canvas pillow underneath it.

Duty.—Police on duty always wear their armlet, and should be careful that their conduct is such as at all times will uphold the credit of the service, as much by personal smartness as by their civility and correct behaviour.

Every constable does usually eight hours' daily duty. At the same time, no fixed rule is laid down, and whether nominally on, or off, duty, his responsibility to the public is the same, and he is bound to prevent and detect crime by all possible means.

Dwelling-Houses.—1. A dwelling-house is one in which a person habitually or usually sleeps.

2. Every one who enters any dwelling-house by night, without breaking in, with intent to commit, although not actually committing, felony therein, or who by day breaks in, is liable to penal servitude. (24 & 25 Vict., c. 96, s. 54.) (*See* BURGLARY, p. 33; and HOUSEBREAKING, p. 96.)

Dying Declarations.—1. In cases of murder or manslaughter, in which the victim is likely to die, a Magistrate should be informed of the facts, and requested to attend to take his or her dying declaration.

2. If there is no time for this, the declaration may be taken by an Inspector or other police officer. A statement made by a dying person concerning the subject under inquiry, in the presence of the prisoner, may be used as evidence.

3. An individual accused by the dying person should have formal notice served upon him of the intention to take the declaration (Form 123 under 30 & 31 Vict., c. 35, s. 6), and have an opportunity of being present when the declaration is made, in order to ask any questions.

4. In every case, for a dying declaration to be received in evidence, the declarant must be shown to the satisfaction of the Judge, to have been in actual danger of death, and to have given up all hope of recovery, at the time the declaration was made. It should therefore commence in this form :—

"I, A. B., having the fear of death before me, and being without hope of recovery, make the following statement."

5. It must then be taken down exactly in the words of the dying person, be read slowly and carefully over to him or her from beginning to end, and then signed by the deponent, before witnesses.

Education.—It is a duty every police officer owes to himself, to advance his education by every means in his power. A badly-educated man cannot have much hope of rising to a superior rank, however good his conduct. Every police officer has many opportunities of improving his education, and acquiring a thorough conception of his duties. If, for instance, he takes this manual, and, paragraph by paragraph, composes questions on the several subjects, and writes down the answers in an exercise book, and then learns them by heart, he will practise himself in writing and composition, he will improve his memory and the arranging power of his mind, at the same time that he will acquire a fair general knowledge of the criminal law. Then he should take opportunities of reading aloud, and of writing reports on imaginary incidents which might occur in the course of duty.

Elections.—1. The disability of the police to vote

at Parliamentary elections in England and Wales was removed in 1887 by an Act of which the author was a joint introducer. In Scotland the power previously existed. It has since been extended to Victoria (Australia). But it does not obtain in Ireland, and does not extend to municipal elections, and doubtfully to County Council elections.

2. It cannot, however, be too strongly urged upon the police where they have been given the franchise, that they should most studiously avoid, for their own security and the credit of the force for impartiality, taking any active part in an election, by public speech, writing, or demonstration. Above all, if on duty in or about a place used for political meeting, they should not express any approval or disapproval of the views enunciated by the speakers. They must remember they are policemen first, and electors afterwards.

Embezzlement.—1. When a clerk or servant, or person employed in such capacity, commits theft, by converting to his own use any money or valuable security, received by him on account of his master or employer, *before it has passed into the possession of the latter*, his offence is called embezzlement. (24 & 25 Vict., c. 96, s. 68.)

2. In cases of embezzlement, there is frequently a desire, rather that the amount of the defalcation should be made good, than that criminal justice should be vindicated.

It is therefore generally desirable that a warrant should be applied for by the defrauded party, as a guarantee that the prosecution will be proceeded with, when the absconding clerk or servant has been arrested.

Empty Houses.—Police should invariably pay the utmost possible attention to uninhabited houses. It is a frequent practice for householders, or their servants, to leave houses empty when at church, or absent on a holiday, without any notice to the police, and this thieves take advantage of. (*See* ATTIC LARCENIES, p. 26.)

Engravings.—When many thousand copies of an individual's portrait or of stolen articles are required for circulation, it is usually best to have the original sketch engraved on wood, when it can be printed off, with the necessary particulars and explanations. (*See* STOLEN PROPERTY, pp. 172 and 193.)

Erasures.—Erasures in accounts or official books are not allowable. Erasures in reports should rarely be made, as, if the report has to be transmitted to a third person, erasures say little for the clearness of the writer's mind, and it will generally be better to write the report again.

Escape of Prisoners.—1. For an officer either voluntarily to consent to, or negligently to allow, the escape of a prisoner from his lawful custody, renders him liable to legal punishment for a misdemeanor.

If by any means, or the neglect of any precaution, a prisoner effects his escape from the police, the officer in fault is usually suspended at once; and unless he succeeds in effecting the recapture within a few days, incurs great risk of dismissal.

2. Prisoners most frequently escape in conduct from one place to another, by distracting the attention of the officer, or by obtaining some slight privilege, such as leaning out of a carriage window for air, and subsequently opening the door, or feigning indisposition and urgent wants. Instances, however, are not wanting of prisoners taking advantage of temporary confusion at a police station, or disorder created by their friends in the passage of the Police Court, and thus to mingle unseen with the crowd, and effect an escape.

3. When police lose a prisoner, they must keep cool, and use every possible exertion to head him by telegraph and mounted messengers. A telegram, if the escape is effected on conveyance to a place, should be at once sent to the officer expecting the arrival, and who very likely has witnesses, and other arrangements in readiness. (*See* AIDING PRISONERS TO ESCAPE, p. 21; PURSUIT OF OFFENDERS, p. 155; and TRAVELLING WITH A PRISONER, p. 179.)

Evidence.—1. Police must give evidence with the strictest accuracy; for the administration of justice must in a great measure depend on the trustworthiness of their evidence.

2. They should habitually make accurate observation of all matters relating to duty, that they may be able to state the whole circumstances.

3. Notes should be made at the time of the particulars of a case to refresh the memory, if necessary, when called on to give evidence, and the original notes should always be kept, even if fair copies are made.

POLICE CODE.

4. Police must not suppress or overstate the slightest circumstance, so as to favour the prosecution or prejudice the prisoner.

5. They should endeavour, as far as possible, to feel indifferent as to the results of cases, and they perform their duty best by stating accurately and without malice or favour all the particulars they know.

6. When the police are sufferers from injuries received, and are giving evidence against those whom they believe to be guilty, it is especially necessary that they should not allow any feelings or wishes, as to the decision of the case, to influence them. (*See* TEMPER, p. 178.)

Greater weight will always be given to the evidence of police, if they state fully and without passion all they know, and make it evident that they are speaking the whole truth.

7. They should be especially careful to state all they know upon the first occasion; for if they afterwards add to their evidence in any material point, it is naturally looked on with mistrust, and is open to suspicion, either as to accuracy or veracity.

8. Any of the police, who wilfully depart from the truth, are utterly unfit for the service.

9. The police must not enter into conversations or statements, when before a Magistrate or Court, upon any matters except such as the charge under investigation makes it their duty to mention.

If the police give improper or unsatisfactory evidence, or any remarks are made respecting the evidence of police by Judges, Magistrates, or juries, the Inspector or Sergeant present should report full particulars to his superior officer.

10. Evidence must in all cases be direct; that is to say—

(*a*) If it refers to a fact alleged to have been seen, it must be the evidence of a witness who says he saw it.

(*b*) If it refers to a fact alleged to have been heard, it must be the evidence of a witness who says he heard it, and if affecting the guilt of the prisoner, must have been uttered in his presence. (*See* HEARSAY, p. 92.)

(*c*) If it refers to a fact alleged to have been perceived by any other sense, in any other manner, it must be the evidence of a witness who says he perceived it, by that sense, in that manner.

(*d*) If it refers to an opinion, or to the grounds on

which that opinion is held, it must be the evidence of the person who holds that opinion on those grounds.

11. Evidence may be given, in any proceeding of any fact in issue, and of any fact relevant to any fact in issue, unless excluded by the Judge as too remote to be material, under all the circumstances of the case.

The word "relevant" means that any two facts to which it is applied are so related to each other that, according to the common course of events, one, either taken by itself, or in connection with other facts, proves or renders probable the past, present, or future existence or non-existence of the other. (*See* CIRCUMSTANTIAL EVIDENCE, p. 42.)

Examination of Witnesses.—1. Witnesses are first examined in chief, then cross-examined, and then re-examined.

2. A witness may, while under examination, refresh his memory, by referring to any writing made by himself at the time of the transaction concerning which he is questioned, or so soon afterwards that the Judge considers it likely that the transaction was at that time fresh in his memory. The witness may also refer to any such writing made by any other person, and read by the witness within the time aforesaid, if when he read it, he knew it to be correct.

Any writing referred to, must be produced and shown to the adverse party, if he requires it; and such party may, if he pleases, cross-examine a witness thereupon.

*****Exercising Horses in the Street.**—Every person who, to the annoyance of the inhabitants or passengers, exposes a horse or other animal for sale, or exercises him up and down a thoroughfare, may be summoned. (POLICE ACTS.)

Exhibit.—An exhibit is the document referred to in an affidavit, and shown to the witness when the affidavit is sworn.

Expenses.—Every detail concerning expenditure in the public service must be accurately kept. This can only be done by entering each item, as it occurs, in the diary or pocket-book. Every purchase or payment of a special character should be supported by a voucher or receipt. Any laxity in keeping accounts is certain to lead to errors, which will cause the account to be questioned.

Experts.—When there is a question on any subject on which a course of special study or experience is necessary to the formation of an opinion, including handwriting, the opinions thereon of persons specially skilled in any such matter are relevant, and the persons are called experts.

Expirees.—An expiree is a person who has undergone a sentence of penal servitude, or of police supervision, but whose sentence has expired.

*Explosives.—1. The term "explosive" means every substance used, or manufactured with a view to produce a practical effect by explosion.

2. The manufacture of explosives must be confined to a factory, either lawfully existing or licensed for the purpose by the Secretary of State, or to a small fireworks factory licensed by the Local Authority. (38 Vict., c. 17.)

3. No explosive can be conveyed in a carriage or boat carrying public passengers in greater quantity than 5 lbs., and certain named explosives not at all, all due precautions being taken for the prevention of accidents by fire or explosion, subject to a penalty.

4. Any officer of police, or officer of the Local Authority, who has reasonable cause to suppose that any offence against the Act is being committed in respect of any carriage (not being on a railway) or any boat conveying, loading, or unloading, any explosive, and that the case is one of emergency, and that the delay in obtaining a warrant will be likely to endanger life, may stop, and enter, inspect, and examine such carriage or boat, and by detention, or removal thereof, or otherwise, take such precautions as may be reasonably necessary for removing such danger, in like manner as if such explosive were liable to forfeiture. Larger powers are vested in any Government Inspector,† Chief Officer of the Police, or Superior Officer of the Local Authority.

Retail dealing with gunpowder.

5. A person desiring to keep explosives must register his name, calling, and premises, in such manner and on

† The Chief Inspector of Explosives is located at the Home Office, London, and to him special inquiries or complaints as to explosives should be addressed.

payment of such fee, not exceeding one shilling, as may be directed by the Local Authority. Such registration is valid only for the person registered, and must be annually renewed by sending by post or otherwise, notice of such renewal to the Local Authority.

6. Gunpowder must not be hawked, sold, or exposed for sale upon any highway, street, public thoroughfare, or public place; if any gunpowder is so hawked, sold, or exposed for sale—

(1) The person hawking, selling, or exposing for sale the same, is liable to a penalty; and

(2) All or any part of the gunpowder which is so hawked or exposed for sale, or is found in the possession of any person convicted under this section, may be forfeited.

7. Gunpowder must not be sold to any child apparently under the age of thirteen years; and any person so selling gunpowder is liable to a penalty.

8. Any person who burns, maims, disfigures, or does any grievous bodily harm to any person by the explosion of gunpowder, or other explosive substance, or causes such to explode, with a like intent, is liable to penal servitude. (*See* CORROSIVE FLUID THROWING, p. 54.)

9. Every person who unlawfully sends or delivers, or causes to be taken or received by any person, any explosive substance, or puts or lays the same at any place, is similarly liable. (24 & 25 Vict., c. 100, ss. 28 & 29.)

10. Great care must be taken in moving or opening any package containing an explosive substance. If found near a railway or dwelling-house, and there is no immediate danger, it should not be moved until the arrival of an expert or superior officer of police, and no one allowed to go near it, for much may depend upon the position in which it is found; and footprints must be carefully secured.

Extortion.—Every one commits felony, who, with a view to extort or gain any valuable thing, from any person whatever—

1. Sends, delivers, utters, or directly or indirectly causes to be received, knowing the contents thereof, any letter or writing—

(*a*) Demanding any valuable thing of any person with menaces, without reasonable and probable cause.

(*b*) Accusing, or threatening to accuse, any other person of any crime punishable by law with death, or penal servitude for seven years or more, or of any assault with intent to commit any rape, or of any attempt or endeavour to commit any rape, or of any infamous crime (sodomy or bestiality).

2. Accuses, or threatens to accuse, any person whatever of any of the above-mentioned crimes.

3. Who, with intent to defraud or injure any other person, compels or induces any person to deal with any valuable security in any improper manner. (24 & 25 Vict., c. 96, s. 44.)

Extradition.—1. Treaties of extradition are in force between the British Empire and the Governments of—

1. France.
2. Germany.
3. Austria-Hungary.
4. Brazil.
5. Spain.
6. Italy.
7. Belgium.
8. The Netherlands.
9. Denmark.
10. Sweden and Norway.
11. Switzerland.
12. Hayti.
13. The United States of America.
14. Grand Duchy of Luxemburg.
15. Salvador.
16. Guatemala.
17. Russia.
18. Mexico.

A treaty of extradition was concluded with the Republic of Honduras on the 6th of January, 1874, but was denounced by that Government in 1877.

(33 & 34 Vict., c. 42.)

2. The treaties usually provide that the subjects of the one Government shall not be surrendered to take their trial for any offence committed within the jurisdiction of the other.

3. When a criminal is known to have fled to any one of the countries with which a treaty of extradition has been concluded, the application for his arrest must be made through the Home Office, and be based upon exactly the same documents, and certified in like manner, as detailed under the heading " Colonies, Surrender of Criminals to and from" (p. 44), substituting the Secretary of State for Foreign Affairs for the Colonial Secretary. A guarantee for the reimbursement of the expenses should also be obtained in the form mentioned.

4. As the majority of fugitives from British and colonial justice betake themselves to the United States

of America, owing to the repeated refusal of Congress to bring their international administration of the law into harmony with the spirit of modern times, it is desirable to bear in mind that in cases in which the extradition of a fugitive is requested from that country, the copies of the depositions upon which the warrant was granted can only be received in evidence, if they are produced by some person able to testify upon oath that, of his own knowledge, they are true copies of the originals.

5. The arrest of a fugitive criminal within the United Kingdom may be effected in two ways:—

(*a*) Under a warrant from a Metropolitan Police Magistrate at Bow Street.

(*b*) Under a warrant issued by any police Magistrate or Justice of the Peace in any part of the United Kingdom, on such information or complaint, and such evidence, or after such proceedings as would in the opinion of the person issuing the warrant justify a similar course if the crime had been committed, or the criminal convicted, in that part of the United Kingdom in which he exercises jurisdiction.

6. Failing the issue of such warrant, which, as before stated, may be granted by any Justice of the Peace, in any part of the United Kingdom, an arrest should not be effected, save in the most urgent and exceptional cases which would be guided by the ordinary law of arrest.

7. On the apprehension of any person under the Extradition Acts, and the treaty with any country, he has to be brought before a Magistrate of the Bow Street Police Court, and this, although the warrant may have been issued by a Justice of the Peace, in some other part of the United Kingdom.

8. The crimes for which extradition is usually granted are the following:—†

(1) Counterfeiting or altering money, and uttering counterfeit or altered money.

(2) Forgery, counterfeiting, or altering and uttering what is forged, counterfeited, or altered.

† Except to or from America, the narrow and old-fashioned treaty with which Government is a blot upon Anglo-Saxon civilisation, and only includes:—1. Murder. 2. Assault with intent to commit murder. 3. Piracy. 4. Arson. 5. Robbery (that is, larceny from the person by violence or menaces). 6. Forgery, or utterance of forged paper.

(3) Murder (including assassination, parricide, infanticide, and poisoning), or attempt to murder.
(4) Manslaughter.
(5) Abortion.
(6) Rape.
(7) Indecent assault, acts of indecency, even without violence, upon the person of a girl under twelve years of age.
(8) Child stealing, including abandoning, exposing, or unlawfully detaining.
(9) Abduction.
(10) Kidnapping and false imprisonment.
(11) Bigamy.
(12) Wounding or inflicting grievous bodily harm.
(13) Assaulting a Magistrate or peace or public officer.
(14) Threats by letter or otherwise with intent to extort.
(15) Perjury or subornation of perjury.
(16) Arson.
(17) Burglary or housebreaking, robbery with violence.
(18) Fraud by a bailee, banker, agent, factor, trustee, or director or member or public officer of any company made criminal by any Act for the time being in force.
(19) Obtaining money, valuable security, or goods by false pretences, including receiving any chattel, money, valuable security, or other property, knowing the same to have been unlawfully obtained.
(20) Embezzlement or larceny, including receiving any chattel, money, valuable security, or other property, knowing the same to have been embezzled or stolen.
(21) Crimes against the bankruptcy laws.
(22) Any malicious act done with intent to endanger persons in a railway train.
(23) Malicious injury to property, if the offence is indictable.
(24) Crimes committed at sea:—
(*a*) Any act of depredation or violence by the crew of a British or French vessel, against another British or French vessel, or by the crew of a foreign vessel not provided with a regular commission, against British or French vessels, their crews or their cargoes.
(*b*) The fact of any person, being or not one of the crew of a vessel, giving her over to pirates.
(*c*) The fact of any person, being or not one of the

crew of a vessel, taking possession of such vessel by fraud or violence.

(*d*) Sinking or destroying a vessel at sea, or attempting or conspiring to do so.

(*e*) Revolt or conspiracy to revolt by two or more persons on board a ship on the high seas against the authority of the master.

(25) Dealing in slaves in such manner as to constitute an offence against the laws of both countries.

The extradition is also to take place for participation, either as principals or accessories, in any of the aforesaid crimes, provided such participation is punishable by the laws of both contracting parties.

Although with Portugal, Greece, and the Ottoman Empire there is no treaty of extradition, fugitives can be generally got back from these countries by diplomatic action, set in motion by like procedure.

***Fairs.**—No fair can be held, save by licence from the Crown, or by virtue of long usage, supposing such a grant.

False Accounting.—1. Every one commits a misdemeanor who being a clerk, officer, or servant, or employed in such capacity, wilfully, and with intent to defraud, destroys, alters, mutilates, or falsifies any book, paper, writing, valuable security or account, which belongs to, or is in the possession of, his employer, or has been received by him for, or on behalf of, his employer.

2. Who similarly makes, or concurs in making, any false entry in, or omits, or alters, or concurs in omitting or altering, any material particular, from or in any such book or any document or account. (38 & 39 Vict., c. 24.)

False Character.—1. Any person falsely personating any master or mistress, their representative or agent, and either personally or in writing, giving any false, forged, or counterfeited character to any person offering himself or herself to be hired as a servant, is liable to a penalty. (32 Geo. III., c. 56, ss. 1 & 6.)

2. Every person is guilty of a similar misdemeanor who offers himself or herself as a servant, falsely asserting or pretending that he or she has served in any place, or who, by means of a false, forged, or altered certificate of his or her character, seeks to obtain or does obtain, or

who falsely and wilfully pretends not to have been hired, or to have been retained in any previous service. (s. 4.)

3. In default of payment, imprisonment with hard labour may be inflicted.

False Declaration.—A person who makes a false affirmation or declaration, instead of taking an oath, is liable to the same penalties as if he took a false oath; for the fact that he took an oath in any particular form is an admission that he regards it as binding on his conscience. (*See* PERJURY, p. 128.)

False Keys.—1. Many houses are broken into by false keys, and more particularly those occupied by persons of small means, which are frequently left vacant.

2. Police should be on the alert against this class of offence, especially on Sunday evenings; and if they notice one or two men going to several houses in which there are no lights, or which may be temporarily empty, should quietly ascertain their business, or endeavour to arrest the delinquents in the felonious act, if any.

3. If opportunity affords, it may be better to let the entry be accomplished rather than to apprehend during the progress of the attempt only, as there is then no doubt of the felonious intent. This principle of not acting prematurely, before the evidence is complete, applies to the majority of offences against property under ordinary circumstances.

False Personation.—Every one commits felony, who falsely and deceitfully personates any person with intent fraudulently to obtain any land, estate, chattel, money, or valuable security. (24 & 25 Vict., c. 98, s. 3, and 37 & 38 Vict., c. 36.)

False Pretences.—1. Every one commits a misdemeanor—

(*a*) Who by any false pretence obtains from any other person anything susceptible of larceny, or any money or valuable security, with intent to defraud.

(*b*) Who, with intent to defraud or injure any other person by any false pretence, fraudulently causes or induces any other person to write or sign any paper in any name, in order that it may afterwards be made, or converted into, or used, or dealt with as a valuable security.

2. A false pretence is a false representation, made either by words, writing, or conduct, that some fact

exists or existed, and notwithstanding that a person of common prudence might easily have detected its falsehood by inquiry, and although the existence of the alleged fact was, in itself, impossible.

3. But the expression "false pretence" does not include—

(*a*) A promise as to future conduct, not based upon a false allegation of an existing fact.

(*b*) Untrue or exaggerated commendation or depreciation of an article to be sold in ordinary course, unless there is a definite false assertion as to some fact capable of being positively determined. (24 & 25 Vict., c. 96, s. 88.)

Fastenings to Houses.—If the fastenings to houses are secure, the difficulty of a felonious entry is much increased. Windows properly bolted, or with some apparatus to prevent their being opened from without, shutters duly barred, with bells attached, and doors secured by a chain and bolts, as well as by a lock, present obstacles that are not likely to be easily overcome.

***Felony.**— Serious crimes are usually termed felonies, but the distinction between them and indictable misdemeanors will probably disappear on the long-hoped-for codification of the criminal law by Statute.

Females.—1. Police on duty must not idle or gossip with females in the streets, or at the doors of houses.

2. The police must not interfere with persons speaking to females in the street, unless annoyance or obstruction is caused.

Fences.—Whoever steals, cuts, breaks, or throws down, with intent to steal, any part of any live or dead fence, or any wooden post, pale, wire, or rail, set up, or used, as a fence, is punishable, for a first offence, by a fine and the value ; for the second by imprisonment with hard labour. (*See* DAMAGE TO PROPERTY, p. 58.) (24 & 25 Vict., c. 96, s. 34.)

***Ferocious Dogs.**—1. Every person who suffers to be at large any unmuzzled ferocious dog, or sets or urges any dog, or other animal, to attack, worry, or put in fear any person, horse, or other animal, may be summoned.

2. A magistrate to whom complaint is made that a

dog is dangerous, and not kept under proper control, may order it to be destroyed, or else that the owner shall keep it under control, subject to a penalty for every day of non-compliance.

Finding.—1. The finder of any article is bound to use due diligence to discover the lawful owner.

2. A finder of lost goods who converts them to his own use commits theft, if at the time when he takes possession of them he intends to convert them, knowing who the owner is, or having reasonable ground to believe that he can be found.

3. Police consulted by persons who have found any small article, and who are unable to go to a station, may take it from them and give a receipt, but they should be requested rather to deposit it themselves.

4. The finder of an article has a right of possession against all persons except the actual owner, provided he has done all he can to discover him.

5. Police on giving back an unclaimed article to the finder should obtain an indemnity in the form given in APPENDIX C., p. 195.

***Fines.**—The Chief Constable of a county, and Watch Committee of any city or borough, may fine any constable not exceeding one week's pay. (22 & 23 Vict., c. 32, s. 26.)

Fires.—1. Until the arrival of the firemen, the police should exert themselves in every possible way for the rescue of persons in danger, and the removal of property conformably with the wishes of the proprietors.

2. The police should clear the street or ground in the immediate vicinity of the fire of all persons not usefully employed, taking care that all the adjoining streets, as far as may be practicable, are kept clear of obstructions by crowds or vehicles, &c., so that the arrival of the engines may not be delayed, or those on business obstructed. Special attention must be directed to the thieves and pickpockets who are usually in the crowd.

3. Much loss is sustained at fires by the unnecessary removal of furniture, especially from houses not actually on fire. The firemen will be best able to judge whether danger is to be apprehended for the adjoining houses.

4. It frequently happens that in the confusion consequent upon a fire persons enter a house, and leave open the doors, which causes an increased current of air to add

greater fury to the flames. The police should prevent this as much as possible; but they must use their discretion in allowing respectable persons to enter, whose sole object is the saving of life or to assist the owner in the removal of articles of value. Improper characters, whose evident object is plunder, must be prevented from entering a house under any circumstances.

5. Every constable must be acquainted with the situation of the fire-escape, Fire Brigade station, the fire-alarm post, and residence of the turncock, nearest to every part of his beat.

6. *Treatment of Burns.*—Apply a mixture of oil and lime-water, or castor oil and collodion; and wrap up the part in cotton-wool, wool, or flannel.

7. *Treatment of Scalds.*—Apply a strongly alkaline solution made with carbonate of soda, lime, or magnesia; and enclose the limb, or part affected, in cotton-wool, excluding air as far as possible.

Fireworks.—1. Every person who casts, throws, or sets fire to any firework in or upon any highway, street, thoroughfare, or public place, is liable to a penalty.

*2. No person can make, sell, or offer, or expose to sale, any fireworks without a license from the Local Authority under the Explosives Act, and no fireworks can be sold to a person apparently under thirteen years of age. (38 Vict., c. 17.)

First Offenders.—By the Probation of First Offenders Act, 1887, brought in and passed by the author, and since enacted in several colonies, sentence may be suspended in the case of a young person guilty of a first offence not the product of a criminal mind, and he may be released conditionally upon probation, and subject to sureties, if his reclamation to an honest life and respectable employment is likely to be attained without imprisonment.

Fits.—Persons found in the streets in fits should be carefully taken to the nearest hospital or registered medical practitioner. (*See* PERSONS FOUND INSENSIBLE, p. 128.)

Fixed Points.—Police on fixed-point duty have great opportunities of rendering service to the public, by the exercise of vigilance in reference to the transit of stolen property, and the passage of suspected persons.

Footmarks.—1. Where any offence has been committed, and the delinquent has escaped, every effort must be made to find something by which his or her identity may be established.

2. This may often be done by footmarks.

3. A model may be taken of a footmark, by pouring plaster of Paris, or Spence's Patent Metal, into it, and allowing it to set.

4. In comparing footmarks with the boot of a person suspected, a separate impression must be made with the boot, by the side of the footprint, instead of the latter being placed in the original mark.

5. Great care must be taken that a footmark is not trampled in or obliterated by rain, and as soon as discovered it should be carefully covered over.

***Footways.**—Every person who does any of the following acts, on any footway may be summoned, or if in view of a constable, and it is necessary, apprehended, being liable to a fine.

(*a*) Drives or rides any animal upon a footway.

(*b*) Makes or uses any slide upon ice or snow.

(*c*) Leaves open any cellar-flaps, coal-plates, trap-doors after notice, and to the danger of the passengers.

(*d*) Places any blind or awning, projecting over the footway, within eight feet of the ground.

(*e*) Neglects to keep swept and clean all footways and water-courses adjoining to the premises occupied.

(*f*) Rolls or carries any cask, wheel, hoop, ladder, plank, or pole, save in loading and unloading.

(*g*) Wilfully causes any obstruction.

Forbearance.—Forbearance and moderation on the part of police, even under great provocation, will always be understood and appreciated by the public, and distinguish a careful officer. (*See* TEMPER, p. 178.)

Foreigners.—1. Foreigners should be invariably treated by the police with the utmost consideration and respect.

2. When foreigners are in custody, pains should be taken to explain the proceedings to them, and every facility given for them to communicate with the Consuls of their respective countries.

Forgery.—1. Forgery is the making of a false

document with intent to defraud, or by which any person may be injured. It may be committed—

(a) By in any way making a document to purport to be, what in fact it is not.

(b) By altering a document without authority in such manner as to alter its effect.

(c) By introducing into a document without authority, whilst it is being drawn up, matter altering its effect.

(d) Signing a document in the name of any person without his authority.

(e) Signing a document in the name of any fictitious person.

2. Uttering—that is, offering, disposing of, or putting off with a knowledge of its character, of a forged document—entails the same penalty as the act itself, viz., penal servitude. (*See* BANK-NOTES, p. 27.) (24 & 25 Vict., c. 98.)

Fortune Telling.—Every person pretending or professing to tell fortunes, or using any subtle craft, means, or device, by palmistry or otherwise, to deceive and impose on any one, may be treated as a rogue and vagabond, and sentenced to imprisonment with hard labour. (5 Geo. IV., c. 83, s. 4.)

Fountains.—Police must prevent, as far as practicable, any damage being done to public drinking fountains, and, if necessary, apprehend the persons so offending.

Fowl Stealing.—Fowl stealing is punishable by penal servitude. (24 & 25 Vict., c. 96, s. 7.)

Fraud.—Fraud is the acquisition of anything by the exercise of deceit.† (*See* FALSE PRETENCES, p. 83.)

Fruit Stealing.—The stealing of fruit or vegetable production growing in any garden, orchard, pleasure ground, or hothouse, is punishable by imprisonment, with or without hard labour, for a first offence. Subsequently it becomes felony, punishable by penal servitude. (24 & 25 Vict., c. 96, s. 36.)

Furious Riding or Driving.—Every person who rides or drives furiously, so as to endanger the life or

† When a man is charged with Fraud, the onus of proof of ownership will be with the prisoner, not the constable, after the original charge is disposed of, with regard to any other property seized than that mentioned in the charge. (*See* p. 141.)

limb of any person, or to the common danger of the passengers in any thoroughfare, may be summoned, or, if absolutely necessary, apprehended, and is then liable to a penalty, or in default to imprisonment. (POLICE ACTS.)

Furniture Removing to Avoid Payment of Rent.—1. As felonies may be attempted during the day by property being removed openly, by men apparently belonging to the premises, the police should learn, in all cases where the inquiry can be made without giving offence, that the removal of the goods has been properly authorised.

2. If goods are removed after sunset and before sunrise, the name of the proprietor and number of the van employed, should be taken.

3. When the police notice the removal of goods, supposed for the purpose of evading the payment of rent, notice should be given to the landlord.

Gambling.—Every person playing or gaming in any street, road, highway, or other place to which the public have access, at, or with, any instrument of gaming, or any coin, card, or token, may be apprehended as a rogue and vagabond. (36 & 37 Vict., c. 38, s. 3.)

Gaming Houses.—A common gaming house is one kept or used for playing therein, at any game of chance, or any mixed game of chance and skill, in which—

(*a*) A bank is kept by one or more of the players exclusively of the others.

(*b*) In which any game is played, the chances of which are not alike favourable to all the players, including the banker, or other person, by whom the game is managed, or against whom the other players stake, play, or bet. (8 & 9 Vict., c. 109.)

Game Licences.—1. Game includes hares, pheasants, partridges, grouse, heath or moor game, black game, and bustards.

*2. Every person taking, killing, or pursuing any game, woodcock, snipe, quail, or landrail, by any means whatever, must take out a proper licence from the Inland Revenue, and produce the same on demand, or declare his name and place of residence, subject to a penalty, for either default, or refusal.

3. No game must be killed out of season, subject to a penalty of £1 and costs for every head.

4. Any person dealing in game without taking out a yearly licence, is liable to a penalty. (*See* GUN LICENCES, below.)

Gossiping.—1. There is no practice more pernicious to the police service, than gossiping to strangers about matters of duty. Idle rumours are readily magnified into positive facts, and, passed from mouth to mouth, may be productive of great harm, as much to individuals as to the administration of justice.

2. The police on duty should not gossip or idle with each other, or with any persons, especially servants at houses on their beats. (*See* Sir H. Hawkins' Advice, p. 10.)

*****Greenyards.**—1. In nearly every parish there is a greenyard or pound, where animals found straying or in possession of prisoners, may be kept at certain charges, about which there should be no doubt.

2. The police are responsible that all animals impounded by them are properly fed and cared for.

Grievous Bodily Harm.—Every one commits a misdemeanor, punishable by penal servitude, who commits an assault occasioning actual bodily harm. (*See* WOUNDING, p. 188.)

Guilty Knowledge.—A person doing an act which he knows to be contrary to law, and likely to produce a certain result, and having a desire to attain that end, is said to have a guilty knowledge.

*****Gun Licences.**—1. Every person using or carrying a gun elsewhere than in a dwelling-house or its immediate vicinity, not being included in the undermentioned exceptions, without taking out either a yearly gun (10s.) or game licence (£3) from the Commissioners of Inland Revenue, procurable at post offices, is liable to a penalty of £10; and any officer of police or Excise may ask to see the licence, or, in default, demand the name and address of the person refusing, and if he declines to furnish them, and he is not known, arrest him.

2. The following persons are exempt from gun (not game) licences:—

(*a*) Those in the police, naval, military, or volunteer services carrying a gun in the performance of duty.

(*b*) Servants carrying guns for masters who have licences.

(*c*) Occupiers of land, using or carrying a gun for the protection of their crops.

(*d*) Gunsmiths, their servants and carriers.

(*See* GAME LICENCES, p. 89.)   (33 & 34 Vict., c. 57.)

Habeas Corpus.—A writ of habeas corpus may be issued by any division of the High Court of Justice. It runs throughout the Queen's dominions, and commands the person to whom it is addressed to produce the body of an individual, and justify his detention.

***Habitual Criminals.**—The register of all persons twice convicted of crime, and their photographs, are kept in the Habitual Criminals' Registry Office, Prisons Department, Home Office. From the books, albums, and records of the Criminal Registry Office, all police officers are entitled to all possible information, either by correspondence or personal application.

Hackney Carriages.—Hackney carriages plying for hire in any town are as a rule annually licensed by the urban authority, and must abide by the regulations laid down under the Town Police Clauses Act, 1889. (*See* CABS, p. 34.)

Handcuffs.—1. Handcuffs should never be used except in cases of necessity, when a prisoner is violent and likely to attempt to escape, or if the number of prisoners to be conveyed, or the special circumstances, render such a precaution necessary to impede a rescue.

2. In conveying a prisoner, prior to conviction, by rail or otherwise, handcuffing must necessarily depend on whether he is likely to attempt to escape, and whether his doing so would be likely to succeed, by reason of his superior strength, the fatigue of the officer, as also on the nature of his offence. Persons in custody for crimes of violence may well be handcuffed, while those apprehended for perjury and like offences should be treated somewhat differently.

3. If handcuffs are unnecessarily put on, and the prisoner is acquitted, he may bring an action and recover damages against the officer.

Handwriting.—1. The greatest care is necessary in dealing with cases in which the question of identity of handwriting is involved, and only the most searching examination by persons who have made the science a subject of long study can be relied upon. At first sight many handwritings appear the same, which, upon a closer scrutiny, are entirely dissimilar.

2. Handwriting should, if possible, be proved by some person—

(*a*) Who has seen the individual whose hand is in question, write.

(*b*) Who has received documents purporting to be written and signed by him in the ordinary course of business.

(*c*) Who has received papers purporting to be written by him in answer to documents written by himself, or under his authority, and addressed to that person.

***Harbouring Police.** — (*See* PUBLIC HOUSES, p. 149, par. 22.)

***Harbouring Prostitutes.**—(*See* PUBLIC HOUSES, p. 149, par. 23.)

***Harbouring Thieves.**—(*See* PUBLIC HOUSES, p. 150, par. 25.)

Hearsay.—Hearsay evidence, whether spoken or written, of a fact, is not admissible. It is extremely difficult to give a good practical definition of what is called "hearsay evidence" as applicable to criminal inquiries. The best, perhaps, is that "hearsay" is not "evidence;" and that "hearsay" means, as its name implies, something which another person—*not* the person charged with an offence—may have been "heard" to "say," not in the presence or hearing of the person charged; and therefore a police officer in a witness-box should be careful to state only facts which have come under his own observation, not the statements of other persons to him of what such other persons have seen or heard.

High Treason.—1. Every one in the British Empire commits high treason who forms and displays by any overt act, or by publishing any printing or writing, an intention to kill or destroy the Queen or the Prince of Wales, or to do Her Majesty any bodily harm, tending to death or destruction, maiming, wounding, or restraint. (11 & 12 Vict., c. 12, s. 2.)

2. Every one commits high treason who, either within

or beyond the realm, actively assists a public enemy at war with the Queen.

3. Every person who, in the case of felony, would be an accessory before the fact is, in the case of high treason, a principal traitor.

*Highways.—1. Every one commits a common nuisance who obstructs any highway by any permanent work or erection thereon, or injury thereto, which renders the highway less commodious to the public than it would otherwise be, or who prevents them from having access to any part of it, by an excessive and unreasonable temporary use thereof, or by so dealing with the land in the immediate neighbourhood of the highway, as to prevent the public from using and enjoying it securely.

2. A highway is any public road, bridge, carriage way, bridle path, footway, or pavement.

3. Persons taking away material deposited by the surveyor for the repair of a highway, are liable to a penalty.

4. Every person who wilfully commits any of the following offences, is liable to a penalty of 40s., in addition to liability to make good the damage occasioned, viz. :—

(a) Rides upon a footpath, or leads or drives any cattle or carriage thereon.

(b) Causes any injury to be done to any highway, or the hedges, posts, rails, walls, or fences thereof.

(c) Pulls down, defaces, or destroys any direction-post or milestone.

(d) Plays at any game on any part of a highway, to the annoyance of any passenger.

(e) Pitches any tent, booth, stall, or stand, or encamps upon any part of a highway.

(f) Puts anything on a highway to injure, or interrupt it.

(g) Suffers any filth or offensive matter to run or flow into or upon a highway from any adjacent building or land.

(h) Makes an open fire, lets off any firework, or discharges any gun or pistol within fifty feet of the centre of a carriage-way, to the injury, interruption, or personal danger of any person travelling thereon.

(i) Obstructs in any way the free passage of any highway.

(j) Allows any waggon or cart to be on any highway

without having on the right, or offside, or upon the offside shaft, his name and place of abode. (5 & 6 Wm. IV., c. 50.)

5. Persons committing any of the following offences, are liable to a fine of £5 (£10 if the offender is the owner himself, in sections *a* to *e*), in addition to any civil action to which they may be liable.

(*a*) Furiously riding or driving, so as to endanger the life or limb of any passenger.

(*b*) Leaving any horse, carriage, waggon, or cart unattended, or by any negligence, or wilful misbehaviour, causing any hurt or damage to any person, horse, cattle, or goods; or leaving any cart or carriage on a highway so as to obstruct the passage.

(*c*) Riding upon any carriage or horse, without having the reins, or some person to guide the horse or horses.

(*d*) Who does not observe the rule of the road—viz., to keep on the left, or near side—on meeting any other waggon, cart, carriage, or beast of burden, or to allow the same to pass him. (5 & 6 Wm. IV., c. 54.)

(*e*) Who in any manner wilfully prevents any person, carriage, or waggon from passing him; or, who by any negligence or misbehaviour, prevents, hinders, or interrupts the free passage, on any highway, of any person, waggon, cart, carriage, horse, mule, or beast of burden.

(*f*) Who erects any steam engine, or machinery belonging to it, within twenty-five yards of any part of any carriage or cart way.

6. No one person must drive more than two carriages, waggons, or carts, with one horse each, on any highway; and then the horse of the hinder vehicle must be attached by a rein, of not more than four feet in length, to the back of the foremost, subject to a penalty of 20s.

7. Offenders against the Highway Act who are known should be summoned. If unknown, they may be apprehended without warrant by any surveyor or person acting under his authority, or any other person witnessing the commission of the offence.

***Home Office.**—All business relating to Police and Constabulary Forces in England, Wales, and Scotland, is transacted at the Home Office.

Homicide.—1. Homicide is the killing of a human being by a human act, but for which the person killed would not have died when he did, and which is directly and immediately connected with his death.

2. A child becomes a human being when it has completely proceeded, in a living state, from the body of its mother, and has had a separate breathing existence even for a single instant.

3. A person is not deemed to have committed homicide when the death takes place more than a year and a day after the injury causing it, counting from the day of infliction inclusive.

4. Homicide becomes murder (p. 117), when death is caused by an act done with the intention to cause death or grievous bodily harm, or that which is commonly known as likely to produce death or grievous bodily harm.

5. Homicide becomes manslaughter (p. 112), when death is unintentionally caused by an omission, amounting to culpable negligence, to discharge a duty tending to the preservation of life; or when death is caused accidentally, by an unlawful act.

***Horse Slaughtering.**—1. No person may keep or use any house for slaughtering any horse or other cattle, not killed for butchers' meat,† without a licence from the County Council, subject to a penalty. (26 Geo. III., c. 71; 12 & 13 Vict., c. 92.)

2. Slaughterers must enter in a book all distinguishing particulars, concerning any horse or other cattle brought for slaughter, and it must be produced when required, by any constable or person authorised by a Magistrate.

3. If any person allows an animal brought for slaughter to leave the place, or to be employed in any manner of work, he is liable to a penalty of forty shillings per day, payable, half to the poor, half to the informer, or else three months' imprisonment with hard labour; as also any person found using, or in possession of, such animal.

4. Any constable may, at all reasonable times of the day, alone, or with any Inspector, enter and inspect all premises licensed for slaughtering, and inspect or take an account of any cattle therein. (7 & 8 Vict., c. 87, s. 4.)

† No person may sell, offer, or keep for sale, any horseflesh for human food, unless over such shop, stall, or place, there is a board legibly and conspicuously indicating that horseflesh is sold there, subject to a penalty of £20. (52 & 53 Vict., c. 11.)

Horse Stealing.—1. Every one commits felony, who steals any horse, or kills it with intent to steal the carcase or skin. (24 & 25 Vict., c. 96, s. 10.)

2. The description of horses stolen should be circulated as soon as possible in the *Police Gazette*, and advertised. Inquiry should be directed at all horse auctions, as well as at fairs.

3. Horses turned out to grass, in the suburbs, are frequently stolen during the night, and may be recovered by police on duty in the early morning on the principal thoroughfares and bridges leading into the metropolis and large towns.

4. Precise information should be sought, and circulated, as to special marks of identity about the stolen horse, either in his appearance or action, or in his feet or shoes.

Hotel Larcenies.—Hotel larcenies are occasionally frequent. The thief usually arrives with only a hand-bag, and leaves unperceived before the guests discover their loss. In cases of suspicion, a close watch should be kept, and the porters cautioned to be watchful. If the thief has effected his escape and can be identified, immediate inquiry should be directed at railway stations, and his description circulated.

Housebreaking.—1. Every one commits felony, who breaks and enters, and actually commits, any felony, in any dwelling-house, or building.

2. The same conditions apply to housebreaking, as to burglary (p. 33), with the exception that the offence must be committed by day—six a.m. to nine p.m.

3. Every one commits felony, who, with intent to commit, though not actually committing, felony, breaks and enters any occupied building.

4. Every one who, being in any such building, commits felony therein, and breaks out of the same, is liable to the same punishment as if he had broken in. (24 & 25 Vict., c. 96.)

*****Housebreaking Implements.**—1. Every one is liable to penal servitude—

(a) Who is found, by night (nine p.m. to six a.m.), armed with any dangerous or offensive weapon or instrument whatever, with intent to break or enter into any dwelling-house or other building whatsoever, and to commit any felony therein.

(*b*) Who is found, by night, having in his possession, without lawful excuse (proof of which excuse lies upon him), any picklock or false key, jemmy, centre-bit, chisel, bradawl, gimlet, or other instrument adapted for housebreaking and forcing windows, doors, or locks.

(*c*) Who is found, by night, with his face blackened, or otherwise disguised, with intent to commit any felony.

(*d*) Who is found, by night, in any building whatsoever, with intent to commit any felony therein. (24 & 25 Vict., c. 96, ss. 58 & 59.)

2. Police on duty in the early morning, between dawn and six a.m., should be on the watch for persons likely to be possessed of housebreaking implements, which are not unfrequently carried in small black hand-bags by persons of respectable exterior. They can only be detected by the exercise, with due discretion, of the power to stop and search any person who may be reasonably suspected of having or conveying, in any manner, anything unlawfully obtained. (*See* SUSPECTED PERSONS, p. 175.)

Humane Society.—The instructions issued by the Royal Humane Society should be acted on immediately, and as far as possible by the police, in cases of rescue from drowning, &c., but medical aid must be obtained as quickly as possible. (*See* p. 181.)

Husband and Wife.—1. The police should not interfere in domestic quarrels, unless there is ground to fear that actual violence is imminent. If the parties are creating any obstruction, or attracting a crowd of persons, they should be cautioned before the law is enforced.

2. The evidence of the husband or wife, of an accused person, or of any person jointly indicted with a prisoner, is not usually admissible, unless the offence under inquiry is that of bodily injury inflicted by one on the other, *or on their child* (52 & 53 Vict., c. 44, s. 7; *see* p. 41), or in divorce proceedings, always provided that no witness is bound to answer any question, tending to show that he or she has been guilty of adultery, unless such witness has already given evidence in the same proceeding in disproof of his, or her, alleged adultery. (32 & 33 Vict., c. 68, s. 3.)

3. Neither a husband nor a wife can give the other

into custody, for aught save personal violence. (*See* MARRIED WOMEN, p. 113.)

Identification of Prisoners.—1. It is of the utmost importance that the identification of a person who may be charged with a criminal offence should be conducted in the fairest possible manner.

2. A person detained on suspicion, and whose identity is in question, should be placed, with not less than five or six others, of as nearly as possible similar appearance as to age, clothes, and position in life. The suspected person may be asked if he is satisfied, and any reasonable request on his part should be acceded to. The witnesses should then be introduced, one at a time, and told to go up to the person recognised. They must not communicate with each other in any way; and after the persons are placed for identification, no police officer should hold any communication with a witness.

3. Identification by bringing a suspected person alone into a room, or by showing him to a witness in a cell, is not a fair mode of identification, and is likely to lead to difficulties and mistakes.

Ignorance of Law.—Every person above fourteen years of age is assumed to be cognisant of the law, and ignorance thereof is no excuse for any unlawful act.

Illegal Arrest.—Police are liable in damages for illegal arrest. (*See* ACTIONS AGAINST POLICE, p. 19; APPREHENSION, p. 22.)

Illegal Pawning.—If any person knowingly and designedly pawns anything, the property of another person, without authority, he is liable to a penalty, in addition to the full value of the pledge, payable to the party injured as compensation and costs. (35 & 36 Vict., c. 93.)

Illegitimate Children.—A father is bound to support his illegitimate children up to thirteen, and, if so ordered, to sixteen years of age. (*See* BASTARDY, p. 28.)

Inciting to Crime.—1. Every one who incites any person to commit any crime is guilty of a misdemeanor whether the crime is or is not committed. (For persuading or proposing to murder, *see* CONSPIRACY, p. 49.)

2. Juvenile offenders are frequently incited to criminal acts, and every effort should be made to bring the guilty party to justice.

Incompetency of Witnesses.—Extreme youth, mental deficiency, the relationship of husband or wife to an accused person, usually render witnesses incompetent. (*See* EVIDENCE, p. 74; HUSBAND AND WIFE, p. 97.)

***Incorrigible Children.**—The parent or guardian of an incorrigible child, under fourteen years of age, may apply to a Magistrate for the child to be sent to an industrial school, and the Magistrate may, after due inquiry, make an order accordingly, but the parent will usually have to contribute 5s. per week towards its maintenance. (*See* INDUSTRIAL SCHOOLS, p. 101.)

***Incorrigible Rogues.**—An incorrigible rogue is a person—

(*a*) Who has been previously convicted as a rogue and vagabond.

(*b*) Who violently resists any constable apprehending him for being a rogue and vagabond, and convicted as such.

(*c*) Who breaks or escapes out of any place of legal confinement before the expiration of the sentence passed on him for being a rogue and vagabond. (5 Geo. IV., c. 83.)

Indecent Assault.—1. An indecent assault is any assault accompanied by acts of indecency.

2. Indecent assault upon any female, or any attempt to have carnal knowledge of a girl under sixteen years of age, even with her own consent, is punishable as a misdemeanor. (*See* DEFILEMENT OF CHILDREN, p. 41.)

3. The offence of indecent assault is not committed on a person above sixteen years of age, if the person voluntarily assented to the commission of the indecent act. An indecent assault may be committed on a prostitute, as upon any other person, though her antecedents may give foundation to the defence that she was a consenting party.

4. An indecent assault upon a male person is punishable by ten years' penal servitude. (*See* ASSAULTS, p. 25; SODOMY, p. 170.) (24 & 25 Vict., c. 100, s. 62, and CRIMINAL LAW AMENDMENT ACT, 1885.)

5. The police must not conceal themselves for the purpose of watching persons supposed to be about to commit indecent offences, but should interfere immediately in any case in which an act is done to justify

it, without waiting for a more serious offence to be committed.

Indecent Exposure.—1. Every person wilfully and obscenely exposing his person in any street, road, or public highway, or in the view thereof, or in any place of public resort, with intent to insult any female, may be apprehended and dealt with as a rogue and vagabond. (5 Geo. IV., c. 83.)

2. Any grossly indecent act done in any open or public place, such as the inside of an omnibus, a roof or garden seen from the windows of several houses, a urinal, or the inside of a public booth, where it may be seen by more persons than one—is a misdemeanor.

3. Men who bathe without any screen or covering so near to a public footpath that exposure of their persons must necessarily occur are guilty of an indictable nuisance.

4. Charges of indecently exposing the person should not be lightly made, especially if it is possible that there is no improper intention.

*****Indecent Prints, Exhibitions, or Songs.**—
1. Every person wilfully exposing to view in any street, road, highway, or public place, or in the window or other part of any shop so situated, any obscene print, picture, or other indecent exhibition, is liable to be apprehended, and dealt with as a rogue and vagabond. (5 Geo. IV., c. 83.)

2. Every person selling, distributing, offering for sale or distribution, or exhibiting to public view any profane, indecent, or obscene book, paper, print, drawing, or representation; or singing any indecent song; or writing or drawing any indecent or obscene word, figure, or representation; or using any indecent language to the annoyance of the inhabitants or passengers, within view of any constable, may be apprehended, and is liable to a penalty. (POLICE ACTS.)

Indemnity.—Whenever property is given up by police about which any question may, by the remotest possibility, arise, an indemnity should invariably be taken from the person to whom it is given up. It may be in the following form, and must be duly stamped :—

"I   , of   do hereby acknowledge to have received from   the following articles, viz :—   , valued at and in consideration thereof, do hereby agree to indemnify and hold harmless the said   and all others his superior officers, from all claims and demands whatsoever to be made in respect of the articles aforesaid, and from all loss, damage, cost, costs of actions incurred or to be incurred by reason of all or any suit, claims, and demands, or by any other matter, cause, or thing, in any way connected with the premises.

As witness my hand this   day of   , eighteen hundred and

Signed

Witnessed by   , of   ."

Impressed Stamp.

Indictments.—1. An indictment is a written accusation against a prisoner of a crime preferred to and presented upon oath by a grand jury.

2. Immediately after a prisoner is committed for trial, the officer in charge of the case, unless there is a prosecuting solicitor, should prepare the instructions for the indictment according to the proper forms, taking care that the names of all witnesses are correctly spelt, and legibly written.

***Industrial Schools.**—1. Any person may apply to a Magistrate for an order for a child, under fourteen years of age, destitute, without home, or means of subsistence, or residing with prostitutes, to be sent to a certified industrial school.

2. Any child above ten, escaping from an industrial school, may be apprehended without warrant and taken before a Magistrate.

3. Any person assisting or inducing a child to escape from an industrial school, or knowingly harbouring or concealing a child who has so escaped, or assisting in so doing, is liable to a penalty, or imprisonment. (*See* REFORMATORIES, p. 157.) (29 & 30 Vict., c. 118.)

Infanticide.—1. Infanticide is the killing of a child after it is born. The main questions to be determined are—

(*a*) If the child was born alive?

(*b*) If so, by what means did it die?

2. If it is proved that death is owing to violence, the question arises as to who is the murderer. Suspicion generally falls on the supposed mother, and it is to be determined—

(*a*) Whether she has been delivered of a child?

(*b*) Whether the signs of a delivery correspond with

the age of the child? At the same time, a woman cannot be compelled against her will to undergo a medical examination for the purpose of ascertaining if such is the case.

3. The cases of infanticide, occurring in large cities, are usually those of children whose bodies are found deposited in the streets and elsewhere, and the mother is unknown. As in the case of abandonment, the covering of the body must be carefully examined for any signs of identity, and any birth marks carefully noted, to facilitate the institution of inquiry at hospitals, lying-in wards, workhouses, and among those who attend poor women in their confinements.

Upon the finding of a dead child or fœtus, all wraps, paper, or clothing should be carefully preserved for examination.

*Infectious Diseases.†—1. Any person, suffering from any dangerous infectious disorder, who enters any public conveyance without notice to the owner or driver, is liable to a penalty, and also to compensate him for causing it to be disinfected.

2. The terms "infectious" and "contagious" (catching), applied to a disease, signify that it is communicable from the sick to the healthy.

The following are the principal infectious diseases:—
Eruptive fevers—measles, small-pox, and scarlet fever. Continued fevers—typhus, typhoid, relapsing, and yellow fevers. Diphtheria, erysipelas, whooping-cough, and cholera.

Informality.—Although informality may seem a trifling thing, it nevertheless vitiates legal proceedings, and in the conduct of public business occasions the greatest inconvenience, trouble, and delay.

Information.—1. For the "information" which should precede the issue of a warrant, see WARRANTS, p. 185.

† By the "Infectious Disease Notification Act," 1889, the Medical Officer of Health in London, and every district which adopts the Act, must be informed of the occurrence of any case of small-pox, cholera, diphtheria, erysipelas, scarlatina, scarlet, typhus, typhoid, relapsing, continued, or puerperal fever, which breaks out. The penalty for default is 40s.; and the duty is incumbent upon the head of the family, the relatives attending the sick person, the occupier of the building, and the medical practitioner.

For "circulating information" concerning persons wanted, and property lost or stolen, see p. 138.

2. Police work is impossible without information, and every good officer will do his best to obtain reliable intelligence, taking care at the same time not to be led away on false issues. Information must not be treasured up until opportunity offers for action by the officer who obtains it, but should be promptly communicated to a superior, and those who are in a position to act upon it. Not only is this the proper course to take, in the public interest, but it will be certainly recognised, both by authorities and comrades, promoting esteem and confidence, which will bring their own reward.

Informers.—1. A police officer who keeps his own counsel, and does not gossip or divulge confidences, will have plenty of informers. The great majority of respectable citizens rightly understand their own interests, and are glad to render assistance to a constable, whom they can trust.

2. In no case must an informer be even indirectly invested with any official character, or be allowed to act, as if actually a police officer.

3. There can rarely be occasion to divulge the name of an informant, and it should be kept secret, as far as possible, both in honour and in the public interest. If a constable is asked, in cross-examination, from whom he derived his information, he should decline to answer, unless directed by the Judge, and similarly if the name of his informer is mentioned, and he is asked if the information came from him.

Injured Persons.—(See ACCIDENTS, p. 18; AID TO THE INJURED, p. 21.)

Inquests.—The holding of inquests on dead bodies is entirely a matter for Coroners to decide, upon notice of the discovery of a dead body or of human remains, although they may be compelled to hold or re-open an inquest by mandamus. (See CORONERS, p. 53.)

Inquiries.—(See MAKING INQUIRIES, p. 111.)

Insanity.—1. Every person is presumed to be sane, and responsible for his acts, until the contrary is proved on his behalf.

2. No act is a crime if the person who does it is, at the time when it is done, prevented by any mental disease.

(a) From knowing the nature and quality of his act.
(b) From knowing that the act was unlawful.
(c) From controlling his own conduct.

*Insects.—1. If any owner, or person, having under his charge, any crop of potatoes or other substances, finds, or knows to be found thereon, the Colorado beetle, in any stage of existence, he must, with all practical speed, give notice thereof to a constable, who will at once inform the Local Authority under the Contagious Diseases (Animals) Act. (40 & 41 Vict., c. 68.)

2. As doubt may often arise, and unnecessary alarm be caused, as to whether a given insect is or is not the Colorado beetle, every effort should be made to secure and convey it, in a closely-stoppered bottle, to the Local Authority.

Inspectors of Police.—It is the duty of Inspectors of Police always to recollect that they are the officers of the force, and that language spoken and acts committed by them assume additional importance in the eyes of the public, than the utterances or deeds of subordinates. They should set an example, to those under them, of zeal, and rectitude of conduct, on and off duty, of civility to the public, obedience to orders, loyalty to superiors, and good feeling towards equals, always recollecting that it is as much their duty to advise and encourage constables as to report them for misconduct; never passing over, however, any want of respect or wilful fault.

Interference.—Police may sometimes provoke assaults on themselves, and incite resistance to their authority by unnecessary interference.

When they have to act, they should do so promptly and with determination, but until then they should abstain from interference.

Interrogation of Prisoners.—Prisoners must not be interrogated by police with respect to the offence for which they are in custody, although anything they may voluntarily say may be listened to and noted without a caution.† (*See* CAUTIONING A PRISONER, p. 38.)

---

† It is to be hoped that a Bill several times introduced and enacted in the House of Lords, but obstructed in the House of Commons, permitting judicial and magisterial interrogation, under due restriction, will eventually become law.

Intimidation.—Every person commits a misdemeanor who, with a view to compel any person to abstain from doing any act which he has a legal right to do—

(*a*) Uses violence, or intimidates him, or his wife, or children.

(*b*) Injures his property.

(*c*) Persistently follows such person from place to place.

(*d*) Hides any tools, clothes, or other property belonging to such person, or deprives or hinders him in the use thereof.

(*e*) Persistently watches or besets the house, or other place where such person resides, or works, or carries on business, or happens to be, or the approaches to such house or place.

(*f*) Follows such person, with two or more other persons, in a disorderly manner, in or through any street or road. (38 & 39 Vict., c. 86.) †

* **Intoxicating Liquors.**—(*See* Codification of the law regarding PUBLIC HOUSES, p. 144.)

Jewel Larcenies.—1. Jewel larcenies are usually effected in towns by entering the house, either by climbing up the portico or through the attic windows of an adjoining empty house, and in the country, by means of a ladder placed against an open window, or one easily forced, during the time the family is at dinner, and the servants probably engaged in another part of the house.

2. Periodical printed cautions sent to the masters of houses likely to be selected, or offering facilities for this class of offence, will be found of value.

3. Care should be taken that ladders are not left about unsecured. Internal alarm bells and mechanical signals will be found even more valuable than locks and bars.

4. The more valuable articles are usually broken up and melted down within a few hours of the offence, but careful inquiry must be made for those of less value and likely to be disposed of intact.

5. Sketches should be prepared as soon as possible of the principal articles for the guidance of the engraver, whose blocks may then be set up with the bills (*see* p.

† Great care and tact must be exercised in carrying out this statute in a period of labour trouble.

193), giving a clear description of the things stolen, and offering, if desired, a reward for their recovery and the conviction of the thief—not as an incentive to the energies of the police, but by way of inducement to pawnbrokers and *bonâ fide* purchasers of second-hand goods to be on the look-out.

Judges.—Police must invariably treat Judges with the utmost deference and respect, and any remark on the action of police made by their Lordships, or Recorder, &c., or Chairmen of Courts of Quarter Sessions, should be carefully taken down by the Inspector, or senior officer on duty in Court, and submitted to the Chief Officer of the Force.

Juries.—1. Grand juries and Coroners' juries may consist of any number more than eleven, and usually consist of twenty-three. They may decide by the majority.

In criminal trials the jury invariably consists of twelve men, who must be unanimous.

2. As the names of the jurymen on the jury panel are called before they are sworn, either the prosecutor or the prisoner may challenge them.

Jurisdiction.—1. Police have only authority to act in the district for which they are sworn in, and if they proceed on duty beyond it, they must be sworn in the fresh district, or else be provided with a warrant, properly endorsed for execution therein. The Metropolitan Police are constables within the counties of Middlesex (including the City of London), Surrey, Hertford, Essex, Kent, Berkshire, and Buckinghamshire, and upon the Thames within or adjoining thereto, as well as within the Royal Palaces of Her Majesty, and ten miles thereof.

2. When offences occurring within one district are reported to police of another, the parties should be invariably referred to the proper force; and officers despatched to make inquiries beyond their own district should usually first seek assistance at the head-quarters of the local force.

Justifying Bail is proving the sufficiency of bail, or sureties, in point of property. (*See* BAIL, p. 27.)

Keeping Observation.—In keeping observation on suspected persons or premises, great care must be taken that attention is not attracted; and unless some arrangement can be made with the occupier of an adjacent or opposite house, or other person, it will generally, in the day-time, be more prudent to keep at some little distance.

Keys of Premises.—1. The police should not receive keys of premises from any person, or have in their possession any skeleton key, without the permission of the Superintendent of the division.

2. If an inhabitant or other person wishes to give a key to a constable, or any superior officer, for the purpose of visiting a house or premises for protection, or calling up any one, the Superintendent should report the case, and no such key must be retained without sanction.

3. Except under special circumstances, police should not be allowed to have the keys of private premises, and in no case ought any additional responsibility be thereby assumed. (*See* ACCESS TO PREMISES, p. 18.)

Kidnapping.—(*See* CHILD STEALING, p. 40.)

Killing.—1. Every person who kills another is presumed to have wilfully murdered him, unless the circumstances are such as to raise a contrary presumption.

2. The burden of proving circumstances of excuse, justification, or extenuation, is upon the person who is shown to have killed another.

Ladders.—1. Care must be taken that ladders left against houses have a plank fastened over them, or are otherwise so secured as not to facilitate a felonious entry.

2. In suburban and rural districts, persons should be cautioned against leaving ladders unsecured in the vicinity of residences. (*See* JEWEL LARCENIES, p. 105.)

3. Ladders should be marked by the police at night.

Lanterns.—1. Accidents having occurred to persons travelling by night on horseback, or in carriages, and particularly in districts where there are no lights, by constables suddenly turning the light of their lanterns full on the persons approaching them, and thus frightening the horses, this practice should be avoided, unless in case of accident, or when desired by the persons concerned.

2. If the light is turned on previously, the constable should let it remain so, until the horse has passed, as turning it off too suddenly may produce the same effect as if it were suddenly turned on.

Larceny.—Larceny is the unlawful taking and carrying away of property fraudulently and without claim of right, with intent permanently to deprive the rightful owner thereof. (24 & 25 Vict., c. 96.)

Leading Questions.—1. Leading questions are those which suggest their answer. In legal proceedings they can only be put in cross-examination, save by permission of the Court.

2. Leading questions put by police officers to persons under the excitement occasioned by a loss of property often provoke misleading and erroneous answers. People should be allowed to tell their own story as far as possible.

Lead Stripping.—1. Lead stripping is a common offence, and not unfrequently committed by workmen, who resort to various devices for carrying it through the streets without attracting attention.

2. Any person stealing, or who rips, cuts, severs, or breaks, with intent to steal, any glass, lead, iron, or any material, or fixture, belonging to any building whatsoever, is guilty of felony. (24 & 25 Vict., c. 96, s. 31.)

Letters.—(*See* CORRESPONDENCE, p. 53.)

Libel.—1. Every one commits a misdemeanor who maliciously publishes by printing, writing, signs, or pictures, defamatory matter (termed a libel) of any person, and which directly, or by insinuation and irony, tend to expose him to public hatred, contempt, or ridicule.

2. To publish a libel is to deliver, read it, or communicate its purport in any other manner, or to exhibit it to any person than the one libelled, provided that the person making the publication knows the contents.

3. A person who sends an obscene letter may be guilty of a misdemeanor, and more especially if addressed to women or young girls.

***Licensed Victuallers.**—(*See* PUBLIC HOUSES, p. 144.)

Limitation of Proceedings.—1. Proceedings under several Statutes are specially limited, but in the majority of indictable offences there is no limitation to the time within which proceedings may be taken; but, on the other hand, the law will admit of no delay after discovery of the offender.

2. In cases which may be disposed of summarily, *and which are not specially limited under a particular Statute,*

as, for example, under the Prevention of Cruelty to Animals Act (p. 56), the information or complaint must be made within six months of the cause arising.

Lithography.—Lithography is of great use in reproducing fac-similes of handwriting, which may frequently be of service in securing the arrest or in establishing the identity of a delinquent.

Loan Office Swindlers.—Frauds are sometimes perpetrated through the medium of fictitious loan offices obtaining advances of money, and various sums from persons seeking to borrow, without any intention or ability to advance them any loan.

* **Local Authority.**— Under a great variety of Statutes—Explosives, Infant Life Protection, Petroleum, Public Health, and many others—Parliament has constituted a Local Authority to grant licences, or authorities to do some lawful act, and to enforce the law. In the great majority of cases the Local Authority is—

In the City of London—the Lord Mayor and Aldermen.

In the Metropolis—the Administrative Council of London.

In a borough—the Mayor, Aldermen, and Burgesses in Council.

In a harbour—the Harbour Authorities.

Elsewhere—the County Council.

Long-Firm Frauds.—1. Long-firm frauds consist in obtaining goods by false pretences from merchants, agriculturists, &c., by a gang of persons who, by giving each other fictitious references, obtain consignments of goods, which they sell, and fail themselves to pay for.

2. The earliest opportunity should be invariably taken of obtaining a warrant against a long-firm swindler.

Lost Property.—1. A description of all articles of which notification is given to the police, of their being lost, should be circulated. If the articles are such as might be presented to a pawnbroker and possess any marks of identity, their description should also be published in pawnbrokers' lists.

2. All articles of property found by the police, or given to them by the finder, should be handed to the Inspector or other officer on station duty at the time, by whom full particulars should be entered in the Occurrence

Book, and the entry be signed by the officer as well as by the person who gives in the property.

***Lotteries.**—1. Every person who publicly or privately opens a lottery of any kind without the authority of Parliament is liable to a fine or imprisonment with hard labour.

2. Any person who promises to pay any money, deliver any goods, or do any act on a contingency, relative to a drawing of any tickets, lots, numbers, or figures, in any game or lottery, or who publishes any proposal for any of these purposes, may be apprehended, and is liable to a penalty, or, in default, to three months' imprisonment with hard labour. (42 Geo. III., c. 119.)

3. Christmas lotteries for distributing game, wine, spirits, &c., are not strictly legal, but unless there is reason to suppose that they are likely to be conducted to the prejudice of the subscribers, it will not be necessary to commence legal proceedings against the promoters.

Lunatics.—1. A constable is required to apprehend a lunatic, or dangerous idiot, wandering at large, whether a pauper or not, and convey him before a Magistrate, who, if satisfied as to the facts, may make an order for him to be received into the county asylum.

2. If any constable or relieving officer has knowledge that any person, although not wandering at large and not a pauper, is nevertheless not under proper care and control, or is cruelly treated or neglected by any relative or person having the charge or care of him, he is required to make an information upon oath to a Magistrate, who may either himself visit and examine such person and make inquiry into the facts, or direct and authorise some registered medical practitioner to do so; and upon his report, in writing, order the alleged lunatic to be brought before a Court of Summary Jurisdiction, which upon due evidence may direct him to be received into the county or other fit asylum, unless it is deemed desirable, in either case, to give him up to his friends to place him as a private patient in a hospital or licensed house, or otherwise have him taken care of.

3. Any lunatic escaping from an asylum, registered hospital, or licensed house, may be retaken within fourteen days by any officer or servant of the institution, or person authorised in writing by the Superintendent, or proprietor. If he remains at large more than fourteen

days, the original proceeding must be repeated. (16 & 17 Vict., c. 97, s. 68.)

Machinery Damaging.—1. Any person, who unlawfully cuts, breaks, destroys, or damages, with intent to render useless, any tool or machinery employed in the preparation or manufacture of any silk, linen, or such like goods, is guilty of felony.

2. Every one commits felony who does any similar act with regard to any agricultural, mining, or other engine. (*See* p. 58.) (24 & 25 Vict., c. 97.)

***Mad Dogs.**—The Commissioners of the Metropolitan and City Police within their respective districts, the county Justices in Petty Sessions, or Mayors of boroughs, if a mad dog, or dog suspected of being mad, is found within their jurisdiction, may make, vary, and revoke an order, placing such restrictions† as they think expedient on all dogs not being under the control of any person; and all persons acting in contravention of the order will be liable to a penalty. (34 & 35 Vict., c. 56, s. 3.) (*See* "Dogs Found," p. 68.)

Making Inquiries.—1. The method of making an inquiry so much depends upon its nature and the antecedent circumstances, that no positive rule can be laid down.

2. Inquiries may be said to consist of two classes:—
(*a*) Those in which there is no necessity for concealment.
(*b*) Those in which secrecy is desirable.

3. In the former case it is always best to state at once the object to a master or a principal, who then, in the majority of instances, takes pleasure in assisting the police.

4. In the latter, too great caution cannot be exercised as to action, appearance, language, and demeanour.

5. But to whichever category the inquiry belongs, and whatever the object, it must be made thoroughly and completely. Officers of short experience are often apt, in their haste to get a duty over, to neglect points which appear to them of no importance, but which may

---

† If a constable sees that the muzzle upon any dog is of such a nature, or is so fixed, as to prevent the poor animal from drinking, or to cause it needless pain and irritation, and so drive it mad, he should respectfully invite the attention of the owner to the circumstance.

actually be of the utmost value in the subsequent conduct of the case. It is far better to enter into too much detail than to allow anything to pass unnoticed.

Malice is a formed design of doing mischief to another person.

Malingering.—Constables who are reported by a Divisional Surgeon as malingering, or feigning sickness, with a view to the avoidance of duty, are most seriously punished; for the injury done to the service is not less great than that done to comrades, who have in consequence to do extra work and so incur additional responsibility.

Manslaughter.—1. Manslaughter is unlawful homicide, without malice aforethought.

2. Homicide, which would otherwise be murder, is reduced to manslaughter, if the act by which death is caused is done in the heat of passion caused by provocation, unless the provocation was sought or voluntarily provoked by the offender as an excuse for killing, or doing bodily harm.

*****Man-traps.**—Any person who sets, causes or suffers to be placed, any spring-gun, man-trap, or other engine calculated to destroy human life, or inflict grievous bodily harm, upon a trespasser or any person coming in contact therewith, elsewhere than in a dwelling-house, for its protection from sunset to sunrise, is guilty of a misdemeanor. (24 & 25 Vict., c. 100, s. 31.)

*****Marine Store Dealers.**—1. Every person buying or selling anchors, cables, sails, old iron, or marine stores of any description, must have his name and designation, "dealer in marine stores," painted distinctly on every warehouse or other place of deposit belonging to him, subject to a penalty of £20. (17 & 18 Vict., c. 104, s. 480.)

2. The purchase of marine stores of any description, from any person apparently under the age of sixteen, entails a penalty of £5 for a first offence, and £20 for any subsequent one. (*See* OLD METAL DEALERS, p. 123.)

Marking Places at Night.—1. All places by which a felonious entry may be effected into premises should be marked by police on night duty, including doors of empty houses next to occupied dwellings, doors and windows insecurely fastened, walls, gates, palings, and ladders placed against premises.

2. Any convenient means of marking may be adopted, *so placed that the marks may be certainly disturbed* by the opening of a door, window, or gate, or persons climbing over a wall or paling, or up a ladder.

3. When a mark is found disturbed, police must at once ascertain the cause.

***Married Women.**—*Married Women's Property Act*, 1870, 33 & 34 Vict., c. 93.—1. The earnings of a married woman are deemed her own separate property, as also deposits by her in the savings bank, inheritances of personal property as next of kin, or pecuniary bequests by deed or will under £200.

2. A married woman cannot commit theft upon things belonging to her husband; but if a person elopes with the wife of another man, and takes property, knowing it to be her husband's, he is in such case guilty of larceny.

3. A married woman cannot usually give evidence against her husband, or his fellow prisoner, except in a case where the infliction of bodily harm on herself is the subject of the charge.

4. If a married woman commits theft, or any other crime, except treason, murder, and robbery, in the presence of her husband, she is presumed to have acted under his coercion, and such coercion may excuse her act.

5. The proof of marriage lies upon a woman charged jointly with a man.

Meetings.—1. Police must not, on any account, meet together for any purpose whatever, except by permission of their superiors.

2. Although the police enjoy the parliamentary franchise, they should, as far as possible, avoid any political meeting, except in the discharge of their lawful duty. The police are the servants of the public at large, not of any political party, or of the advocates of any particular opinions. Whatever the individual views of police officers may be, and however they may vote, they should not give active expression to them, either on duty or off duty, so long as they remain in the public service. (*See* ELECTIONS, p. 72.)

Memorials.—1. Nothing can be more improper or subversive of discipline than for police to seek for the redress of any grievance, or the grant of some advantage or indulgence, by memorial, and it is the bounden duty of every Superintendent, Inspector, Sergeant, or constable, to whose knowledge it comes that such a document is in contemplation, or in course of preparation to bring those concerned in it before a superior officer without hesitation or delay.

2. The just request or complaint of every individual invariably meets with attentive consideration, but any action akin to attempted coercion, by amalgamation, cannot be treated otherwise than insubordination, and be visited by the severest punishment.

Memory.†—1. Extreme accuracy is of such importance in criminal cases, that police must not trust to their memories, but enter at once in their pocket-books and diaries, the particulars of all inquiries made, and the circumstances attendant upon each occurrence. The statement of a prisoner, in relation to the charge for which he is in custody, must more especially be reduced to writing at the earliest practicable moment, and, if possible, be read over to the prisoner and signed by him. It should be taken to the trial and produced, if called for.

2. A witness may, while under examination, refresh his memory, by referring to any writing made by himself at the time of the transaction concerning which he is questioned, or so soon afterwards that the Judge considers it likely that the transaction was at that time fresh in his memory. The original notes, even if copied, should never be destroyed, for cross-examination may be adversely directed to such destruction. An expert may refresh his memory by reference to professional treatises.

3. Any writing so used must be shown to the adverse party, if he requires it, and cross-examination may be founded thereon.

Menaces.—(See DEMANDING PROPERTY WITH MENACES, p. 60; and ABUSIVE LANGUAGE, p. 18.)

*****Metropolitan Police.**—1. The Metropolitan Police Force‡ was first established in 1829, by the Statute 10

† See also p. 72.
‡ The headquarters of the Metropolitan Police have since 1829 been at Scotland Yard, but will be moved in the course of 1890 to a fitting pile of buildings, erected at a cost of £200,000, on the Thames Embankment, close to Westminster Bridge, the Houses of Parliament, and the Home Office.

Geo. IV., c. 44, but it was not until 2 & 3 Vict., c. 47, that it assumed its present functions. It consists now (October, 1889) of 30 Superintendents, 842 Inspectors, 1,389 Sergeants, 12,012 constables—a total strength of 14,273, with 362 horses, distributed into four districts, twenty-two land divisions, five dockyard divisions, and one River Thames division.

2. The rates of pay range from 24s. per week to upwards of £565 per annum, with allowances. Every constable of ability, good education, perseverance, zeal, and sobriety, may rise to the rank of Divisional Superintendent, the pay, emoluments, and position of that office.

3. The Metropolitan Police therefore offers to young men a career which is to be secured in few other callings without capital. It also provides a pension, for those who have served upwards of fifteen years, besides medical attendance, and very economical lodging for single constables.

Miscarriage.—(*See* ABORTION, p. 17.)

Misconduct of Police.—1. The following are the faults most likely to be committed, and against which young constables should particularly guard, for entries on the defaulter sheet in the first years of service will materially reduce the possibility of eventual promotion and selection for the prizes of the service:—

(1) Drunkenness.
(2) Drinking on duty.
(3) Taking off the armlet to obtain drink from a publican.
(4) Insubordination.
(5) Disobedience of direct orders.
(6) Infringement of the General Orders, and Regulations, and the Periodical Orders issued to the particular force, with which every constable of every force is bound to make himself acquainted, and to know thoroughly.
(7) Disrespect to a superior officer.
(8) Unnecessary interference.
(9) Using unnecessary violence to a prisoner.
(10) Incivility, or use of improper language.
(11) Giving information to any person concerning orders received, or the progress of a case, without authority.
(12) Conveying information, either directly or in-

directly, which may delay the execution of a warrant or service of a summons.

(13) Leaving a fixed point or beat improperly. Inattention on a fixed point, or not properly working a beat.

(14) Neglect of duty, in not taking prompt steps to secure the arrest of an offender.

(15) Neglect of duty, in not discovering doors and windows open at night, or the effecting of a felonious entry.

(16) Neglecting to mark exposed places at night.

(17) Talking and gossiping on duty.

(18) Soliciting a gratuity.

(19) Accepting any gratuity without reporting it.

(20) Absence without leave, or malingering.

(21) Absence from section house and roll call.

(22) Quarrelling with comrades.

(23) Unpunctuality for parade.

(24) Slovenly dress and appearance.

(25) Bringing in, or taking, an improper charge.

(26) Taking any unusual step, or leaving the district, without authority.

(27) Neglecting to obtain necessary names, addresses, and particulars, in a criminal case, or case of accident.

(28) Neglecting to assist persons injured or taken ill in the street.

(29) Incurring debts.

(30) Bringing discredit on the police force, or causing any injury to the public service in any way.

*2. The Metropolitan Police are subject to the following disciplinary punishments, for misconduct:—

(1) To be charged before a Magistrate (Police Acts), involving dismissal, in addition to any imprisonment, with hard labour, which may be inflicted, and forfeiting all right to gratuity or pension.

(2) Dismissal.

(3) Suspension, forfeiting all pay and service while it continues.

(4) Reduction in rank.

(5) Reduction in class.

(6) Placing at foot of the class.

(7) Fines extending from 1s. to several days' pay, usually not more than five.

(8) Removal from the reserve, or special duty.

(9) Forfeiture of leave.

(10) Severe reprimand and caution.

(11) Caution.

Misdemeanor.—A misdemeanor is a crime or offence of less degree than felony, such as libels, conspiracies, assaults, &c., which are of lower account than murder, burglary, arson, &c., which are felonies.

Misdemeanant.—1. A misdemeanant is a person who has been convicted of a misdemeanor.

2. They are of the first, the second, and the third class, according to their offence, and their prison treatment varies accordingly.

Mistakes.—Every one is liable to make mistakes, even with the best intention and every desire to do right. It is always better for a police officer to make known his error before it is found out, for it may not then be too late to repair the mischief. A mistake may be rectified if taken in time, but if allowed to go on it soon becomes irreparable and perhaps culpable.

Murder.—(*See* CONSPIRACY, p. 49.) 1. Murder is unlawful homicide with malice aforethought, and its punishment is death. (24 & 25 Vict., c. 100, s. 9.)

2. When a dead body, or part of a dead body, is found, whereof the cause of death was evidently due to foul means, the constable whose attention is first called thereto should on no account move it or anything surrounding it; or allow any other person to do so; or in any way confuse footmarks in its vicinity until the arrival of an Inspector or other superior officer, for whom, and for a Surgeon, a message should be sent, *always provided* that the murderer is not known, and that no immediate step can be taken to secure his arrest; or that public decency is not offended, and that the station is within a reasonable distance.

3. As soon as the Inspector arrives (or if delay is impossible, the Sergeant or constable), he must make, in conjunction with the Surgeon, a minute and careful examination—

(*a*) For any footmarks about the body, which should be modelled or covered over before fresh imprints are made by the Surgeon and police.

(*b*) Of the position of the body.

(*c*) Of the condition of its clothing.

(*d*) Of the position of the wound, and judging by the body and the clothing, in what way, and from which quarter, and with what instrument, and under what circumstances it was probably inflicted.

(e) Whether the murderer has left his weapon or any trace of his identity in the vicinity of the body.

(f) Whether there is in the pockets, or about the person of the deceased, any paper or article disclosing his identity, if unknown, or the name of his probable murderer, or any circumstances pointing in any particular direction.

The senior officer of police present must allow no person to approach the place where the crime was committed, or suffer any article about the deceased to be moved, until its exact position has been carefully noted. If a search is necessary, such as to find a similar bullet to that by which the fatal wound was inflicted, or an article corresponding to one left apparently by the murderer near his victim, it cannot be made too speedily or thoroughly.

These are all points, information upon which may be of priceless value in the after adjustment of evidence, but which can only be secured immediately on discovery.

4. If parts only of a body are found in some receptacle, they should on no account be taken therefrom, or disturbed in their position, save under the direction of the surgeons, when they should be taken out very carefully, and every point immediately committed to paper.

5. It is impossible to pay too much attention to details, or to make too careful memoranda, in cases of murder. In a celebrated case, the inquiry was much thwarted by the limbs having been shaken out of the receptacle containing them, and the consequent impossibility of subsequently ascertaining what relation a scrap of paper, having a date on it, bore to the body—whether it was so near it as to have been probably laid there by the murderer, or simply blown in by the wind.

6. In cases of supposed murder there are five things to prove:—

(a) That some definite person is dead (unless the act of killing was witnessed, when the murderer could be tried and executed, although the name of his victim was unknown).

(b) That the death was otherwise than in the course of nature.

(c) That death took place within a year and a day from the commission of the fatal act.

(d) By whom the death was caused.

(*e*) That it was caused by the felonious act of the prisoner, and of malice aforethought.

7. Every one is guilty of felony who attempts to commit murder by any means whatever.

Mutiny.—Mutiny in the naval and military forces is an offence of which Courts-Martial have cognisance.†

Neatness.—Neatness should be a point of study for every police officer as much in his own person and clothing, as in the station and section-house and the official reports he has to make, and the books he has to keep.

Necessity.—An act which would otherwise be a crime may be excusable if done only to avoid consequences which would otherwise have inflicted irreparable evil, and provided that the act was absolutely necessary both in its origin and its degree.

***Neglect of Duty.**—1. Every constable guilty of any neglect or violation of duty is liable to a penalty of £10, or, in the discretion of the Magistrate before whom he is charged, to one month's imprisonment, with hard labour. (Police Acts.)

2. Except in aggravated cases, however, Chief Officers of Police generally deal themselves with reports for neglect of duty, but police must remember that the former alternative exists.

3. The Chief Constable of any county police force, and the Watch Committee of any city, borough, district, or place, is and are empowered to suspend any constable, within their respective jurisdiction, whom he, or they, shall think remiss or negligent in the discharge of his duty, or otherwise unfit for the same. The Chief Constable or Watch Committee is and are also empowered, at his or their discretion, to fine any such constable in a sum of money not exceeding one week's pay, and to reduce such constable from a superior to an inferior rank, such fine or reduction in rank to be in addition to any other punishment to which the constable may be liable. (22 & 23 Vict., c. 32, s. 26.)

Newspapers.—1. Police must not on any account give any information whatever to gentlemen connected with the press relative to matters within police knowledge, or relative to duties to be performed or orders

† In the police service "insubordination" is mutiny, and it is one of the most serious and fatal offences which can be committed.

received, or communicate in any manner, either directly or indirectly, with editors or reporters of newspapers on any matter connected with the public service, without express and special authority. (*See* OFFICIAL SECRETS, p. 123.)

2. The slightest deviation from this rule may completely frustrate the ends of justice, and defeat the endeavour of superior officers to advance the welfare of the public service. Individual merit will be invariably recognised in due course, but officers who without authority give publicity to discoveries, or the progress of a case, tending to produce sensation and alarm, show themselves wholly unworthy of their posts.

Notes.—Notes made at the time of, or soon after, an occurrence or criminal inquiry may be referred to in giving evidence, but the practice is not desirable, as the opposite party has a right in such case to examine them, and to cross-examine upon their contents. Notes, *which should be invariably made, and never destroyed,* should be read over before going into Court, rather than in the witness-box.

Nuisances in Streets.—1. Attention should be directed to the courts, lanes, alleys, and places in the densely populated, and other parts of divisions, where the drainage is neglected, where dead animals are found lying, or where an accumulation of decayed vegetable matter, offal, or filth, is collected or laid.

*2. Every person who in any street or public place in the Metropolitan Police District, or in any urban district, does any of the following acts, is liable to a penalty, and should be summoned, if after caution the act is repeated.

(*a*) Beats or shakes any carpet, rug, or mat, except door-mats before 8 a.m.

(*b*) Throws or lays any dirt, litter, ashes, or offensive matter on any street, except sand or ashes in time of frost to prevent accidents, or litter to prevent the freezing of pipes or noise in case of sickness, provided they are removed as soon as the occasion ceases.

(*c*) Allows any offensive matter to run into any street.

(*d*) Keeps a pig-sty to the front of any street.

(*e*) Fails to keep sufficiently swept and cleansed, all footways and watercourses adjoining the premises occupied or owned.

(*f*) Leaves open, to the danger of passengers in any thoroughfare, the entrance to any vault, cellar, or underground room, without a sufficient fence or handrail, or a light after sunset.

(*g*) Who leaves the covering of any such vault or cellar defective, without taking the above precautions to warn and prevent persons from falling thereinto.

(*h*) Who sets up any projection or blind from any window or other part of a house or shop, or exposes anything for sale, so as to hang over any carriage-way or foot-way, and to cause any annoyance or obstruction. (*See* COMMON NUISANCE, p. 46.)

Numbers on Collars and Helmets.—The numbers of police on their collars and helmets must not be concealed in any way. They are worn for the purpose of reference and identification; and persons wishing to take or ascertain the number of any Sergeant or constable, must not be obstructed. If the number is asked for, it should be given immediately.

Oath.—1. Witnesses are required to swear to the evidence they give in a Court of Justice, as an outward symbol that they are about to speak in the presence of God.

2. A witness has nothing to fear in cross-examination, if he really desires to speak only the plain truth, taking care that he understands the questions, weighing well each answer before giving it; being cautious never to speak positively as to dates or persons, if there can be the smallest shadow of a doubt; well considering how solemn a thing an oath is, and resolved to give evidence without malice or personal motive.

3. Every one is guilty of felony who administers, or aids or assists in the administration of an oath, purporting to bind any person to commit treason or murder; or who takes any such oath or engagement without absolute compulsion. (*See* PERJURY, pp. 15 and 128.)

Obscene Publications.—1. Every one commits a misdemeanor who without justification—

(*a*) Publicly sells, or exposes for public sale or to public view, any obscene book, print, picture, or other indecent exhibition.

(*b*) Publicly exhibits any disgusting object. (14 & 15 Vict., c. 100, s. 29.)

2. Every person who sells, distributes, or offers for sale or distribution in the streets, any profane, indecent,

or obscene book, paper, print, drawing, or representation (in the Metropolitan Police District, it must be to the annoyance of an inhabitant or passenger) may be apprehended without warrant, if the offence is committed within view of the constable, and is liable to a fine. (POLICE ACTS.)

3. Obscene words or figures painted, written, or chalked on walls, doors, pavements, &c., should be defaced by the police, and the offenders charged if possible. Threatening words or figures should also be quietly erased.

Obstructions.—1. Every person wilfully causing any obstruction in any public footpath or thoroughfare or crossing, by means of any cart, carriage, sledge, truck or barrow, or any horse or other animal, or by any other means, may be summoned (or apprehended if not known), and is liable to a fine; and, similarly, if after being made acquainted with the regulations framed for regulating the route of horses, carriages, carts, and persons, on any public occasion, wilfully disregards them, or does not conform himself thereto. (POLICE ACTS.)

2. Persons who wilfully, and after caution, continue to cause an obstruction in the public streets, or squares, are further guilty of behaviour whereby a breach of the peace may be occasioned, exposing them to arrest, and an additional penalty.

Obstruction of Justice and Police.—1. Every person commits a misdemeanor who obstructs, or in any way interferes with, the execution of any legal process, or obstructs any constable in the execution of his duty, which includes keeping the highways, roadways, and pavements clear for the lawful passage without hindrance or annoyance of all Her Majesty's subjects. (24 & 25 Vict., c. 100, ss. 18 & 38.)

2. The giving of information that a warrant is about to be applied for, or has been issued against a particular person, comes within the former definition, if its execution is in the smallest degree thereby delayed. (*See* CONSPIRACY, p. 49; DISSUADING WITNESSES FROM TESTIFYING, p. 66.)

Obtaining Money or Goods by False Pretences.—1. Persons who obtain either money or goods by false pretences may be received into custody, on being charged by a private person of respectability, or apprehended without warrant if the offence is committed in the presence of a constable, or if he is in fresh pursuit. (See FALSE PRETENCES, p. 83.)

2. Every person going about as a gatherer or collector of alms, or endeavouring to procure charitable contributions of any nature or kind under any false or fraudulent pretence, is liable to imprisonment with hard labour. (5 Geo. IV., c. 83, s. 4.)

Official Secrets.—1. Any person who acts as a spy in or about any fortress, arsenal, factory, dockyard, camp, ship, or other place belonging to Her Majesty, and without lawful authority takes any sketch or plan, or acquires any document, model, or information, and communicates, or intends to communicate, it directly or indirectly to a foreign State, is guilty of felony and liable to penal servitude for life, or in any other case is guilty of a misdemeanor and liable to imprisonment with or without hard labour and to a fine.

2. Any person who by reason of his holding or having held an office (including a contract, or employment with a contractor) under any department of the Government of the United Kingdom or of any of Her Majesty's possessions, and obtains control over any document, or acquires any information which he wilfully communicates to any person (including a newspaper reporter) to whom the same ought not in the public interest to be communicated, is guilty of a breach of official trust, and punishable by penal servitude for life if the communication is to a foreign state, or by fine and imprisonment in any other case. The person inciting another to commit any such offence is likewise guilty of a misdemeanor. (52 & 53 Vict., c. 52.)

3. There can be no doubt that the Metropolitan Police, the Royal Irish Constabulary, and Colonial Government Police, come under these provisions, and in all probability the members also of Provincial Constabulary Forces, for they are to a certain extent under the Home Office. It therefore behoves every police officer to be additionally careful not to communicate to any person, or to the press, information in his possession, the disclosure of which might frustrate the ends of justice.

***Old Metal Dealers.**†—Any dealer in old metals

† The repeal of the Old Metal Dealers Act was contemplated by the Stolen Goods Bill lately before Parliament (1882).

who, either personally or by any servant or agent, purchases, receives, or bargains for any metal, whether new or old, in any quantity, at one time, of less weight than hereunder stated, is liable to a penalty, viz.:—

		Not less than
Lead, or any composite thereof	... ...	... 112 lbs.
Copper, ,, ,, ,,	... ...	... 56 ,,
Brass, ,, ,, ,,	... ...	... ,,
Tin	... ...	... ,,
Pewter	... ...	... ,,
German Silver ...	... ...	... ,,

(24 & 25 Vict., c. 110, s. 3.)

Open-air Preaching.—The police should not interrupt, or in any way interfere with, persons preaching in the open-air, unless actual obstruction of the public thoroughfare be caused at the time, or some specific nuisance to the public or to persons residing at the spot is thereby occasioned.

Opinions.—1. The "opinions" of witnesses are rarely receivable in evidence, even in the case of medical persons and scientific experts, who should endeavour rather to point out facts, and let the jury form their own opinion thereon.

2. Opinions can usually be combated; and in the same way that it is dangerous to give expression to an opinion in the witness-box, it is unwise for police to give any definite opinion to persons aggrieved and others as to the motive for committing the crime, the method of its commission, and its authors.

3. Police should listen to other people's opinions and their reasons for them, forming their own private conclusion, and acting accordingly.

Orange Peel.—1. The police should remove pieces of orange peel when seen on the pavement, frequent accidents occurring by passengers slipping thereon.

2. If orange peel is wilfully and continually thrown on a pavement, with the evident design of causing annoyance and exposing the public to danger, the delinquent may be apprehended, and charged with throwing rubbish on a thoroughfare. (*See* HIGHWAYS, p. 93.)

Orders.—The orders of a superior officer should be immediately obeyed, without hesitation or delay. If a subordinate has any ground of complaint, it can only be preferred, or attended to, after obedience. (*See* MIS-CONDUCT OF POLICE, p. 115; MUTINY, p. 119.)

*Ownership.—Where property in possession of the police is claimed by any person whose ownership appears in the least open to question, he should be either called upon to prove his title by documents or satisfactory evidence, or else to apply to a Magistrate. (*See* DISPUTED OWNERSHIP OF PROPERTY, p. 66; INDEMNITY, p. 100.)

Parading for Duty.—Police must parade for duty precisely at the hour ordered, and with all their clothing and appointments clean, properly put on, and in good order.

Parochial Authorities and Visitors.—Police should study the wishes of parochial authorities, as far as possible, and facilitate in any way they properly can the benevolent actions of the clergy and other visitors of the sick and poor, who, by providing for their necessities, improve the moral and physical condition of the people, and lessen the tendency to commit crime.

*Pawnbrokers.—1. A pawnbroker who does any of the following things is liable to a penalty :—

(1) Takes an article in pawn from any person appearing to be under the age of twelve years, or to be intoxicated.

In the Metropolitan Police District the age is sixteen years, instead of twelve years.

(2) Purchases or takes in pawn or exchange a pawn ticket, issued by another pawnbroker.

(3) Employs any servant, or apprentice, or other person under the age of sixteen years to take pledges in pawn.

(4) Under any pretence purchases, except at a public auction, any pledge while in pawn with him.

(5) Suffers any pledge while in pawn with him to be redeemed with a view to his purchasing it.

(6) Makes any contract or agreement with any person pawning, or offering to pawn, any article, or with the owner thereof, within the time of redemption, for its purchase, sale, or disposition.

(7) Sells, or otherwise disposes of any pledge pawned with him, except at such time, and in such manner, as authorised by the Act.

2. Every person is liable to a penalty, who—

(*a*) Offers to a pawnbroker an article by way of pawn, being unable or refusing to give a satisfactory account of the means by which he became possessed of the article.

(*b*) Wilfully gives false information to a pawnbroker as to whether an article offered by him in pawn to the pawnbroker is his own property or not, or as to his name and address, or as to the name and address of the owner of the article.

(*c*) Not being entitled to redeem, and not having any colour of title by law to redeem a pledge, attempts or endeavours to redeem the same.

3. Where a pawnbroker reasonably suspects that an article has been stolen, or illegally or clandestinely obtained, he may seize and detain the person and article, or either of them, and deliver them to a constable, to be conveyed before a Justice. (Pawnbrokers' Act, 1872; 35 & 36 Vict., c. 93.) (*See* ILLEGAL PAWNING, p. 98.)

***Pawnbrokers' Lists.**—1. To every pawnbroker and established second-hand goods dealer in the Metropolitan and City Police Districts, as well as in most towns, is issued daily a list of all articles stolen or lost *possessing any distinctive mark of identity*.

2. The lists contain a description of such articles stolen in the provinces as are reported to Criminal Investigation Department by constabulary forces, *if they possess any recognisable marks*.

3. The lists should be prepared with great care, and in such manner as to secure, if possible, the attention of pawnbrokers and their assistants, by omitting all unnecessary words—thus, "Gold Locket: mark of identity, A. E. T."—and giving engravings of special articles.

***Pedlars.**—1. Pedlar means any hawker, pedlar, petty chapman, tinker, caster of metals, mender of chairs, or other person who, *without any horse or other beast bearing or drawing burden*, travels and trades on foot, and goes from town to town, or to other men's houses, carrying to sell, or exposing for sale, any goods, wares, or merchandise, or procuring orders for goods, wares or merchandise, immediately to be delivered, or selling or offering for sale his skill in handicraft.

2. Any person who acts as a pedlar without having obtained a certificate authorising him so to act is liable to a penalty.

3. Any police officer may call upon a pedlar to produce

and show his certificate, and allow him to examine his pack or box. Any person acting as a pedlar who refuses to show his certificate, or has none, or refuses or attempts to prevent inspection of his pack, may be arrested, and is liable to a penalty. While it is very desirable that this power should be exercised with great discretion, it is necessary to remember the great facilities a pretended pedlar may have, especially in rural districts, for petty larceny. (34 & 35 Vict., c. 96; 44 & 45 Vict., c. 45.)

4. Licences are not required for the sale, in legally constituted public fairs or markets, of fish, fruit, or vegetables.

Pencils and Pocket-books.—Every police officer should be at all times provided with a pencil and pocket-book, to make notes of inquiries, record the names and addresses of persons to be summoned, and of witnesses to any accident, and to carry the photographs of persons whose apprehension is sought.

Pensions.—1. The granting of pensions to the police is dependent upon the regulations of each force. The author and other members of Parliament have done their best to induce successive Governments to pass a Superannuation Act, but the difficulty is much increased by the extension of local government, and the joint control of the constabulary acquired by provincial county councils. The best course now will be for each locality to promote its own Bill, and follow the example of Lincolnshire, the West Riding of Yorkshire, the City of London, &c.

2. An association exists to provide employment for pensioners of the Metropolitan and City Police who are anxious for it. Reliable men for almost any kind of duty, with the guarantee of their pension for good conduct, can be met with on application to the Secretary, Police Pensioners' Employment Association, Queen's Hall, James Street, Westminster, London. Telegraphic address—"Police Pensioners, London."

* **Performances in the Streets.**—Every person who, to the annoyance or obstruction of the inhabitants, exhibits any show or public entertainment in a thoroughfare, is liable to a penalty, and may be apprehended if necessary, and the offence is committed within sight of the constable to whom complaint is made. (POLICE ACTS.)

Perjury.—1. Perjury is a wilfully false assertion, upon oath or affirmation properly administered, in any legal proceeding, on a matter material to the issue or likely to affect the result.

2. Subornation of perjury consists in procuring some person to make a false assertion upon oath or affirmation in such manner as to cause him actually to commit the perjury.

3. Perjury and subornation of perjury are misdemeanors, and every one who commits either is liable to penal servitude. (2 Geo. II., c. 25, s. 2.) (*See* SIR H. HAWKINS' ADVICE, p. 15.)

Personation.—Every one commits felony who falsely and deceitfully personates any person, with intent fraudulently to obtain any land, estate, chattel, money, valuable security, or property. (37 & 38 Vict., c. 36.)

Persons Found Insensible.—1. Insensibility is the suspension of the functions of animal life, except those of respiration and circulation.

2. Insensibility is likely to be mistaken for drunkenness, and it must be remembered that the conditions may be complicated with each other and with the effects of drink, and that no single sign can be relied on in forming a conclusion on the condition of the patient.

3. When a person is found insensible, the following points should be observed:—

(*a*) The position of the body and its surroundings.
(*b*) The cause of insensibility.

4. Place the body on the back, with the head inclined to one side, the arms by the sides, and extend the legs.

Examining the head and body, pass the fingers gently over the surface, and search for wounds, bruises, swellings, or depressions.

Observe the state of the respiration, whether easy or difficult; the presence or absence of stiffness; and the odour of the breath.

Petitions.—1. Police should not in any way, either directly or indirectly, assist in preparing or obtaining signatures to any petition to Parliament, or to a Secretary of State, or to a Lord-Lieutenant or Governor, or to a chief officer of police, in respect of any matter, within the discretion of Parliament, or affecting the police service, or any persons in it, or any matter of police duty, or affecting the prosecution of offenders or the sentences inflicted upon them.

2. Proper representations invariably secure for opinions, wishes, or views the consideration they deserve. (*See* MEMORIALS, p. 113.)

Photography.—1. The utility of photography in the pursuit of criminals, or the identification of dead bodies, cannot be over-estimated. At the same time great caution is necessary, for there is frequently much similarity between the photographs of wholly different people.†

2. The photographs of all persons sentenced to penal servitude in Great Britain are taken prior to liberation and registered at the Home Office and Convict Office, Great Scotland Yard, in addition to a copy being affixed to the descriptive form sent from the prison to the police of the district, into which the convict has elected to be released.

3. The Secretary of State has decided that, upon the application and at the cost of police, the Governors of Her Majesty's prisons should cause the photographs to be taken of prisoners whose names are furnished to them.

4. This enables the police to secure for future reference the photograph of a person convicted of a serious offence, but sentenced to imprisonment only. Officers in charge of cases, who consider that the photograph of the prisoner should be taken, should make a recommendation to that effect through the proper channel.

Pickpockets.—1. The greatest vigilance is necessary on the part of police for the detection of pickpockets, and every effort should be made to apprehend them while the hand is absolutely in the pocket of the person robbed, or the stolen property is still in their possession; for although an arrest for attempting to pick pockets is perfectly legitimate, there are so many channels open for successful defence to the charge, in the absence of corroboration, that it is better under ordinary circumstances to wait.

† A system is under trial with the Paris police to remedy these defects of photography, by careful measurement of the different parts of a prisoner's body by means of ingenious instruments, and their tabulation under various heads.

2. Pickpockets frequent railway stations, race meetings, and fires, and often take advantage of any crowd, or of the unguarded way in which watches and purses are carried, especially by ladies.

3. Observation for pickpockets is better kept at a short distance above or behind a crowd, and when those persons whose movements are suspicious have been signalled out, the officer must endeavour to get as near them as possible without attracting their notice.

Placards and Printed Bills.—The police should notice all bills or placards posted up, and pamphlets or handbills distributed in the streets, and anything of an obscene, immoral, unusual, or offensive nature should be reported, and a copy if possible obtained.

*Poaching.—1. Every one commits a misdemeanor who by night unlawfully takes, or destroys, any game (hares, pheasants, partridges, grouse, heath, or moor game, black game, and bustards) or rabbits in any land, whether open or enclosed; or by night unlawfully enters or is upon any such land with any gun, net, engine or other instrument, for the purpose of taking or destroying game.

2. Any person found committing such offence may be apprehended and handed over to a constable by the owner or occupier of the land, or person having the right of sporting thereon, or any assistant, gamekeeper, or servant of such person.

3. If a poacher assaults, or offers any violence to, a person thus authorised to apprehend him, he is guilty of a misdemeanor.

4. "Night" means the interval between the end of the first hour after sunset and the beginning of the last hour before sunrise.

5. Any constable in any highway, street, or public place, may search any person whom he has good cause to suspect of coming from any land, where he has unlawfully been in search or pursuit of game, or any person aiding or abetting such person and having in his possession any game unlawfully obtained, or any guns, nets, or instruments used for taking or killing game. He may also stop and search any cart, or other conveyance, in or upon which he has good cause to suspect that any such game, or any such article or thing, is being

carried by any such person, and if any such game or article be found, it may be seized, and the person summoned before a Court of Summary Jurisdiction. (9 Geo. IV., c. 69.)

Poisons and Poisoning.—1. Poisons are substances capable of destroying life.

2. The points to be kept in view in cases of poisoning are—

(*a*) To get rid of the poison by encouraging vomiting.

(*b*) To counteract the effects of the poisons by antidotes, which will mechanically, or chemically, render the poison harmless.

(*c*) To remedy the effects produced, and obviate the tendency to death, by stimulants, artificial respiration, and exciting the excretory organs.

3. *Emetics.*—Emetics are remedies used for the purpose of causing vomiting. The safest and readiest are—

(*a*) Irritating the back of the throat with the finger or a feather.

(*b*) Large draughts of tepid water, containing a tablespoonful of salt or mustard.

(*c*) One or two tablespoonfuls of ipecacuanha wine, in water.

The stomach pump cannot be used except by a surgeon, but a safe substitute can be found in a piece of gutta-percha tubing, provided the patient is not in an insensible condition. Take three yards of elastic gutta-percha tubing, about half an inch in diameter; make the patient swallow from fifteen to twenty inches of it; raise the free end above his head, and pour down a pint of water, or as much as the stomach will receive. Then lower the free end and it will empty itself; repeat the filling and emptying as often as is thought necessary. (Shepherd's Handbook.)

4. In a case of suspected poisoning, police must take care that not only all bottles and boxes containing medicine and medicinal matter, all food or drink prepared for the sufferer and not used, and the receptacles in which they were served, are seized, but also that all evacuations of the deceased, by vomit or otherwise, are preserved intact for medical analysis. This can only be secured by placing them in a locked room, under constant charge of a constable, and the vessels in which

substances for analysis are placed must be first thoroughly washed with clean water, and only removed under strict medical direction. Pocket handkerchiefs and pillow cases used by the person believed to have been poisoned should also be scientifically examined, if secured before washing, for expectoration tainted with poison.

*5. If it is only after burial that suspicious facts come to light, the Home Secretary may be applied to on affidavit for an order to exhume the body.

6. Every person offering, exposing for sale, or selling any grain, seed, or meal which has been dipped in poison, or with which any poison has been so mixed as to render it calculated to destroy human life, is liable to a penalty, and similarly any person knowingly and wilfully sowing any poisoned seed.

Poisoning Animals.—1. If any person wilfully and unlawfully administers, or causes to be administered, to any horse, cattle, or domestic animal any poisonous or injurious drug or substance, he is liable to a penalty, or imprisonment, unless he shows some reasonable excuse, or is the owner of the animal or his agent. (39 & 40 Vict., c. 13.)

*2. Every person who knowingly and wilfully sets, places, or causes to be laid upon any land any flesh or meat which has been mixed with poison, or impregnated with any poisonous ingredient calculated to destroy life, is liable to a penalty, unless it be for the destruction of rats and small vermin in a dwelling-house, or enclosed garden or drain, protected so as to prevent any dog entering, or within any rick or stack. (27 & 28 Vict., c. 115, s. 2.)

Police Districts.—1. A police district in any county or division of a county, or any city, borough, or town maintaining a separate police force, and the Chief or Head Constable thereof is the chief officer of police.

*2. The City of London, and the liberties thereof, form the City Police District, and the chief officer is the Commissioner of Police in the City.

3. The Commissioner of Police of the Metropolis is the chief officer of the Metropolitan Police District.

*"**Police Gazette.**"— 1. The *Police Gazette*,

London, is issued gratis, twice a week, viz., on Tuesdays and Fridays, to the police forces of the kingdom.

2. A request for the arrest of any person must be authenticated by the signature of a Superintendent of Police, or of a Chief Officer, or his immediate deputy, if no warrant has been issued.

3. Stolen animals, and property, should be described as concisely as is possible, giving prominence to special marks of identity.

4. Announcements for insertion in the *Police Gazette*, and applications for copies to be regularly supplied, should be addressed to

The Editor of
The *Police Gazette*,
Metropolitan Police Office,
London, S.W.

***Police in Private Employ.**—The Chief Constable of any county, with the approval of the Justices of the county in General or Quarter Sessions assembled, may on the application of any person or persons showing the necessity thereof, appoint and cause to be sworn in, any additional number of constables at any place within the limits of his authority, at the charge of the person or persons by whom the application is made, but subject to the orders of the Chief Constable, and for such time as he shall think fit.

***Police Stealing or Embezzling.**—Any police officer who steals or embezzles any chattel, money, or valuable security entrusted to, or received, or taken possession of by him by virtue of his employment, or in any manner fraudulently applies or disposes of the same or any part thereof to his own use and benefit, or for any purpose whatsoever, except for the public service, is liable to fourteen years' penal servitude. (24 & 25 Vict., c. 96, s. 69.)

***Police Supervision.**—1. When any person is convicted of felony, or of any of the undermentioned misdemeanors, viz. :—

(1) Uttering false or counterfeit coin.
(2) Possessing counterfeit gold or silver coin.
(3) Obtaining goods or money by false pretences.
(4) Conspiracy to defraud.

(5) Being found by night armed, with intent to break into a dwelling-house.

(6) Being found by night, without lawful excuse, with housebreaking implements.

(7) Being found by night with face blackened, &c., with intent to commit felony.

(8) Being found by night in any dwelling-house or building, with intent to commit felony.

And a previous conviction for any felony or for any such misdemeanor is proved against him, the Court, in addition to any other punishment, may direct that he be subject to the supervision of the police for any period not exceeding seven years, commencing immediately on the termination of the term of penal servitude or imprisonment. (34 & 35 Vict., c. 112, s. 8.)

2. A person under sentence of police supervision is under precisely the same conditions as a convict on licence (*see* p. 52), except that he has no licence to produce. (*See* PREVENTION OF CRIME ACTS.)

Portico Larcenies.—Portico larcenies are committed by climbing up the portico, at an hour when the family and servants are not likely to be about, and the entry is much facilitated in summer by the window over the portico being often carelessly left open. (*See* ATTIC LARCENIES, p. 26.)

Post Letters.—Every one who steals a post letter bag, or post letter from a post letter bag or from a post office, from an officer of the post office, or from a mail, or who steals any chattel, money, or valuable security from or out of a post letter, or who stops a mail, with intent to rob or search the same, is guilty of felony, and, similarly, any person feloniously receiving any article stolen by such means. (7 Wm. IV.; 1 Vict., c. 36.)

Post Office.—1. The attention of police should be directed to the various attempts that are made to intercept letters posted in pillar letter boxes. Constables should carefully and frequently, especially at night, examine the apertures of the boxes on their beats, by running their fingers, as far as possible, round the inside, and should they discover that any device, trap, or sticky substance, has been inserted, they should *not* remove it, but keep careful and quiet watch, to endeavour to discover the offender until visited by the Sergeant, who will send immediate information to the station.

2. Postmen, or drivers of mail-carts, &c., guilty of any act of drunkenness, negligence, or other misconduct, whereby the safety of a post letter bag or post letter may be endangered, or who collect, receive, convey, or deliver a letter otherwise than in the ordinary course of post, or who give any false information of an assault or attempted robbery upon them, or who loiter on the road, or wilfully mis-spend their time, so as to retard or delay the progress or arrival of a post letter bag or post letter, and drivers of mail-carts who improperly carry a passenger, are liable to a penalty or to imprisonment.

3. Police noticing the commission of any of these offences by postmen and mail-drivers, should report the circumstances, with all particulars, and the matter should be officially notified to the Postmaster-General, except in the case of drunkenness, when, if absolutely necessary, the postman may be detained, and a notification sent to the nearest post office.

4. Police should cultivate a friendly feeling with the Post Office officials by all possible means.

Power of Attorney.—A power of attorney is a writing authorising another person to do any lawful act in the stead of another, and is either general or special.

* **Prevention of Crime Acts.**—1. The Prevention of Crime Acts, 1871 and 1879, are those under which convicts on licence and persons under sentence of police supervision are required—

(a) To report themselves to the police within forty-eight hours of their arrival within a police district.

(b) To report themselves every month to the police.

(c) To notify to the police their changes of address.

(d) To get their living by regular means and honest employment.

2. The seventh section of the Act of 1871 provides, that if any person has been already twice convicted of a crime, *the first conviction having been proved at the trial of the second indictment,* he is, within seven years of the expiration of the last sentence, liable to twelve months' imprisonment with hard labour if—

(1) He is proved to the satisfaction of a Court of Summary Jurisdiction to be getting his livelihood by

dishonest means, having been apprehended on the written authority of the chief officer of police.

(2) If, on being charged, he refuses to give his name and address, or gives a false name and address.

(3) If he is found in any place, whether public or private, under such circumstances as to satisfy the Court before which he is brought that he was about to commit or to aid in the commission of any offence punishable on indictment or summary conviction, or was waiting for an opportunity to commit or aid in the commission of any offence punishable on indictment or summary conviction.

(4) If he is found in or upon any dwelling-house, or any building, yard, or premises being parcel of or attached to such dwelling-house, or in or upon any shop, warehouse, counting-house, or other place of business, or in any garden, orchard, pleasure ground, or nursery ground, or in any building or erection in any garden, orchard, pleasure ground, or nursery ground, without being able to account to the satisfaction of the Court before which he is brought, for his being found on such premises.

In either of the two latter cases he may be arrested without warrant.

3. Under the sixteenth section of the Prevention of Crime Act, 1871, a chief officer of police may authorise in writing the entry by a constable upon any premises in search of stolen property, in either of the following cases:—

(1) Where the premises are, or within the preceding twelve months have been, in the occupation of any person who has been convicted of receiving stolen property or harbouring thieves.

(2) When the premises are in the occupation of any person who has been convicted of any offence involving fraud or dishonesty, including unlawful possession, and punishable by penal servitude or imprisonment.

The chief officer of police may give the authority, without specifying any particular property, if he has reason to believe generally that the premises are being made a receptacle for stolen goods.

In the exercise of such authority any constable may search and seize and take any property he may believe to have been stolen, in the same manner as he would be authorised to do if he had a search warrant, and the property seized corresponded to the property described in the search warrant.

Previous Convictions.—1. When a prisoner is arrested for a serious offence, every effort should be made to ascertain his former character, and if any previous convictions are recorded against him.

2. The description of the prisoner, and any other facts serving to identify him, should be circulated in Informations, and if necessary in the *Police Gazette* and *Hue and Cry,* or in papers corresponding thereto. The attention of warders, and police visiting remand prisons, may be especially called to him by the officer in charge of the case. The records at the Convict Office, and in the Habitual Criminals' Registry, Home Office, should be searched, if possible; and, finally, if a photograph can be obtained, it may be transmitted on a descriptive route form to the Governors of prisons, and the several constabulary forces, for the inspection of warders and police.

3. All these measures, except the prisoner's being seen in visiting prisons, are applicable to a prisoner under remand in any part of the country.

4. When a previous conviction is found, it must be proved against the prisoner. This is done by its being included in the indictment before a true bill is found by the grand jury (the Clerk of Arraigns or Clerk of the Peace being notified to that end), and the prisoner being called upon to plead thereto after the verdict of the jury, and before sentence. If the prisoner denies his identity, a person who was either present at his conviction or saw him in prison must be called, and *in any case a certificate of the previous conviction must be put in.*

5. A certificate of a previous conviction is obtained at the office of the Clerk of Arraigns of the Central Criminal Court, or Clerk of the Peace of the county in which he was convicted. At the former the certificate is given free of charge, elsewhere the fee is five shillings.

6. The Magistrates should always be informed of a previous conviction, and if they then direct its proof it will be necessary to produce—

(*a*) A witness who was present at the former trial, or who saw the prisoner when undergoing imprisonment for the previous offence.

(*b*) A certificate of such conviction, signed by the Clerk or proper custodian of its records.

The previous conviction is then placed on the depositions, which are sent direct from the Police Court to the office of the Clerk of the Peace.

7. A certificate of the previous conviction is invariably required before the sentence of a convict on licence or person under police supervision for a breach of the Prevention of Crime Acts.

*Printed Informations.—1. Informations describing persons whose apprehension is sought, and their crime; property stolen, lost, or found; persons and animals lost and found, are compiled and printed at the Metropolitan Police Office, and issued to every station in the Metropolitan and City Police Districts four times a day (9.30 a.m., 12.30 p.m., 6.30 p.m., and 10.30 p.m.), except Sunday, when they are issued twice.

2. The 12.30 p.m. issue contains everything relating to criminal matters, and must be especially studied by every officer desiring to do good work.

3. The descriptions of persons wanted by constabulary forces, of persons in custody concerning whom the Criminal Investigation Department has been communicated with, and of property stolen, &c., are circulated in the 1.30 issue.

Prisoners.—1. In apprehending a person, and making him or her a prisoner, no more violence should be used than is absolutely necessary for the safe custody of the prisoner.

2. The usual plan is to seize the right arm and keep hold of it until the prisoner is in the station, to prevent the possibility of escape. When a prisoner is once in custody, he must never be lost sight of for a single instant on any pretence whatsoever, and he should not be released except by direction of a Magistrate, or on the responsibility of an officer in charge of a police station.

3. If a prisoner resists, the constable is bound to endeavour to detain him, taking care not to inflict any avoidable injury.

4. If the constable is likely to be overpowered, he may draw his truncheon and use it, taking care to avoid striking any one on the head. The arms and legs should

be aimed at to disable a prisoner, as the parts of the frame least likely to suffer serious injury.

5. The constable may also spring his rattle or blow his whistle, which will bring assistance; but extreme measures should not be resorted to except where all other attempts have failed, and a prisoner is likely to escape through the constable being ill-used and overpowered.

6. Prisoners who are very violent, or who are charged with very serious offences, should, if necessary, be handcuffed.

7. No conversation should be held in the hearing of prisoners, nor should improper language or taunting remarks be used towards them.

8. All possible facility should be given for prisoners to send for bail, and to communicate with their friends, but no letter must be sent without the officer on duty first satisfying himself that it contains nothing in the nature of a warning to accomplices, or prejudicial to the interests of justice.

9. When prisoners in wet clothes are brought to a police station, inquiry should be made as to whether they wish their wet clothing dried. If they do so, it should be done, as far as practicable.

10. Prisoners should be supplied with clear water to drink.

11. Necessary refreshments for prisoners may be purchased out of money taken from them, providing the charge against them does not relate to the money. The amount expended for refreshments must be entered in the prisoner's property book.

12. When it is necessary for prisoners to have refreshment, either at their own or at the public expense, no beer or spirits whatever should be given to them, or admitted into the cells, but only tea or coffee, with such eatables as are usual.

13. A solicitor, or a clerk authorised to act for him, may be allowed to communicate with a prisoner in the custody of the police at a station, if the prisoner wishes it, but no interview should be allowed a person who seeks to be retained for the prisoner's defence, without any instructions to that end. Facility, as far as practicable, should be given that the communication may not be overheard by any one; but care must be taken that

the prisoner shall not escape, and, if necessary for the purpose, one of the police may keep the prisoner in sight during the communication.

14. A statement made by a prisoner when charged at a station must be accurately written down at the time by the Inspector or Sergeant on duty, and reported to the Magistrate who hears the case.

15. If prisoners are insensible, or appear to be ill or injured in any way, although they do not complain, a Surgeon should be sent for immediately. This course relieves the police of responsibility, and should be strictly observed. The police incur heavy responsibilities by deviation from this rule. (*See* also DRUNKEN PERSONS, p. 70.)

16. An Inspector or Sergeant, on commencing his tour of duty in charge of a police station, should on each occasion receive from the Inspector or Sergeant whom he relieves a statement of the number of persons then confined, and with him visit the cells, and make a personal inspection of each prisoner. The Inspector or Sergeant, for his own security, ought to see that the prisoners are in a proper state when he commences his tour of duty. (*See* PRODUCTION OF A PRISONER AS A WITNESS, p. 142; SEARCHING A PRISONER, p. 165.)

*Prisons.—1. The whole of the prisons in the United Kingdom were brought under the control of the Secretary of State for the Home Department by the Prisons Act, 1877.

2. Every person who, contrary to the regulations of the prison, brings or attempts by any means whatever to introduce into any prison any spirituous or fermented liquor or tobacco, and every officer of a prison who suffers any spirituous or fermented liquor or tobacco to be sold or used therein, contrary to the prison regulations, is liable to imprisonment or a penalty, or both, and if a prison officer to dismissal as well.

3. Every person who, contrary to the regulations of a prison, conveys or attempts to convey any letter or other document, or any article whatever not allowed by such regulations, into or out of any prison, may be apprehended by any one, and is liable to a penalty of £10, and dismissal, if an officer. (*See* WARDERS, p. 185.) (28 & 29 Vict., c. 126, s. 37.)

Prisoner's Property.—1. All articles taken from a prisoner, as either possibly relating to the charge, or because by means of them he may inflict some injury on himself, should be entered in a prisoner's property book, which ought to be kept at every station.

2. Property taken from prisoners must not be returned to them, or handed to any other person, until the Magistrate's decision is known.† (*See* pp. 66 and 100.)

3. If the prisoner is discharged, the property may usually be restored to him on his signing the book.

4. Property relating to a charge, which is found and brought to a police station subsequent to a charge being entered, should be accurately described in the prisoner's property book.

5. The prisoner's property book should be invariably sent to the Court with the charge-sheet, *and the Magistrate may be asked if any special property, or any small sum of money, found on the prisoner, may be handed to the prisoner, or to some person designated by him in writing.*

Private Parties, Balls, &c.—Private individuals desiring the services of the police, *in the regulation of traffic*, &c., at private entertainments, should write to the Superintendent of the division wherein they reside, specifying the number of men required. A regulated charge is usually made for such services, which are, as a rule, assigned to constables as extra duty.

Privileged Communications.—A privileged communication is that which a witness cannot be compelled to divulge. Communications made in the public interest for the prevention or detection of crime (cases quoted in Taylor on "Evidence," 7th Ed., Vol. I., p. 792) enjoy the same privilege as those which take place between a husband and wife during marriage, or between a client and his legal adviser, or in the *bonâ fide* discharge of a duty. (*See* COMMUNICATIONS TO POLICE, p. 46.)

*****Prize Fights.**—1. The police have legal authority to apprehend, detain, and charge before a Magistrate, any person or persons against whom evidence can be produced that he or they intended to be concerned as a

† When a constable exercises his discretion in taking possession of property, the moment he has so taken possession, his discretion ceases, and he must not give it up to any one, save by order of a Court or of his superior officer. (*See* Reg. *v.* Ryan and D'Eyncourt, 21, Q., B.D., 109.)

principal or accessories in a prize fight in any part of the kingdom.

2. Police hearing that persons are in training, or preparing to fight, or are accessory to an intended prize fight, must immediately report the circumstances.

3. Evidence to identify them and prove the intention may be obtained by all proper means.

4. Boxing matches may be in the nature of prize fights, if taking place for a wager, and between noted combatants. The proprietors of places in which matches of this particular character, not merely amateur meetings, are announced to be held, should be cautioned that they will be held strictly responsible if any infringement of the law takes place, and police should attend the match, and similarly caution both principals and seconds, against whom, as well as against all persons present, proceedings may be taken according to the circumstances of the case.

5. In giving cautions in these and similar cases, police should be careful to speak in general terms only, and not be drawn into any statement, as to how far a person may go without overstepping the boundary of the law.

Procurators Fiscal.—Procurators Fiscal are the public prosecutors in Scotland, where the criminal procedure is not the same as in England, Wales, and Ireland.

Production of a Prisoner as a Witness.—When the evidence of a prisoner in custody is necessary to the ends of justice in any case, civil or criminal, application on affidavit must be made to the Home Secretary, or a Judge at Chambers, for the issue of a warrant, or order, under his hand to bring up the prisoner. (Form, Appendix E.)

Promotion.—1. All promotions in the Metropolitan Police, and most other forces, up to the rank of Superintendent, are made from the next rank below.

2. When vacancies in the higher ranks occur, and directions are given for men to be recommended for promotion, those best qualified in all respects are selected, seniority of service being duly considered.

3. Police should not endeavour to obtain promotion by the intervention of private persons. Such requests seldom advance the object desired, but rather retard it, as evidencing a spirit to endeavour to secure selection by favour rather than by merit. Any officer who wishes for

early advancement has frequent opportunities of attracting the notice of his superiors by some action evidencing zeal, ability, and judgment, by strict attention to duty, sobriety, and a smart appearance, and respectful demeanor.

*4. In order to provide the most meritorious and fit men to fill the superior ranks in the police, any constable or officer promoted from one force to another, either of a county or borough, who has served in his last force for seven years, may, for the purposes of superannuation, reckon as service in the force to which he is promoted one half of the period of his previous service, provided that the promotion is made, in the case of a county constable, on the recommendation of the Chief Constable, with the sanction of the Court of Quarter Sessions, and in the case of a borough constable, on the recommendation of the Head Constable of the borough, with the sanction of the Council, and that in both cases the service is formally certified at the time of the promotion. (22 & 23 Vict., c. 32, s. 19.)

Prostitutes.—1. There is frequently considerable difficulty in dealing with prostitutes in the absence of any private complaint or express statutory provision regarding them. The latter is not unfrequently found in some local enactment. The exercise of great tact and patience in the matter is in any case necessary. Prostitutes cannot legally be taken into custody simply because they *are* prostitutes; to justify their apprehension they must commit some distinct act which is an offence against the law.

*2. Under the Vagrant Act (section 3) every common prostitute wandering in the public streets or public highways, or in any place of public resort, and behaving in a riotous or indecent manner, is deemed an idle and disorderly person, and liable to one month's imprisonment with hard labour.

3. Under the Metropolitan Police Act (2 & 3 Vict., c. 47, s. 54) every common prostitute, or night-walker, loitering, or being in any thoroughfare, or public place, for the purpose of prostitution or solicitation, *to the annoyance of an inhabitant or passenger who will charge her, and attend the Police Court to give evidence*, is liable to a penalty of 40s.

4. Under the Town Police Clauses Act (10 & 11 Vict.,

c. 89, s. 28) every common prostitute or night-walker, loitering and importuning passengers, for the purpose of prostitution, is subject to a similar fine, or fourteen days' imprisonment in default.

5. The police have no power to interfere with men and women talking together in the streets, so long as they behave themselves properly, and are not assembled together, in such numbers as actually to cause obstruction in the thoroughfares: but if it is absolutely necessary to interfere, then it must be done civilly and firmly, without any offensive language or manners.

Provision of Necessaries.—1. Every person who takes charge of another, or under whose care another may actually be, is under a legal duty to provide for him or her the necessaries of life, and is criminally responsible for the neglect of that duty, if the person to whom it is owing is, from age, health, insanity, or any other cause, unable to withdraw himself from the control of the person from whom it is due.

2. If a person delegates the discharge of this duty to another, and furnishes the means, it is the legal duty of the latter to provide the necessaries of life, and of the former to use ordinary care that the duty delegated is properly performed.

Public Occasions.—On all public occasions care must be taken not to interfere with the enjoyment of the people by imposing any unnecessary regulation, or any absence of good temper on the part of the police, and the traffic should always be left open as long as possible.

***Public Houses** (Licensing Acts, 1872-74; 35 & 36 Vict., c. 94; 37 & 38 Vict., c. 49).

LICENSING.

1. Every person selling or exposing for sale by retail any intoxicating liquors must be duly licensed, but Clubs do not require to take out a licence for such sale *to members only, for consumption on the premises.*

2. In both Counties and Boroughs the Justices appoint a Licensing Committee. (Act 1872, s. 37.) In Middlesex and Surrey the Annual General Licensing Meetings are held within the first ten days of March; elsewhere between August 20 and September 14.

3. Every person intending to apply for a new licence

must, at least twenty-days before, give notice in writing to one of the overseers of the parish and to some constable therein, setting forth his name and address, and a description of the licence for which he intends to apply; and within twenty-eight days before must affix and maintain, between 11 a.m. and 5 p.m., a like notice on the premises in question, and on one of the doors of the church or chapel of the district, and advertise the same in some paper circulating in the district, not more than four weeks and not less than two weeks before the intended application. (Act 1872, s. 40.)

4. The renewal of a licence cannot be opposed unless notice has been served upon the holder, at least seven days before the commencement of the General Annual Licensing Meeting, or the renewal has been adjourned to allow the holder to be present. (Act 1872, s. 42.) Such notice must be in duplicate, must state in general terms the grounds of objection, and may be in the following form :—

*To*_____

*of*_____

I_____ (Rank and Name) _____ of the _____ (Force) _____, do hereby give you notice that, with the approval of _____, it is my intention at the General Annual Licensing Meeting to be held for _____ at _____ on the _____ day _____ next, to oppose the renewal of the Licence which you now hold for the sale by retail of Intoxicating liquors at _____ in the said Licensing District; and that the following is a statement in general terms of the ground on which the Renewal of such Licence will be opposed (that is to say) :—

*Dated*_____

*Signed*_____

5. A person intending to apply for the transfer of a licence must, fourteen days before, serve a notice of his intention upon one of the Overseers of the Parish, and upon the Superintendent of Police of the District. (Act 1872, s. 40.)

6. Licensing Justices should be furnished with full information concerning the applicants for new licences or transfers; and this may be conveniently done in the under-mentioned form.

Licensing District for the   Division,
County of   ,   18 .
Result of Police Inquiries upon application under the Licensing Acts for a New Licence or a Transfer.

Name of Applicant, and Situation of House and Sign (if any).	APPLICATION: State whether for Transfer or Temporary Authority ("Protection Order"), or for New Licence, and whether an Inn ("Licensed Victuallers"), or Beerhouse ("off," or "on"), or "Wine" or other Licence.	Where and when Application will be heard.	In the case of Transfer or "Protection Order," Name, Residence, and Occupation of incoming tenant.	Licensed Houses in Previous occupation of incoming Tenant or proposed Holder, and description of Licence.	Convictions of incoming Tenant or proposed Holder by Magistrates, and Nature and Date of Offence, and Date of Conviction.	Charges and Complaints other than Convictions.	Witnesses forthcoming if required.

Signature and Date.

When applicants reside beyond the district, the form can be sent for the last columns to be filled in by the Chief Officer of Police in the district in which the applicant formerly resided.

7. A Protection Order, or Temporary Licence, may be granted by a Magistrate after the usual police inquiry to an intending applicant for a Transfer of an Intoxicating Liquors' Licence; but if it is not granted at the next Special Licensing Session, the house must be immediately closed.

8. An occasional licence may be granted by the Commissioners of Inland Revenue, the consent of a Justice of the Peace being first obtained, *to any person already licensed to sell intoxicating liquors,* to sell the like articles at any other place than on the licensed premises, for not exceeding three consecutive days at one time. (26 & 27

Vict., c. 33, s. 20.) Notice of the grant of the occasional licence must be given at the Police Station nearest the place of sale, that such steps may be taken for the preservation of order as are reasonable under the circumstances.

9. Every holder of a licence must, within a reasonable time after demand, produce it for the perusal of a Justice of the Peace, constable, or officer of the Inland Revenue, subject to a penalty of £10. (Act 1872, s. 64.)

10. Licences may be taken out for six days, or provide for closing at night one hour earlier than would otherwise be required, the duty being abated one-seventh in respect of each such abridgment. (Act 1874, s. 8.)

CLOSING.

11. All premises in which intoxicating liquors are sold by retail must be closed as follows:—

(*a*) Within the metropolis (that is, within the City of London, the jurisdiction of the London County Council, or four miles from Charing Cross), between 12.30 a.m. and 5 a.m., except on Saturday evening, when they must be closed at midnight. On Sunday they may be open from 1 p.m. to 3 p.m., and from 6 p.m. to 11 p.m.

(*b*) Without the metropolis, but in the Metropolitan Police District, and in populous places of over 1,000 inhabitants, the hour of closing is 11 p.m. on every night except Sunday, when it is 10 p.m., and of opening on week days, 6 a.m.

(*c*) In country districts the hour of closing on all days is 10 p.m., and of opening 6 a.m., except on Sundays, when it is 12.30 p.m.

(*d*) Public houses, wherever situate, must be closed on Sunday afternoon from 3 (or 2.30 p.m., according as the hour of opening is 12.30 or 1) until 6 p.m.

The same rules prevail as to Christmas Day and Good Friday and the days before as for Sunday and Saturday.

Any Police or Stipendiary Magistrate, or any two Justices, may order public-houses to be closed for any time if a riot is anticipated. (*See* RIOT, p. 161.)

12. In the Metropolitan Police District the Commissioner of Police (elsewhere, two Justices) may, for the accommodation of persons attending any public market, or following any lawful calling, or on special occasions (but not persons attending a theatre), grant to

any licensed victualler an order exempting him from the provisions as to closing on such days and during such time as may be specified.

13. Before an application is submitted for an exemption order, inquiry should be made as to the hours for which it is required; the nature of any proposed entertainment; the general mode in which the house is conducted; whether an order or licence has been granted on any former occasions, and, if so, whether there has been any complaint.

14. Whenever an order of exemption is granted, a notice thereof is to be affixed in a conspicuous position outside the premises.

OFFENCES.

15. Any person selling or exposing for sale by retail any intoxicating liquor, without being duly licensed to sell the same, or at any place where he is not authorised by his licence to sell the same, is liable for a first offence to a penalty of £50, or one month's imprisonment with hard labour; for a second, to a penalty of £100, or to three months' imprisonment, and to be disqualified from holding a licence for five years; for a third offence, to a penalty of £100, or six months' imprisonment with hard labour, and to be disqualified for any term, or for ever, from holding a licence. (Act 1872, s. 3.)

16. If a person not licensed to sell intoxicating liquors to be consumed on the premises permits such to be done by any purchaser, he is liable for a first offence to a penalty of £10; for a second, to £20. (Act 1872, s. 5.)

17. Any licensed person selling any description of *spirits*, for drinking on the premises, to a person apparently under sixteen years of age, is liable to a penalty of 20s. for a first offence, and of 40s. for a second or subsequent offence. (Act 1872, s. 7.)

18. Any person making or using any internal communication between any licensed premises and any unlicensed premises used for public entertainment or resort, is liable to a penalty of £10 for each day, and shall forfeit his licence. (Act 1872, s. 9.)

19. If any licensed person permits drunkenness or any violent, quarrelsome, or riotous conduct to take place on his premises, *or sells any intoxicating liquor*

to a drunken person, he is liable to a penalty of £10 for a first offence, of £20 for a second. (Act 1872, s. 13.)

20. Any person who, during the time at which premises for the sale of intoxicating liquors are directed to be closed, sells any intoxicating liquor, or opens or keeps open his premises for the purpose, or allows any intoxicating liquor, although purchased before the hours of closing, to be consumed on such premises, is liable to a penalty of £10 for the first offence, and of £20 for a second. Inmates and lodgers in the house may, however, be supplied at all times, as well as persons arriving at or departing from any station by railroad (Act 1872, s. 24), and no licensed victualler is liable to any penalty for supplying intoxicating liquors after the hours of closing to private friends *bonâ fide* entertained by him at his own expense. (Act 1874, s. 30.)

21. If any licensed person has in his possession on the premises in respect of which his licence is granted, any description of intoxicating liquor which he is not authorised to sell, unless he can account for the same to the satisfaction of the Court, he will be liable to a penalty of £10 for a first offence, and to £20 for a second. (Act 1872, s. 10.)

HARBOURING POLICE.

22. If any licensed victualler or publican, or his servant, harbours, or knowingly suffers to remain on his premises, any constable, during any part of the time appointed for such constable being on duty, unless for the purpose of keeping or restoring order or in the execution of his duty; or supplies any liquor or refreshment, whether by way of gift or sale, to any constable on duty, unless by authority of some superior officer of such constable; or bribes or attempts to bribe any constable, he is liable, for a first offence, to a fine of £10, for a second, to a fine of £20, and in either case to have the conviction recorded on his licence. (Act 1872, s. 16.)

HARBOURING PROSTITUTES.

23. If any licensed person knowingly permits his premises to be the habitual resort of or place of meeting of reputed prostitutes, whether the object of heir so resorting or meeting is or is not prostitution,

if he allows them to remain thereon longer than is necessary for the purpose of obtaining reasonable refreshment, he is liable for a first offence to a penalty of £10; for a second, to £20 (Act 1872, s. 14); and if he allows his premises to be a brothel, he shall incur the latter penalty, forfeit his licence, and be disqualified for ever from holding one. (Act 1872, s. 15.)

24. The question as to the time sufficient for obtaining reasonable refreshment has been the subject of much controversy, but convictions have followed in several cases in the metropolis where it has been shown that known prostitutes resorted to certain places night after night, that they remained longer than was necessary for the service of the refreshments ordered, that it was evidently but a colourable pretext for remaining, and that they went in alone and came out accompanied by men. If prostitutes promenade about the public room in which refreshments are served, or are guilty of any unseemly conduct, proof thereof will generally show an infringement of the statute.

HARBOURING THIEVES.

25. Every person who occupies or keeps any lodging-house, beer-house, public-house, or any place of public entertainment or resort, and knowingly lodges or harbours thieves or reputed thieves, or knowingly permits or suffers them to meet or assemble therein, or knowingly allows the deposit of goods therein, having reasonable cause for believing them to be stolen, is liable to a penalty of £10, or to four months' imprisonment, with or without hard labour, in default; and in addition may be required to enter into recognisances, with or without sureties, in £20 for twelve months, or in default be imprisoned for three months, besides forfeiting his licence. (34 & 35 Vict., c. 112, s. 10.) A publican who permitted thieves to assemble in his house at a meeting to collect money for the defence of a prisoner, although not in pursuance of any unlawful design, was held rightly convicted. (Marshall v. Fox, L. R., 6 Q.B., 370.)

GAMING.

26. Every licensed victualler who suffers any gaming or unlawful game to be carried on, including the playing

of cards, billiards, bagatelle, or skittles, *for money or beer*, even among his private friends in his private room (Passen *v.* Rhymer, 29 & 7 M.C. 189), is liable to proceedings under the Act for the Suppression of Betting Houses (16 & 17 Vict., c. 119), and to a further penalty for the first offence of £10, and for any subsequent offence of £20. (Act 1872, s. 17.)

27. If any person defaces or obliterates any record of a conviction on his licence, he is liable to a penalty of £5. (Act 1872, s. 34.)

28. Every licensed person must have painted and fixed on the premises in respect of which his licence is granted, in such form as the Licensing Justices may direct, his name, and, after "licensed," such words as may express the nature of the licence, subject to a penalty of £10 for a first offence, and £20 for any subsequent one. (Act 1872, s. 11.)

29. Most offences by licensed persons against the Licensing Acts must, unless the convicting Magistrates otherwise direct, be recorded on the licence of the person convicted. If any two convictions for offences against the Intoxicating Liquors Acts are recorded, and the licensed person is convicted a third time, his licence will be forfeited, and he shall be disqualified for five years, and the premises in respect of which his licence was granted will, unless otherwise ordered, be disqualified from receiving a licence for two years. (Act 1872, s. 30.)

DUTIES AND POWERS OF POLICE, &C.

30. Any constable may, for the purpose of preventing or detecting the violation of any of the provisions of the Licensing Acts, which it is his duty to enforce, at all times enter upon any licensed premises, and may examine every room and part of such premises. Refusal to admit him, demanding to enter in the execution of his duty, on the part of the licensed victualler or by any person acting by his direction or with his consent, entails a penalty of £5, or £10 for a second offence. (Act 1874, s. 16.) This right of entry must, however, be entirely subject to the regulations of the force to which the constable belongs.

31. A constable, on receipt from a Justice of a search

warrant granted on information on oath of intoxicating liquor being sold or kept for sale at any unauthorised place, may enter with force and search the place, and seize any intoxicating liquor therein, and supposed to be in such place for unlawful sale, and the vessels containing it. Any person at the time on the premises shall, until the contrary is proved, be deemed to have been there for the purpose of illegally dealing in intoxicating liquors, and failing to answer satisfactorily the questions put to him by the constable, or to give his correct name and address, may be apprehended without warrant, and is liable to a penalty of £5. (Act 1874, s. 17.)

32. Any constable may demand the name and address of a person found on licensed premises during the time they are required by law to be closed, and such person is liable to a penalty of 40s. The constable may require evidence of the correctness of such name and address; and if such person refuses to furnish his name and address, or such evidence, he may be apprehended without warrant, and is liable to a penalty of £5; and to a like sum if, by falsely representing himself to be a traveller or a lodger, he obtains or attempts to buy or obtain any intoxicating liquor during unauthorised hours. (Act 1872, s. 25.)

33. The police have the same powers with respect to premises for which an occasional licence has been granted, and the same obligations as to public order are incumbent upon the person obtaining an occasional as an annual licence.

34. Police should enter licensed premises when required so to do by any licensed person, his agent, or servant, and on demand expel or assist in expelling from the licensed premises any person "who is found" drunken, violent, quarrelsome, or disorderly, and any person whose presence on the premises would subject the licensed person to a penalty under the Licensing Act, 1872; and may use such force as may be required for the purpose. (Act 1872, s. 18.) Any person committing an assault in the presence of the constable, or who assaults the police in ejecting any person, should be taken into custody. The duty of the constable ceases on reaching the threshold or limits of the house; but circumstances may arise to make it desirable to proceed against the person so expelled for drunkenness, or for

some subsequent offence in the public thoroughfare against the Police Acts.

35. The evidence necessary for the police to adduce in support of a charge of selling at an unlawful hour will be proof that a sale, or transaction in the nature of a sale, actually took place; and proof of consumption or intended consumption of intoxicating liquor on premises to which a licence is attached, by some person other than the occupier of or a servant in such premises, is evidence that such liquor was sold by or on behalf of the holder of the licence to the person consuming or being about to consume it. (Act 1872, s. 62.) Notice should be given to the defendant (either in the summons or separately in writing) to produce his licence. If he fails to produce it, verbal proof of the name and description outside the house will doubtless be regarded by Magistrates as sufficient proof of the holding of the licence.

36. All notices and documents required by the Licensing Acts to be served or sent may, unless otherwise expressly provided, be served and sent by post, and until the contrary is proved, evidence that the letter containing the notice or document was prepaid and properly addressed is conclusive of service and receipt. (Act 1872, s. 70.)

37. In every licensing district a register of licenses is kept by the Clerk of the Licensing Justices, and any police officer may inspect it at any reasonable time without fee, or any ratepayer on payment of one shilling. The register should be carefully searched whenever a Licensed Victualler or Beer House Keeper is summoned by police for an offence against the Licensing Acts. If it is found that a conviction is recorded against the defendant, a copy thereof certified by the clerk should be obtained and produced at the first hearing, and if a conviction follows, where costs can be allowed, application should be made to include therein the fee paid for the copy of the conviction.

38. In all cases of appeal against a conviction by Magistrates under the Licensing Acts, the police should be represented by counsel, and in the Metropolitan Police District the Inspector concerned immediately submits the usual forms for legal aid.

39. In the Metropolitan Police District the following rules prevail as to licensed persons:—

(*a*) No communication is made in writing or verbally concerning their characters and antecedents except through the Commissioner.

(*b*) All cases in which sufficient causes of complaint exist to justify their being brought before the Justices are reported to the Commissioner at least fourteen days prior to the meeting of the Justices.

(*c*) In the event of irregularities occurring at public-houses, a report is to be made to the Commissioner, and the Superintendents may apply for permission to caution the landlords that a repetition of such irregularity *might* lead to the renewal of their licenses being opposed by police.

(*d*) The Commissioner considers all such cases previous to the Annual Licensing Meetings, so that (if thought desirable) notice and grounds of objection to the renewal of the licence may be given to the holder, pursuant to the provisions of the Licensing Acts.

(*e*) The Superintendents who have transmitted any such report as above mentioned, on or immediately before the 8th February, where the licensed premises are situate in Middlesex or Surrey, and on or immediately before the 1st August when the premises are situate elsewhere, furnish the Commissioner with the date of every such report, and make any additional observations on the case as are expedient, especially on the subsequent general conduct of the licensed victualler.

(*f*) The police are cautioned to be watchful for the commission of offences or irregularities on licensed premises, and to report the same. They should, moreover, be on their guard never to be drawn into accepting drink, or any gift whatever from a licensed victualler, for the first yielding to such temptation sacrifices for ever their independence as officers of the law. It is the practice of some unprincipled publicans to leave a pot of beer in some place on a constable's beat. Such a man should be the object of especial watchfulness, for his aim must be to infringe the law, to bribe the constable to close his eyes, and to render him unfit to discharge his duty.

Public Prosecutor. — By the Prosecution of Offences Act 1879 the office of Director of Public Prosecutions was established. If a failure of justice is

likely to occur in an important case in England and Wales, either from want of funds, or the unwillingness of persons to prosecute, or from an attempt to compound the offence and withdraw from the public duty of punishing it, the whole facts should be submitted to
  The Director of Public Prosecutions,
      Treasury Chambers,
         Whitehall,
           London.

Pursuit of Offenders.—1. Rapidity of action is the great essential in the pursuit of offenders. It is absolutely necessary to use every effort to get in advance of the person whose arrest is sought. To this end it has to be considered, in what direction the delinquent has escaped, or is likely to fly, and by what means, he will seek to conceal the course taken. Every probable or possible route should be blocked as far as possible, and artifice may well be resorted to in the pursuit. (*See* BURGLARY, par. 7.)

2. If a photograph and the handwriting of the culprit can be obtained, it may be engraved and reproduced, and distributed in such thousands, with the offer of a suitable reward, as will ensure active attention.

3. Telegrams, but better still letters, accompanied by photographs, and full particulars as to companions, luggage, &c., should be despatched to all likely places of flight and passage.

Queen's Evidence.—An accomplice in a crime may be accepted as a witness against his companions in guilt, but his evidence must be corroborated.

Questioning.—1. A person can only be questioned respecting the commission of a crime, so long as there is no intention to arrest him. (*See* p. 65.)

2. From the moment, it has been determined to arrest, no question must be asked respecting the offence without a strict caution. (*See* p. 38.)

3. Police officers must be careful not to give offence in the questions they are obliged to put in making inquiries. The exercise of a little tact will prevent this; and if it is explained to them, most persons will understand that success is rendered almost impossible by any

reticence of information. A clue may often be found in what passes for a fact of no importance.

Raffles.—(*See* LOTTERIES, p. 110.)

Railways.—1. Every person commits felony—

(*a*) Who does any injury to a railway, or any bridge or viaduct passing over or under it, with intent and so as thereby to render it dangerous or impassable.

(*b*) Who does, or causes anything to be done, with intent to obstruct, upset, overthrow, injure, or destroy any engine, tender, or truck used on any railway, or who—

(1) Puts, places, casts, or throws anything whatever across any railway.

(2) Takes up, removes, or displaces any rail, sleeper, or other thing belonging to any railway.

(3) Turns, moves, or diverts any points or other machinery belonging to a railway.

(4) Makes, shows, hides, or removes any signal or light upon or near to any railway. (24 & 25 Vict., c. 97.)

2. A person likewise commits felony who throws anything at a carriage used upon any railway, with intent to injure or endanger the safety of any person therein or thereon, or in or upon any other engine or carriage forming part of the same train. (24 & 25 Vict., c. 100, s. 33.)

3. Police travelling by railway on duty are conveyed at special rates, on production of their authority.

Rape.—1. Rape is the act of having carnal knowledge of a woman, without her conscious permission, or by permission extorted by force or fear of immediate bodily harm.

2. Every one is guilty of felony who commits rape. (24 & 25 Vict., c. 100, s. 63.)

3. A woman who alleges a rape to have been committed upon her can only be examined by a surgeon with her consent.

Receipts.—The forgery of any receipt for money or for goods is a felony. (24 & 25 Vict., c. 98, s. 23.)

Receiving Stolen Goods.—1. A person is said to receive stolen goods as soon as he obtains control over them from the person who delivers them.

2. If goods are received by a wife or servant, in the absence of the husband or master, the latter does not

become a receiver, unless he does any act approving of the receipt of the goods which he knows to have been unlawfully obtained.

3. Knowingly receiving any property whatsoever, the stealing, taking, or otherwise obtaining whereof is a felony, is itself felony. (24 & 25 Vict., c. 96.) (*See* p. 156.)

4. Knowingly receiving any property so obtained, converted, or disposed of, as to amount to a misdemeanor, is itself a misdemeanor.

Recognisances.—1. A recognisance is an obligation acknowledged in due form (*see* BAIL, p. 27) to do a certain thing therein named.

2. If the condition of a recognisance entered into either by a party, or his bail, is broken, the recognisance is forfeited, and on its being estreated the parties become debtors to the Crown for the sums in which they are respectively bound.

Reformatories.—Every person who knowingly assists, directly or indirectly, an offender to escape from a reformatory school, or induces him to escape, or knowingly harbours, conceals, or prevents any offender who has escaped from returning to school, or assists him in so doing, is liable to a fine, or to imprisonment with hard labour. (29 & 30 Vict., c. 117.)

*****Refreshment Houses.**—1. No person can open a house for public refreshment, resort, and entertainment, between ten in the evening and five in the morning, without an Excise licence.

2. Refreshment houses must close at the same hour as public-houses. (*See* p. 147.)

3. Every person licensed to keep a refreshment house, knowingly suffering any unlawful games or gaming therein, or allowing prostitutes, thieves, or drunken and disorderly persons to assemble or continue in or upon his premises, is liable to a penalty. (23 Vict., c. 27, s. 6; 24 & 25 Vict., c. 91, s. 8.)

Registers.—Every person commits felony who in any way whatsoever tampers with any register of births, baptisms, marriages, deaths, or burials authorised or required by law for the time being to be kept.

Registration of Births and Deaths.—1. It is the duty of the father and mother of a child born alive, and, in default of them, of the occupier of the house, of each person present at the birth, and of the person having charge of the child, to register its birth within forty-two days.

2. A person finding a living new-born child exposed is bound to give all possible information to the Registrar within seven days.

3. It is similarly the duty of the relatives of a person dying in any house, the persons present at the death, the occupier of the house, or of the person causing the deceased to be buried, to register the death within five days, and likewise of the person finding a body elsewhere than in a house, and therefore of Police finding a dead body. (37 & 38 Vict., c. 88.)

Regulating Traffic.—1. Police employed in the regulation of traffic should be careful not unnecessarily to check a line, and to take only the most favourable opportunities for doing so.

2. The coolest judgment must be preserved, that none of the convergent streets may become unduly blocked.

3. The police should not take hold of the bridles of horses, either to stop or back them; such conduct being likely to cause accidents, and provoke an assault on the police. The names and addresses of coachmen and drivers who fail to comply with the directions received should be taken, with a view to their being summoned for obstruction. (*See* CARRIAGES, p. 36; PUBLIC OCCASIONS, p. 144.)

4. Care must always be taken to keep the crossings as clear as possible, and to render all needful assistance to passengers.

Regulations.—In the same way that every man is bound to know the law, or, as the maxim runs, "Ignorantia juris non excusat" (Ignorance of the law does not excuse), every police officer of whatever grade is bound to know all the regulations of the service to which he belongs, and if he infringes or deviates from them without reasonable cause, must take the consequences.

Remands.—1. A prisoner charged with an indictable offence may be remanded from time to time by Courts of Summary Jurisdiction, not exceeding eight days at a time, by a Police or Stipendiary Magistrate, or by any one Justice, to the next practicable sitting of a Petty Sessional Court.

2. Whenever it is intended to institute inquiry in London, with respect to the antecedents of prisoners, within constabulary districts, such a remand should be invariably applied for as will leave at least five clear days for the inquiry in the Metropolitan Police District; that being the very shortest period in which it can be *properly* done in so vast an area, amid an invariable pressure of business from internal requirements, and requests from all parts of the kingdom and the Continent. (*See* CORRESPONDENCE, p. 53.)

Reports.—Every report should be legibly written on one side of the paper only, and arranged in numbered paragraphs if the subject is in any way involved. Full particulars should be given, without, however, going into excessive detail. Slang terms must not be used. Statements should be shown by "inverted commas," the pages be numbered, and the report must be signed by the officer by whom it is made, attaching the rank he holds to his signature, and be submitted through the proper channel.

Requests to Apprehend.—1. The arrest of persons wanted by other police forces, on charges of felony, may be effected, *if there is no doubt as to their identity*, without warrant, the prisoner being detained until an officer from the other jurisdiction, summoned by telegraph, arrives to conduct him thereto—such officer being invariably despatched by the first train, and the hour of his arrival being telegraphed.

2. In requesting search for a person whose apprehension is sought, the fullest information must be given, and nothing omitted which may serve to identify the delinquent. *If a warrant has been issued, the fact must be stated; and if the accused is likely to be found, it should be transmitted, accompanied by a declaration as to the signature of the issuing Justice, under the Summary Jurisdiction Act,* 1879, *s.* 41, *rule* 45.

Rescue from Custody.—Every one commits high treason, felony, or misdemeanor, who rescues a prisoner in lawful custody on such a charge.

Resignation.—1. No police officer can withdraw

himself from his duties without giving proper notice in writing, or under special circumstances.

2. When an officer leaves the service either on resignation or dismissal, all articles of appointment must be delivered up to the Superintendent in proper repair, any pay due being retained to make good the deficiency. (*See* ABSCONDING FROM DUTY, p. 17.)

Resisting Police.—1. Every one is guilty of a misdemeanor who assaults, resists, or wilfully obstructs any peace officer in the due execution of his duty, or any person acting in aid of such officer.

2. A person who obstructs, or in any way interferes with, or knowingly prevents the execution of any process, by giving information or otherwise, is guilty of a misdemeanor. (*See* p. 122.)

Reward Bills.—1. No bill offering a reward should be distributed by police, or by their authority, unless it distinctly states—

(*a*) The amount of the reward.

(*b*) The precise conditions on which it will be paid.

(*c*) The name and address of the person responsible for the payment.

2. No reward can be offered in a criminal case for the recovery of stolen property, unattended by the apprehension and conviction of the guilty party, but a reward may be offered for private information leading to the conviction.

*3. Rewards are only very exceptionally offered by Her Majesty's Government, in cases of especial gravity, involving murder, attempted murder, or a wholesale destruction of property by incendiarism, *and when the identity of the criminal is clear.* The offer may be accompanied by an assurance of a recommendation for the Queen's most gracious pardon of any accomplice, not being the actual perpetrator of the crime, and such pardon may be also offered without a reward if the Home Secretary is applied to.

4. Police should never offer a reward, or have reward bills drawn up, without the written authority of the person who undertakes to be responsible for the payment of the amount. (Form of a reward bill is given in the Appendix.)

*Rewards for Exertions in Assisting Justice.
—Courts of Assize or the Central Criminal Court may order compensation from public funds to those who have been active in the apprehension of persons guilty of murder, or attempted murder, procuring abortion, rape, burglary, housebreaking, arson, robbery, cattle stealing, or felonious receiving, or who have shown extraordinary courage, diligence, or exertion therein.

Rewards to Police.—1. When police distinguish themselves *by special zeal, ability, or courage*, they may be commended or granted a pecuniary reward.

*2. The Court of General or Quarter Sessions for any county, and the Watch Committee, subject to the approbation of the Council for any borough, may, upon the recommendation of the Chief Constable of any county police force, or of the Superintendent of the Police for the borough, grant to any constable in the county or borough out of the police rate or borough fund, a gratuity in money not exceeding £3, in respect of and as a reward for any meritorious act done by the constable in the execution of his duty.

Riot.—1. A riot is an unlawful assembly (consisting of three or more persons), which has actually begun to execute the purpose for which it assembled, by a breach of the peace, and to the terror of the public.

2. Every person convicted of riot is guilty of a misdemeanor.

Riot Act.—1. Whenever twelve persons or more are unlawfully, riotously, and tumultously assembled together, to the disturbance of the public peace, it is the duty of the Justices of the Peace or of the Mayor, Bailiffs, or other head officers, of a city or town corporate, to make, or cause to be made, a proclamation in these words, or like in effect:—

"*Our Sovereign Lady the Queen chargeth and commandeth all persons being assembled immediately to disperse themselves, and peaceably to depart to their habitations, or to their lawful business, upon the pains contained in the Act made in the first year of King George for preventing tumultuous and riotous assemblies. God save the Queen.*"

2. All persons commit felony who—

(*a*) Wilfully and knowingly oppose, obstruct, let, hinder, or hurt any person who begins to make or goes to make the said proclamation, whereby such proclamation is not made; or

(*b*) Who remain or continue together unlawfully, riotously, and tumultuously, for one hour after the proclamation aforesaid was made ; or, if they know that its making was hindered, for one hour after it would have been made if it had not been hindered.

Riotous Demolition of Houses, &c.—All persons are guilty of felony who, being riotously and tumultuously assembled together, to the disturbance of the public peace, unlawfully and with force demolish, or pull down, or destroy, any building, machinery, or mining plant, or begin to do so. (24 & 25 Vict., c. 97, s. 11.)

Robbery.—Robbery is the offence of stealing from the body, or in the immediate presence of the person from whom the thing is taken, by actual violence intentionally used to overcome or prevent his resistance, or by threats of injury to his person, property, or reputation.

***Rogues and Vagabonds.**—1. Any person may be treated as a rogue and vagabond who commits any of the following offences, viz.:—

(*a*) Pretends or professes to tell fortunes, or uses any subtle craft, means, or device, by palmistry or otherwise, to deceive and impose on any of Her Majesty's subjects ;

(*b*) Wanders abroad, and lodges in any barn or outhouse, or in any deserted unoccupied building, or in the open air, or under a tent, or in any cart or waggon, not having any visible means of subsistence, and not giving a good account of himself;

(*c*) Wilfully exposes to view in any street, road, highway, or public place, or in the window, or other part of any shop, or other building situate therein, any obscene print, picture, or other indecent exhibition ;

(*d*) Wilfully, openly, lewdly, and obscenely exposes his person in any street, road, or public highway, or in the view thereof, or in any place of public resort, with intent to insult any female ;

(*e*) Wanders abroad and endeavours, by the exposure of wounds or deformities, to obtain or gather alms;

(*f*) Goes about as a gatherer or collector of alms, or endeavours to procure charitable contributions of any nature or kind under any false or fraudulent pretence;

(*g*) Runs away and leaves his wife, and his or her child or children chargeable, or whereby she or they or any of them, become chargeable to any parish, township, or place;

(*h*) Has in his custody or possession any picklock, key, crow, jack, bit, or other implement, with intent feloniously to break into any dwelling-house, warehouse, coach-house, stable, or outbuilding;

(*i*) Is armed with any gun, pistol, hanger, cutlass, bludgeon, or other offensive weapon, or has upon him any instrument with intent to commit any felonious act;

(*j*) Is found in or upon any dwelling-house, warehouse, coach-house, stable, or outhouse, or in any enclosed yard, garden, or area, for any unlawful purpose;

(*k*) Is a suspected person or reputed thief frequenting any river, canal, or navigable stream, dock or basin, or any quay, wharf or warehouse, or any avenue leading thereto, or any street, or any highway, or any place adjacent to a street or highway, with intent to commit felony. (5 Geo. IV., c. 83, s. 4; VAGRANT ACT.) (*See* SUSPECTED PERSONS, p. 175.)

Sacrilege.—Every one commits felony who breaks and enters any church, chapel, meeting-house, or other place of divine worship, and commits any felony therein, or who having committed any felony therein, breaks out. (24 & 25 Vict., c. 96, s. 50.)

Saluting.—1. Police officers of all ranks should salute all members of the Royal Family, the Home Secretary, and their own principal officers, whenever they address or pass them whether in uniform or plain clothes.

2. All Inspectors, Sergeants, and constables salute a Superintendent on passing, either in uniform or plain clothes.

3. Sergeants and constables salute an Inspector in uniform.

4. The salute should be invariably acknowledged.

5. Police in plain clothes should not salute in *military*

fashion, which is only to be done when the helmet or forage cap is on the head, but take off their hats as in civil life.

6. Police engaged in actual detective duty must on no account recognise a superior or other police officer, if there is the smallest possibility of their being thereby themselves identified. (*See* ATTENTION, p. 26.)

7. Police marching in a body do not salute, but the word "Eyes right" or "left" is given by the Inspector or Sergeant in charge, on passing a member of the Royal Family or a superior officer.

*8. Police on duty on any special occasion, when Her Majesty the Queen, or any member of the Royal Family is present, do not salute when the Royal Personage passes, but stand at attention and keep a sharp look-out that advantage is not taken of the opportunity to pick pockets, break the ranks, or approach the Royal Carriage.

Sanitary Hints. (*Promulgated by the Vestry of St. George's, Hanover Square.*)—1. Keep cisterns and waterbutts clean and covered.

2. Cleanse drains, sinks, closets, and urinals, charge traps with water, and see that the closets are kept in working order, to avoid enteric (typhoid) fever, diarrhœa, and other diseases. See that the waste pipes of sinks, and especially the waste pipe of the drinking-water cistern, do not go directly into the soil pipe or drain; they should end in the open air over a trapped gully.

3. Empty dust-bins weekly, and keep them covered; do not throw vegetable matter into them—it is better to burn it.

4. Attend to ventilation and avoid overcrowding. At least 300 cubic feet of space are required for each person, and the air in this space must be frequently changed; a slit through the wall, just over the lintel of the door, will admit plenty of fresh air into a room without draught.

5. Be temperate in eating and drinking.

6. Place a patient sick of an infectious disease into a room apart from others, removing carpets, curtains, and unnecessary furniture, or send the person to a special hospital. No child of a family in which there is a case of infectious disease should be sent to school.

7. Vaccinate healthy children at the earliest possible

age, and advise re-vaccination above the age of fifteen years.

Searching a Prisoner.—1. A prisoner apprehended for homicide or any offence involving fraud or dishonesty, should be searched as soon as practicable after he or she is charged; and all weapons, valuable property, documents, books, or memoranda taken from him or her, carefully labelled, to be used as evidence if occasion requires, great care being taken both on the way to the station and at the station, that by no artifice, he or she succeeds in destroying, tearing, swallowing, or hiding anything whatsoever bearing on his or her offence. Money not connected with the offence charged should not be taken from a prisoner.

2. The prisoner's house, lodgings, and effects should also be searched with the same object, and by two officers if possible.

3. Any knives, or any articles whereby self-injury might be inflicted, should be invariably taken from persons in custody for drunkenness.

4. The clothes and boots of a prisoner apprehended for murder should be at once replaced by others, that they may be examined for traces of blood. The clothes should be immediately wrapped up in clean paper and sealed, and be delivered to the Surgeon by the constable who removed them from the prisoner and who sealed the packets.

5. *Women must be employed to search female prisoners.*

Search Warrants.—Search warrants can only be obtained under the provisions of a particular statute, or upon the oath of a credible witness that there is reasonable cause for suspecting that property stolen or unlawfully obtained is concealed in some place within the jurisdiction of the Magistrate to whom the application is made.

Secrecy.—The first duty of a police officer is to maintain absolutely secret (except from his superiors) all information he becomes possessed of, in his official capacity. Gossiping, even without any such intention, may wholly defeat the ends of justice, and be the cause of the greatest mischief. (*See* pp. 90 and 123.)

Seduction. — Unlawful intercourse, procured by threats, false pretences, or the administration of drugs, is criminal. There is also a remedy by civil action for damages for the loss sustained by the father in the service of his daughter. (*See* DEFILEMENT, p. 60.)

Sergeants.—1. A Sergeant should report every case of misconduct on the part of constables to the Superintendent or Inspector at the earliest opportunity.

2. He should not become familiar with constables, but instruct them in the duties they have to perform, and so conduct himself as to secure the respect of those over whom he is placed, having no dealings or money transactions of any kind with them.

Servants.—1. Police should notice and report to their Inspector irregularities of servants in improperly admitting persons to or letting them out of their masters' houses at unreasonable hours, especially when families are out of town, and the houses are left in charge of the servants.

2. Police on duty must not gossip with servants, or loiter near houses with that object, or accept refreshment, or any other gifts whatever from servants.

3. Police in towns should notice persons going about at an early hour in the morning collecting bottles, &c., from servants. The bottles so sold are frequently the property of the master, and an opportunity is thus afforded for committing felony and enabling servants to dispose of other property of their masters. Constables must act as circumstances appear to require, either in apprehending, or cautioning the persons in question.

4. When inquiring into burglaries and other offences, police must be careful not to accept in the absence of sufficient grounds the theories which are frequently thrust upon them of complicity of some of the servants with the thieves.

5. If there is any cause whatsoever to suspect that a larceny has been effected by any person in a house, and even in cases where there is no evidence to point to the thief, and if it is desirable to establish whether any one in the house was concerned, the best course will be for the entire household to be summoned to be questioned separately as to their movements, and then, before any one is allowed to go into any other part of the house, for the master to state that, in order to free the servants,

and all others in the house from suspicion, he suggests that they should *all* allow their things to be searched without delay.

6. Consent being obtained, every floor should be occupied by a police officer, or some independent person, to prevent any one entering a room before it is searched. In company with the owner of the stolen property and the person whose things are being examined, the most minute search should be made. Such a proceeding will rarely be resented by the servants if, as in fairness to them, every member of the family and every guest submits to the same ordeal. It is of great value, as then it will be established, or otherwise, that the missing articles have not been mislaid, as is so often the case with petty domestic larcenies, and also that the thief must be looked for outside the house.

7. It must be remembered that stolen articles, and especially jewellery or money, may be secreted between mattresses, in writing-cases, work-boxes, and baskets, between the leaves of books, the folds of clothes and linen, underneath table-covers, in boots and shoes, and also in water-closets.

8. Police cannot search a servant's boxes without his or her consent, which should be usually obtained by the master or mistress.

9. A police officer, in making inquiry into the antecedents of servants, must take care that it is done in such a manner as neither to injure their present position nor their future prospects. Above all, accusations must not be made without ample grounds, or expression given to individual suspicion.

***Sessions, Assizes, or Central Criminal Court Sittings.**—1. On arrival at the Court, the Inspector or Sergeant, if there be one concerned in the case, and if not, the constable who has charge of the case, must find the prosecutor and witnesses, and keep them together to go to the Clerk of Indictments; and after the bill of indictment is prepared, all the witnesses should be kept in readiness to go before the grand jury. Should the prosecutor or a witness be absent before the bill is found, the Inspector, Sergeant, or constable in charge of the case, must inform the Clerk of Arraigns or Clerk of the Peace accordingly, that the bill may not be ignored by the grand jury from the absence of the prosecutor or witness.

2. After a true bill has been found, the police in charge of the case must keep the prosecutor and witnesses together to appear in the Court at any moment the case may be called on, and the police must not leave without permission from the proper officer of the Court, and the other witnesses should, as far as possible, be prevented from doing so.

3. The list of cases for trial posted in the Court must be frequently referred to for information, but the police and other witnesses should bear in mind that cases are sometimes called on out of their order on the list for trial.

4. Should any witness be absent when the case is called on for trial, the police must inform the Judge or Chairman of such absence; and all witnesses should be reminded that the Court will refuse his expenses to any person improperly absent.

5. The whole of the property and duplicates of property in pawn taken from the person or lodgings of a prisoner, or found anywhere, if believed to have been in the possession of the prisoner or to relate to any charge against him, should be taken to the Court, and in readiness to be produced before the Court as soon as the case comes on; and if in parcels, to prevent delay they should be opened. If property is of such bulk or weight that it cannot be brought, explanation must be given to the Court.

6. The inspector on duty at the station should in every instance keep an account of all articles taken from a prisoner or seized, and secure and mark the property in the presence of the officer engaged in the case, so that the latter may be enabled to swear that each article is the same as that first seized by him.

7. The police must not drink with, or provide or pay for, or in any way interfere with providing refreshment for witnesses, unless in any special case by express authority.

8. No police officer should recommend a prosecutor to employ legal aid in any case, or interfere in any way with procuring legal aid, either for a prosecutor or a prisoner.

9. All property in the hands of the police which

belonged to a person convicted, must be delivered up immediately to the Superintendent of the division.

10. If any question is raised, during or after a trial, as to whom any property in the hands of the police should be given up, application should be made by the police concerned, to the Judge to make an order, respecting the disposal of such property. If such order is not made, a full report of the circumstances, with the name of any person claiming the property, should be made.

11. In all cases of property, given up to any person by direction of the Judge, a receipt enumerating each article should be taken by the police.

12. At the conclusion of a trial the police who were engaged in the case, should go immediately to the office of the Clerk of Arraigns or County Treasurer to sign the necessary list of witnesses having claims for expenses.

13. The police should not incur any expenses in conveying witnesses to any trial without authority.

14. The whole of the police attending Sessions as prosecutors, witnesses, or on any other duty, should appear in proper uniform, except those allowed to wear plain clothes.

Sheep Stealing.—Every one who steals any ram, ewe, sheep, or lamb, or wilfully kills any such animal, with intent to steal the carcase, skin, or any part thereof, is guilty of felony. (24 & 25 Vict., c. 96, s. 10.)

Ships.—1. Any person unlawfully and maliciously setting fire to, casting away, or in any wise destroying a ship or vessel, is guilty of felony.

2. Any person unlawfully and maliciously damaging any ship, or vessel, with intent to destroy the same, or render her useless, is guilty of felony, whether the vessel is in a complete or unfinished state. (24 & 25 Vict., c. 97, s. 44.)

Shooting.—Every one is guilty of felony who, with intent to maim, disfigure, or disable any person, or to do some other grievous bodily harm, or to prevent any lawful apprehension or detention, shoots at any person, or by actually drawing a trigger, or in any other manner, attempts to discharge at any person any kind of loaded arms. (24 & 25 Vict., c. 100, s. 18.)

Shutters.—Shutters insecurely fastened must be noticed by the police on night duty and duly marked.

Simple Larceny.—Simple larceny is theft without any circumstances of aggravation.

Slander.—Slander is not an offence within the operation of the criminal law, unless the words are calculated, both in themselves and in their use, to provoke an immediate breach of the peace. (*See* ABUSIVE LANGUAGE, p. 18.)

Slang Terms.—Slang terms must never be used by police in any official matter, whether in reports or letters, in addressing a superior, or any person, including a prisoner, and above all they must not be used in giving evidence.

__Slides in the Streets.__—Every person who makes or uses any slide upon ice or snow in any street or other thoroughfare, to the common danger, is liable to a penalty, and may be summoned; or if not known, and the offence is committed within sight of a constable, apprehended. (POLICE ACTS.)

Smuggling.—1. Every person concerned in importing or unshipping goods liable to duty for which duty has not been paid or secured; knowingly harbouring or possessing the same; or concerned in any fraudulent evasion, or attempt at evasion, of the duties, laws, or restrictions upon the import of goods, is liable to a penalty, and treble value of the goods. (39 & 40 Vict., c. 36, s. 186.)

2. Offenders may be arrested without warrant, immediate information being conveyed to the Secretary to the Board of Customs.

3. Every one is guilty of a misdemeanor who assaults, resists, or obstructs any person duly employed for the prevention of smuggling in the execution of his duty, or in seizing any goods liable to forfeiture under the Customs Acts, or aids, abets, or assists therein.

Sodomy.—1. Every one who carnally knows any man or animal commits sodomy, and is guilty of felony. (24 & 25 Vict., c. 100, s. 61.)

2. Every male person is guilty of a misdemeanor, who commits any assault with intent to commit sodomy, or any indecent assault with any male person, in public or

private, or procures or attempts to procure the commission thereof. (CRIMINAL LAW AMENDMENT ACT, 1885.) The police cannot compel persons to submit themselves for medical examination.

Soldiers.—1. Police should constantly endeavour to maintain the most friendly feeling with soldiers of the army, militia, and volunteers, and with sailors of the Royal and Colonial Navy, quartered or stationed in any particular place.

2. The police must not enter into conversation with soldiers while on sentry, unless their duty makes it necessary to do so.

3. If a sentry on his post charges a person with committing an offence, such person should be taken to the police station, and detained there until the soldier can attend to sign the Charge Sheet. Notice should be sent to the guard-room, as soon as possible, that the person is at the station, and that the sentry is to come there.

Special Constables.—Every special constable has, throughout the entire jurisdiction of the Justices appointing him, all such powers, authorities, advantages, and immunities, and is liable to all such duties and responsibilities, as any constable duly appointed. (1 & 2 Wm. IV., c. 41.)

Special Duties.—1. The smartest, best-conducted, and most reliable men are invariably selected for special duties.

2. Police employed on detached special duty, are still under the orders of their own officers, and subservient to all the regulations of the service, and they should not perform acts inconsistent with police functions.

Stations.—1. Strict order, discipline, and cleanliness should be observed at police stations.

2. Irregularities, noises, or disturbances by prisoners or others within or in the neighbourhood of stations, must be checked as much as possible, so as to prevent annoyance to the inhabitants.

3. Persons coming in a proper manner to the door of a police station should be admitted by the constable, without inquiry as to the nature of their business, if they state that they wish to see the Inspector or Sergeant on duty.

4. Persons not connected with the police service,

should not be permitted to remain at a police station longer than is absolutely necessary for completion of the business they come upon.

5. Any person guilty of any violent or indecent behaviour in any police office or station house, is liable to a penalty.

*Stolen Property.†—1. The facilities at present afforded by English law for the tracing and recovery of stolen property are very inadequate, and the large class of offences in which the evidence of identity hinges entirely upon the possession of or dealing with the stolen goods necessarily remain to a great extent unpunished, despite the utmost exertions of the police.

2. But, nevertheless, nothing must be omitted to convey full descriptions to pawnbrokers and all persons to whom the articles are likely to be offered for sale. Especial prominence should be given to all articles having marks of identity, or which are not susceptible of being melted down or having their identity destroyed.

3. In all cases where property of importance, either from its intrinsic value or as a means of tracing criminals, is stolen or lost, a sketch of the same should be obtained, if possible, for informations and reward bills, and forwarded to the engraver with the full written description. (*See* REWARD BILLS, p. 160.)

Stone Throwing.—1. Every person who wantonly throws or discharges (from a catapult or otherwise) any stone or other missile to the damage or danger of any person is liable to a penalty, and may be apprehended without warrant, if the act is committed within sight of a constable. (POLICE ACTS.)

2. Police on duty on bridges under which steamers pass, must be particularly on the alert against attempts to drop stones into the funnels—a practice attended with the greatest danger, and demanding the strict enforcement of the law. (*See* RAILWAYS, p. 156.)

Street Music.—Any householder within the Metropolitan Police District, personally, or by his servant, or by any police constable, may require any street musician

† A measure promoted by the author was for some years before Parliament on this subject, but the opposition of the Pawnbrokers' Associations was too strong for it to pass the House of Commons, as it had twice done the Upper House.

or street singer, to depart from the neighbourhood of the house of such householder, on account of the illness, or on account of the interruption of the ordinary occupations or pursuits, of any inmate of such house, or for other reasonable or sufficient cause; and every person, who sounds or plays upon any musical instrument, or sings in any thoroughfare or public place near any such house, after being so required to depart, is liable to a penalty not exceeding 40s., or imprisonment not exceeding three days. Offenders may be arrested by a constable, if charged by a private individual, who will go to the station and enter into a recognisance to prosecute. (27 & 28 Vict., c. 55, s. 1.)

Stretchers.—1. A stretcher is simply a light portable bed for carrying the sick; it is composed of a framework of poles, with a piece of canvas stretched between them as a mattress.

A variety of things will answer as substitutes for a stretcher—such as doors, window shutters, ladders, or hurdles.

2. To place a man on a stretcher with three bearers—

(*a*) The three men should fall in facing the feet of the injured man, and be numbered off from the right.

(*b*) Put the foot of the stretcher at the man's head, in a line continuous with his body.

(*c*) Nos. 1 and 2, one at either side, locking hands underneath the shoulders and hips, raise the patient, carry him forward over the stretcher, and then lower him on to it.

(*d*) No. 3 takes charge of the injured portion (*limb* or *head*), and steadies it with a hand on either side of the wound.

(*e*) Nos. 1 and 2 then take their places at the head and foot of stretcher, lift and carry off, while No. 3 walks at the side of the stretcher as a safeguard to the patient, and as a relief to No. 1 or 2 if necessary.

3. Rules for carrying a stretcher—

(*a*) Carry the stretcher in the hands, or suspend it by straps over the bearers' shoulders.

(*b*) Never allow the stretcher to be placed on the shoulders.

(*c*) Bearers to march in broken step, and not in time.

(*d*) Avoid all jolting, crossing fences, ditches, &c.

(e) The pace to be about twenty inches.

(f) In ascending, the patient's head to be in front, and in descending, behind.

Subpœnas.—1. A subpœna is a writ commanding attendance in Court, on a certain day therein named, under a penalty. In criminal cases, the subpœnas are usually either to give evidence, or to produce documents.

2. Subpœnas are either issued by the Crown Office, or the Clerk of the Peace, of a county or sessional jurisdiction. The former have force throughout the United Kingdom, the latter within the jurisdiction of issue only.

Suicide.—1. A person who kills himself in a manner which in the case of another person would amount to murder, is guilty of murder, and every person who aids and abets any person in so killing himself is an accessory before the fact, or a principal in the second degree, in such murder.

2. Persons who attempt to commit suicide, should be apprehended and charged with the misdemeanor, if that course is authorised. If at the time of apprehension, any injury has been inflicted, medical aid should be obtained, or the person be conveyed to a hospital, according to the circumstances of the case.

3. If persons cannot be removed and charged, on medical grounds, they should be kept under the observation of police, as may be necessary to prevent their escape, and they should be charged when sufficiently recovered. (*See* TREATMENT OF PERSONS RESCUED FROM DROWNING, HANGING, AND SUFFOCATION, p. 181.)

Note.—In cases where the throat has been cut, the head should be supported, and the patient kept perfectly still, until the arrival of medical aid, the bleeding being stopped by all possible means.

*****Summary Jurisdiction.**—1. A Court of Summary Jurisdiction consists of the Lord Mayor, or any Alderman of the City of London, or any Metropolitan Police Magistrate or any Stipendiary Magistrate sitting alone, or otherwise of two Justices. Every case must be heard, tried, determined, and adjudged in open Court.

2. The judicial power of Magistrates in England and Wales is now mainly regulated by the Summary Jurisdiction Act 1879 (42 & 43 Vict., c. 49), extending Jervis's Act (11 & 12 Vict., c. 42).

Summonses.—1. A summons is a magisterial order to appear in Court, with reference to a matter named therein, at a given time.

2. Upon any information or complaint, not necessarily upon oath, to a Magistrate having jurisdiction within the place, wherein any person is suspected to have committed any indictable offence or act contrary to law, and whereof a Court of Summary Jurisdiction can take cognisance, such Magistrate may, if he thinks fit, issue a summons against such person.

3. A summons must be served upon the person to whom it is directed by delivering the same to the party personally, or if he cannot be found, then by leaving the same with some person for him at his last or most usual place of abode, the constable serving it attending before the Court of Summary Jurisdiction to depose, if necessary, to such service.

4. If the person so served does not appear in obedience to the summons, a warrant may be issued for bringing him before the Court of Summary Jurisdiction to answer the charge in the information or complaint, and to be further dealt with according to law.

5. Whenever the facts of any alleged offence are open to any doubt, or the offence is not of a grave character involving imprisonment, or against a person not likely to abscond, who would be materially injured in his reputation or occupation by a process of arrest, a summons should be applied for, in preference to a warrant.

***Superannuation Fund.**—The question of police superannuation is still undecided. (*See* PENSIONS, p. 127.)

Suspected Persons.—1. The law gives very great powers to police in dealing with suspected persons; but it must always be remembered that an arrest for some actual offence is far more satisfactory than a charge on mere suspicion. Apprehension, therefore, of prisoners as suspected persons cannot be encouraged, and if of frequent occurrence suggests the inference that the officer effecting them possesses little skill in keeping discreet observation. At the same time, it may often happen that an evil-disposed person becomes aware of his being watched, and endeavours to escape. Such circumstances may then justify arrest as a suspected person, for there is the corroboration of a series of suspicious acts; but an officer must remember that if the apprehension is not justified by the circumstances, a civil action may be brought against him.

2. Every person stopped as possibly conveying stolen property should be treated with the utmost civility, whatever his antecedents, and it should, if necessary, be explained that the exercise of this legal right by the police affords the surest protection for all honest citizens, and especially during the last hour of night duty, and the first hour of the day duty—5 to 7 a.m.

3. In some cases too great caution cannot be exercised as regards a person suspected of a larceny; but in others the point will be much more satisfactorily settled by going at once to the individual, and asking, with befitting civility, if, as a proof that no suspicion can attach to him, he will allow his house or boxes to be searched.

4. Any person found in, or upon, any dwelling-house, warehouse, coach-house, stable or outhouse, in any enclosed yard, garden, or area, for any unlawful—not merely an immoral—purpose, may be apprehended as an idle and disorderly person. (5 Geo. IV., c. 83, s. 4.)

5. Any constable may likewise apprehend every suspected person or reputed thief frequenting any river, canal, or navigable stream, dock, or basin, or any quay, wharf, or warehouse near or adjoining thereto, or any street, highway, or avenue leading thereto, or any place of public resort, or any avenue leading thereto, or any street, highway, or place adjacent, with intent to commit felony.

6. Every person wandering abroad, and lodging in any barn or outhouse, or in any deserted or unoccupied building, or in the open air, or under a tent, or in any cart or waggon, not having any visible means of subsistence, and not giving a good account of himself or herself, may also be thus charged.

7. Any constable or peace officer may take into custody without warrant any person whom he shall find lying or loitering in any highway, yard, or other place during the night, and whom he shall have good cause to suspect of having committed or being about to commit any felony, and shall take such person, as soon as reasonably may be, before a Justice, to be dealt with according to law. (24 & 25 Vict., c. 96, s. 104.)

8. Accusations or imputations against the character

of any one must not be made by police, except in the furtherance of the law, and for the prevention of fraud. (See PREVENTION OF CRIME ACTS, p. 135; ROGUES AND VAGABONDS, p. 162.)

Suspensions.—1. Police are usually suspended for absence without leave, insubordination, drunkenness on duty, violence, allowing a prisoner to escape, or any gross neglect of duty, or disobedience of orders. (See p. 115.)

2. The Chief Constable of any county, or the Watch Committee of any borough, is empowered to suspend any constable, within their respective jurisdiction, whom they think remiss or negligent in the discharge of his duty.

Telegraph and Telegrams.—1. The telegraph, if properly utilised, is of the utmost value in the detection of crime. If the arrest of any person is sought, of whom a good and recognisable description can be given, a multiple telegram should be sent to every adjacent force on the route he may possibly have taken, so as to block his escape as far as possible.

2. When serious burglaries occur in provincial districts, the fact should be notified by telegram to all the neighbouring towns. It is sometimes assumed that the thieves have betaken themselves to the capital, whereas the probability is quite as great of their seeking refuge in nearer and more unsuspected places. Nevertheless in England a telegram should be sent to the Criminal Investigation Department as soon as possible, and a superior officer is always on duty at Scotland Yard to take immediate steps, and to convey the information to all quarters of the Metropolitan and City Police Districts by means of the telegraph, printed informations, and the pawnbrokers' lists.

3. While telegrams may be brief, it is very important that they should be perfectly clear, and state distinctly who they are from and what is wanted, as ambiguity must necessarily lead to delay and confusion.

4. Any person who cuts, breaks, throws down, destroys, injures, or removes anything whatever, being part of, or used in or about any electric or magnetic telegraph, or in the working thereof, or prevents or obstructs, in any manner whatever, the sending, con-

veyance, or delivery of any communication by telegraph, is liable to imprisonment with hard labour.

Temper.—*No police officer can properly discharge his duty without the most perfect command of temper.* The necessity for this command of temper cannot be too strongly impressed upon the police, and particularly on young constables, who may be prone to consider invidious or idle remarks or abuse reflecting upon or addressed to themselves as an aggravation of an offence, and it may occur that in stating the particulars of a charge at the station, or in giving evidence in respect thereto when before the Magistrate, such stress is laid upon the personal matter, as might possibly lead to the impression that the latter was the actual offence committed. A constable must not be moved or excited by any language or threats, however insolent; the cooler he keeps himself, the more power he will have over his assailant. Idle or silly remarks are unworthy of notice, and if the persons making them see that they have no effect upon the constable, they will soon desist.

Forbearance and moderation will always be understood and appreciated by the public, the magistrates, and police authorities. (*See* CIVILITY, p. 42.)

Tenants, Damage by.—(*See* DAMAGE TO PROPERTY, p. 58.)

Testimonials.—While the existence of the most friendly feeling from the public towards the police is most desirable, the acceptance of a testimonial by any officer still serving in the locality is inconsistent with the varied duties of police officers in enforcing the law, for it puts them under an obligation towards the inhabitants of a district, or their friends.

Threats.—1. If a person threatens another with immediate personal violence, a constable may interfere and prevent a breach of the peace. (*See* ABUSIVE LANGUAGE, p. 18.)

2. Every one is guilty of felony, who accuses or threatens to accuse, any person whatever of treason, felony, or any crime punishable by penal servitude for seven years or more, with the view of extorting any valuable thing from any person whatever. (24 & 25 Vict., c. 96, s. 47.)

3. The same penalty attaches to any similar accusation or threat to accuse any person of attempted rape, or of any infamous crime—threats which, above all others, should be at once boldly met. (*See* EXTORTION, p. 78.)

4. A person who with menaces or force demands any valuable thing, of any person, with intent to steal the same, is also liable to penal servitude, whether the thing demanded is received or not.

Threatening Letters.—1. Every one commits felony who sends, delivers, utters, or directly or indirectly, causes to be received, knowing the contents thereof, any letter or writing demanding or intending to gain, any valuable thing of any person with menaces, or by accusation or threatened accusation of any crime punishable by more than seven years' penal servitude, attempted rape, or any infamous crime.

2. Every person commits felony who maliciously sends, delivers, or utters, or directly or indirectly causes to be received, knowing the contents thereof (24 & 25 Vict., c. 96, s. 44)—

(*a*) Any letter or writing threatening to kill or murder any person. (24 & 25 Vict., c. 100, s. 16.)

(*b*) Any letter or writing threatening to burn or destroy any house, barn, or other building, or any rick or stack of grain, hay, straw, or other agricultural produce, whether in or under any building or not, or any ship or vessel, or to kill, maim, or wound any cattle. (24 & 25 Vict., c. 97, s. 50.) (*See* EXTORTION, p. 78; HIGH TREASON, p. 92.)

Ticket-of-Leave Men.—(*See* CONVICTS ON LICENCE, p. 52.)

Tolls.—Police in uniform are exempt from tolls.

Tramways.—Any person who wilfully places any stones, dirt, wood or refuse, or other material on any part of a tramway, or who does, or causes to be done, anything in such manner as to obstruct any carriage using a tramway, or knowingly aids or assists in the doing of any such thing, is liable to a penalty. (33 & 34 Vict., c. 78, s. 50.)

Travelling with a Prisoner.—1. Police conveying an unconvicted prisoner by rail to the jurisdiction within which the offence for which the apprehension has been effected was committed, should, while taking every precaution to prevent escape, not impose any avoidable indignity.

2. If the prisoner is a powerful man in custody for a crime of violence, or is of notorious antecedents, or disposed to give trouble, or if the journey is long, or through many tunnels, it will be better to handcuff him, but otherwise it will usually be sufficient for the officer to take the prisoner's arm while on the platforms, taking care when in the train that he does not succeed in escaping by some pretext, through an open window or door. It is always safer for a single officer to travel in a compartment having other male passengers, than by himself. (*See* HANDCUFFS, p. 91.)

3. If by any accident a prisoner does escape, the officer in charge must immediately, and on his own responsibility, send telegrams to all surrounding places. (*See* ESCAPE OF PRISONERS, p. 74.)

***Treason-Felony.**—Every one is guilty of treason-felony who expresses any intention by an overt act, or by publishing any writing or printing—

(*a*) To depose the Queen, her heirs or successors, from the style, honour, and royal name of the Imperial Crown of the United Kingdom or of any other of Her Majesty's dominions or countries; or

(*b*) To levy war against Her Majesty, her heirs or successors, within any part of the United Kingdom, in order by force or constraint to compel her to change her measures or counsels, or in order to put any force or constraint upon, or in order to intimate or overawe both Houses or either House of Parliament; or

(*c*) To move or stir any foreigner with force to invade the United Kingdom or any other of Her Majesty's dominions or countries under the obeisance of Her Majesty, her heirs and successors. (11 & 12 Vict., c. 12.) (*See* HIGH TREASON, p. 92.)

***Treasure Trove.**—Money or coin, gold, silver, plate, or bullion found hidden in the earth or other private place, the owner thereof being unknown, belong to the Crown, and every one commits a misdemeanor who conceals the finding thereof, whether the offender found such treasure himself, or received it from a person who found it, but was ignorant of its nature;

but the Lords Commissioners of Her Majesty's Treasury pay, on behalf of the Crown, the full bullion value, if the finding is properly notified.

Treatment of Persons Rescued from Drowning,† Hanging, or Suffocation.—1. *Treatment to restore natural breathing—*

(*a*) To maintain a free entrance of air into the windpipe.—Cleanse the mouth and nostrils; open the mouth; draw forward the patient's tongue, and keep it forward; an elastic band over the tongue and under the chin will answer the purpose. Remove all tight clothing from about the neck and chest.

(*b*) To adjust the patient's position.—Place the patient on his back on a flat surface, inclined a little from the feet upwards; raise and support the head and shoulders, on a small firm cushion, or folded article of dress, placed under the shoulder-blades.

(*c*) To imitate the movements of breathing.—Grasp the patient's arms just above the elbow, and draw the arms gently and steadily upwards, until they meet above the head (this is for the purpose of drawing air into the lungs); and keep the arms in that position for two seconds. Then turn down the patient's arms, and press them gently and firmly for two seconds against the sides of the chest (this is with the object of pressing air out of the lungs. Pressure on the breast-bone will aid this).

Repeat these measures alternately, deliberately, and perseveringly, fifteen times in a minute, until a spontaneous effort to respire is perceived, immediately upon which, cease to imitate the movements of breathing, and proceed to induce circulation and warmth.

Should a warm bath be procurable, the body may be placed in it up to the neck, continuing to imitate the movements of breathing. Raise the body for twenty seconds in a sitting position, dash cold water against the chest and face, and pass ammonia under the nose. The patient should not be kept in the warm bath longer than five or six minutes.

(*d*) To excite inspiration.—During the employment of the above method, excite the nostrils with snuff or smelling-salts, or tickle the throat with a feather. Rub

† Illustrated instruction boards are issued by the Royal Humane Society, 4, Trafalgar Square, London.

the chest and face briskly, and dash cold and hot water alternately on them.

2. *Treatment after natural breathing has been restored.*

(*e*) To induce circulation and warmth.—Wrap the patient in dry blankets, and commence rubbing the limbs upwards, firmly and energetically. The friction must be continued under the blankets or over the dry clothing.

Promote the warmth of the body by the application of hot flannels, bottles or bladders of hot water, heated bricks, &c., to the pit of the stomach, the armpits, between the thighs, and to the soles of the feet. Warm clothing may generally be obtained from bystanders.

On the restoration of life, when the power of swallowing has returned, a teaspoonful of warm water, small quantities of wine, warm brandy-and-water, or coffee should be given. The patient should be kept in bed, and a disposition to sleep encouraged. During reaction large mustard plasters to the chest and below the shoulders will greatly relieve the distressed breathing.

3. *Hanging.*—Remove all constrictions from the neck and chest, and employ artificial respiration as for drowning.

4. *Suffocation.*—Remove the patient into fresh air, undo clothing, and employ artificial respiration as in drowning.

Trees.—Every one is guilty of felony who steals or who unlawfully cuts, breaks, roots up, or otherwise destroys or damages, with intent to steal, the whole or any part of any tree, sapling, or shrub, or any underwood, if the value of the property stolen, or the amount of the injury done exceeds £5, or exceeds the value of £1 if the article or articles stolen or damaged grow in any park, pleasure ground, garden, orchard, avenue, or any ground adjoining or belonging to any dwelling-house. (24 & 25 Vict., c. 96, s. 32, & c. 97, s. 21.)

*****Trespass.**—1. Any person who commits any trespass by entering or being, in the day-time, upon any land, in search or pursuit of game, woodcocks, snipes, quails, land-rails, or rabbits, is liable to a penalty. (1 & 2 Wm. IV., c. 32, s. 30.) (*See* POACHING, p. 130.)

2. Any such trespasser may be apprehended without warrant, and taken before a Justice within twelve hours,

if, at the instance of any person having the right to kill game upon the land, or his agent, keeper, or servant, he refuses to quit, or give his correct Christian name, surname, and exact place of abode. A person found in any enclosed yard, garden, or area, for any unlawful purpose, may be apprehended as an idle and disorderly person. (5 Geo. IV., c. 83, s. 4.)

3. A mere entry upon the land of another not in search of game, &c., is not a criminal offence, but one for which an action will lie and damages may be claimed, but refusal to leave on request may constitute conduct tending to provoke a breach of the peace.

4. Although as a general rule the police should not apprehend, or unnecessarily interfere with, any person unless some specific act has been committed by which the law has been broken, there are some exceptional occasions on which the police may aid others in the assertion of their civil rights. If a police constable or other officer is requested by a householder to aid in turning out a person improperly there, although in law that person is simply a trespasser, the officer may, when he can place reliance on the statement of the applicant, properly give his assistance; as, for example, when the master of a family finds a person in his house, who, having entered peaceably (with or without the connivance of a servant) refuses to leave on request, the constable may act in the master's aid and remove the person from the house, using no more force than is necessary for that purpose.

5. On such occasions a constable should only act in the presence, and on the express application of the lawful occupier, and after the person has refused to leave on a formal request made to him in the presence of the constable.

6. The constable should himself use persuasion before putting hands on the person. He must also bear strictly in mind that he is not to take the person into custody, but to leave him perfectly free as soon as the street or public road is reached; for although the intruder in such a case is wrongfully in the house, he has not in law been guilty of any breach of the peace or any offence punishable summarily or otherwise, and the intervention of the police is, strictly speaking, not in the character of a peace officer, but rather as a private person aiding the

occupier, and in law acting as his servant for that special purpose.

7. The police must use great care in discriminating between such a case as that above mentioned and cases of real dispute as to the right of possession, and where it is neither necessary nor desirable to interfere.

Truncheons.—Truncheons are supplied to the police to enable them to protect themselves if violently attacked. If a constable is likely to be overpowered, he may draw his truncheon and use it, taking care to avoid striking any one on the head. The arms and legs should be aimed at to disable a prisoner, as the parts of the frame least likely to suffer serious injury. *The use of the truncheon must not be resorted to, except in extreme cases, when all other attempts have failed, and a prisoner is likely to escape, or be rescued, through the constable being ill-used and overpowered.*

Unlawful Drilling.—1. All assemblies are unlawful which are held in order that the persons assembled may train or drill themselves, or be trained or drilled, to the use of arms, or for the purpose of practising military movements or evolutions without lawful authority.

Every person commits felony who—

(*a*) Is present at, or attends any such unauthorised assembly, for the purpose of training or drilling any other person to the use of arms, or the practice of military exercise, movements, or evolutions; or

(*b*) Who trains or drills any other person to the use of arms, or the practice of military exercise, movements, or evolutions; or

(*c*) Who aids or assists therein.

2. Every person commits a misdemeanor, who attends, or is present at any such assembly, for the purpose of being, or who at any such assembly, is trained, or drilled, to the use of arms, or the practice of military exercise, movements, or evolutions. (60 Geo. III. & 1 Geo. IV., c. 1.)

Uttering.—(*See* COUNTERFEIT COIN, p. 55; FORGERY, p. 88.)

Vaccination.—The parent, or other person having the charge, of any child must have it vaccinated within three months from its birth, subject to a penalty.

*Vagrancy.—1. Every person who being able, wholly or in part, to maintain himself or herself, or his or her family, by work or by other means, and wilfully refusing or neglecting so to do, by which refusal or neglect he or she, or any of his or her family whom he or she may be legally bound to maintain, shall have become chargeable to any parish, township, or place, may be apprehended as an idle and disorderly person, and is liable to one month's imprisonment with hard labour. (5 Geo. IV., c. 83.)

2. Every person wandering abroad, and lodging in any barn, or outhouse, or in any deserted or unoccupied building, or in the open air, or under a tent, or in any cart or waggon, not having any visible means of subsistence, and not giving a good account of himself or herself, may be charged as a rogue and vagabond. (*See* BEGGARS, p. 29; DESERTING FAMILIES, p. 63; ROGUES AND VAGABONDS, p. 162.)

Valuable Securities.—Every one who steals for any fraudulent purpose, destroys, cancels, or obliterates the whole or any part of a valuable security, commits felony, of the same nature and degree, as if he had stolen any chattel of the same value, as that to which the valuable security relates. (24 & 25 Vict., c. 96.)

Warders.—It is of great importance that the most perfect cordiality should at all times prevail between police officers and the warders of prisons. The latter see prisoners for so much longer than police, that they are far more likely to recognise them if re-arrested; and it is therefore better for warders to prove convictions, independently of the loss of time involved by this being done by police.

Warrants.—1. A warrant is an authority, under hand and seal, to some officer to arrest an offender to be dealt with according to law, or to commit him to prison, to search premises, or to levy distress for the non-payment of a legal penalty.

2. A warrant of arrest can only be issued, in the first instance, upon an information upon oath or affirmation. The information, containing the name, address, and occupation of the deponent, the date and place of

commission of the offence, the name or description of the accused, and the exact charge, is drawn out by either the applicant, his solicitor, or the clerk at the Police Court, the police officer, if any, engaged in the case, giving every possible assistance.

3. Warrants are not necessary for an apprehension to be made in cases of felony, occurring within a Police District, if the offender is still within the jurisdiction, but they should be invariably applied for—

(*a*) In cases in which the presumption is strongly in favour of the delinquent's having absconded beyond the jurisdiction; as the existence of a warrant enables steps to be taken to secure his extradition if gone abroad, and to effect his apprehension in other places.

(*b*) In cases in which there is any suspicion that the aggrieved person has some other object in view than the furtherance of the law; embezzlement being often within this category.

(*c*) In cases of misdemeanor, when an apprehension is not effected at the time of its commission.

4. A warrant of arrest may be executed either by night or day, and it does not become void by the death of the issuing Justice.

5. A warrant must be read over to the prisoner it is intended to arrest thereon, and after execution it is returned to the Court.

*6. The warrant of a Metropolitan Police Magistrate does not require to be backed. It extends over the whole of the United Kingdom and the Channel Islands. The warrant of the Lord Mayor and the Aldermen of the City of London does not require endorsement for execution in the counties of Middlesex, Surrey, and Hertfordshire (nor of Justices of those counties within the City), but a warrant issued by any other Magistrate requires endorsement beyond the area of his own jurisdiction, unless an offender be taken in close pursuit within seven miles of the county border.

7. If a warrant has been issued, the fact should be stated in all communications requesting the arrest of the offender; and if sent by post to another force for execution, it should invariably be accompanied by a declaration of signature, under the Summary Jurisdiction Act, section 41, rule 45. (*See* APPENDIX H; BACKING WARRANTS, p. 26.)

*Wife's Protection Order.—A wife deserted by her husband may at any time after such desertion, apply to a Court of Summary Jurisdiction, for an order to protect any money or property she may acquire by her own lawful industry, and property which she may become possessed of after such desertion, against her husband or his creditors, or any persons claiming under him. (*See* p. 113.) (20 & 21 Vict., c. 85, s. 21.)

Wilful Damage.—(*See* DAMAGE TO PROPERTY, p. 58.)

Wills.—Every one commits felony who either during the life of the testator, or after his death, steals, or for any fraudulent purpose, destroys, cancels, obliterates, or conceals, the whole or any part of any will, codicil, or other testamentary instrument, whether it relates to real or personal estate, or to both. (24 & 25 Vict., c. 96, s. 29.)

*Withdrawal from Prosecution. — 1. In all criminal cases in England and Wales where a prosecutor withdraws from a charge, except by leave of the Court, or fails to appear to support it, a remand should be applied for by the police, for the facts to be submitted to the Director of Public Prosecutions. (*See* PUBLIC PROSECUTOR, p. 154.)

2. A prisoner arrested in consequence of the well-founded complaint of an individual, who, nevertheless, declines to charge when the result he sought has been attained, and in spite of there being *primâ facie* evidence of guilt, should be charged by the officer arresting him, a remand being applied for, and a witness summons to secure the prosecutor's attendance, application being made for legal aid if necessary ; as the furtherance of public justice is the object for which police forces are established.

Witnesses.—1. The attendances of witnesses residing in England may be secured at Police Courts by witness summonses, elsewhere by subpœnas. (*See* p.174.)

2. A witness summons addressed to a person residing beyond the jurisdiction in which it is issued, must be endorsed† prior to service, whether issued by a Metropolitan Police Magistrate, or other Justice, and to this

† This applies also to Scotland, and to the process of any Scotch Court of Summary Jurisdiction. (44 & 45 Vict., c. 24, s. 4.)

end should be accompanied by a declaration of signature, under section 41, rule 45 of the Summary Jurisdiction Act, 1879.

3. As in the case of subpœnas, a reasonable amount must be tendered for expenses on the service of a witness summons beyond the district.

4. In all cases where a person is committed for trial, the prosecutor and every witness is bound over, by recognisance, to prosecute and give evidence. A witness refusing to be so bound, may be committed for safe custody until the trial.

5. If a witness disobeys a summons, and no just excuse is offered for the neglect or refusal, after proof of its due service, a warrant may be issued, to bring and have such person at the appointed time and place; or if even in the first instance a Justice is satisfied by evidence, upon oath or affirmation, that it is probable such person will not attend to give evidence without being compelled to do so, a warrant may be issued instead of a summons.

6. If any witness refuses to be examined upon oath or affirmation concerning the premises, or refuses to take such oath or affirmation, or refuses to answer such questions concerning the premises, as may be put to him, he may be committed to prison.

7. If any person is dangerously ill, and in the opinion of some registered medical practitioner not likely to recover, and is able and willing to give material evidence relating to any indictable offence, or relating to any person accused of such offence, any Justice may take his statement on oath. (*See* COMPETENCY OF WITNESSES, p. 47; DISSUADING WITNESSES FROM TESTIFYING, p. 66; DYING DECLARATIONS, p. 71; EVIDENCE, p. 74; PRISONERS AS WITNESSES, p. 142.)

Woods.—Any person unlawfully and maliciously setting fire to any wood, whether standing or cut down, any plantation of trees, or to any heath, gorse, furze, or fern, wheresoever the same may be growing, is guilty of felony. (*See* ARSON, p. 25.) (24 & 25 Vict., c. 97, s. 16.)

Wounding.—1. Every person who by any means whatever, unlawfully and maliciously wounds, or causes any grievous bodily harm to any person is guilty of felony.

2. In wounds, the bleeding should be first stopped by

compression on the nearest artery. The parts should next be washed carefully with cold water, and strips of adhesive plaster put on. If internal organs protrude through a wound, they should be returned, and the sufferer not moved, until the arrival of medical aid. (24 & 25 Vict., c. 100, s. 18.)

Wrecking.—1. Every one who prevents or impedes any person being on board of or having quitted any ship or vessel in distress, wrecked, stranded, or cast on shore, in his endeavour to save his life, or prevents or impedes any person in his endeavour to save the life of any person so situated, is guilty of felony.

2. Any person who assaults an officer in the execution of his duty, in or concerning the preservation of any vessel in distress, of any vessel, goods, or effects wrecked, stranded, cast on shore, or lying under water, commits a misdemeanor. (24 & 25 Vict., c. 100.)

3. Every one who plunders or steals, any part of any ship or vessel wrecked, stranded, or cast on shore, or any goods, merchandise, or article of any kind belonging to any such ship, or vessel, is guilty of felony. (24 & 25 Vict., c. 96, s. 64.)

APPENDIX A.

Form of Reward Bill.

£100 REWARD.
Burglary and Attempted Murder.

WHEREAS, at 11.30 a.m. on Sunday, the 31st of May, a person was shot at with a pistol by one of two men (tall, and wearing a short pea-jacket with a velvet collar, probably now having a bullet-hole in the left arm), who effected an entrance into

, stealing two purses — the one containing 7s. silver and a Turkish pound; the second, a Bank of England five-pound note, No. 80,790, and stamped Charles Cammell & Co., memoranda with reference to cutlery work, a season ticket on the Great Northern Railway from Sheffield to London, in the name of Edward Johnson, and a gold cross of the above shape, with alternate diamonds and sapphires;

AND WHEREAS, on Monday, the 1st of June, at 2 a.m., a constable was shot with a revolver and wounded by John Brown, formerly of 6, Adam Street, Manchester (whose description is given below), whom he found secreted on enclosed premises, at ;

£100 REWARD

Will be paid by Her Majesty's Government to any person (other than a person belonging to a Police Force in the United Kingdom) who shall give such information as shall lead to the discovery and conviction of the said John Brown; and the Secretary of State for the Home Department will advise the grant of Her Majesty's most gracious

PARDON

to any accomplice or offender in either instance, not being the person who actually fired either shot, who shall give such evidence as shall lead to a like result.

DESCRIPTION.—Age 30, height about 5 ft. 11 in., complexion pale, thin features, full sandy whiskers, slight moustache, no beard (it will probably have grown since); dress, dark trousers, a short pea-jacket with a velvet collar, dark tweed cloth hat.

Note.—John Brown has a twitch in the left eye when speaking, and a dark mole on the neck below the right ear. He is tattooed on the right elbow with a heart and the word "Dinah." He has an American accent, knows most of the towns in the United States, where he was at one time employed as a billiard-marker, and if excited makes frequent use of the expression "you bet."

Information to be given to   or at any Police Station.

Police Office,   *Signature and*
(Date.)   *Designation.*

£10 REWARD.
Police Notice.

Description, likeness, and handwriting† of Charles John Henry, *alias* Smith, Baxter, Evans, Parker, Brooks, Perkins, &c., whose apprehension is sought on a warrant for fraud, and obtaining goods by false pretences.—Age 33, height 5 ft. 6 in., complexion fresh, hair and moustache and whiskers brown, short beard, oval face, aquiline nose, eyes blue, blinks when speaking, two abscess scars left side of neck, cut corner of left eye, two upper front teeth deficient, stammers slightly, and usually wears dark clothes and tall hat (maker, Heath, London). Was convicted at the Central Criminal Court on 3rd April, 1871, for forgery, and sentenced to eighteen months' hard labour as Charles Henry Smith; and again at the Central Criminal Court on 21st September, 1875, for fraud, and sentenced to two years' hard labour as Charles Baxter, *alias* Charles Smith. Takes shops, answers advertisements of provincial traders, and, under the pretence that he is a general dealer, and an agent for French houses, obtains goods of all kinds fraudulently from different parts of the country.

A REWARD OF £10 will be paid by Henry Mathews, of No.   ,   , to any person giving such information as shall lead to the apprehension and conviction of the above.

Information to

† The engraving of the handwriting is omitted from this edition.

APPENDIX B.

Form of Information for a Warrant.

Metropolitan Police District or County of (as the case may be) to Wit. } The information of taken on oath this   day of   in the year of our Lord One Thousand Eight Hundred and Ninety   at in the County of   , before me the undersigned, one of the Magistrates of   sitting at   aforesaid, against

charged with embezzlement (or as the case may be)

†This deponent, *John Jones*, on his oath saith as follows :—I am a draper, and carry on business at   . Between 14th July and 18th November last I had in my service one Henry Brown, of
He was paid by weekly wages, and one of his duties was to collect debts due to me, and each day to pay over the sum collected to me at the above address. On 1st September last, Henry Williams, of   was indebted to me in the sum of £4 16s., for goods supplied. The receipt for this amount, produced by Mr. Williams, is in the handwriting of the aforesaid Henry Brown, but the money was never accounted for by him. He is not now in my employment.

Henry Williams on oath saith : I reside at   . On 1st September last I was indebted to the deponent John Jones in the sum of £4 16s., and on that date paid the amount to his collector, Henry Brown, whose receipt I produce.

Information—Fraud.

William Brown on oath saith : I reside at   and am a licensed victualler. On the 27th October last a customer, named Henry Williams, whom I have not since seen, and whose address is unknown to me, came to my house and asked for change, for the cheque produced, marked A, and attached hereto. It is for the sum of £8 10s., and is drawn on the Holborn Branch of the London and County Bank, in the name of James Fletcher, and made payable to the order of Henry Williams, who endorsed it in my presence. Believing the cheque to be genuine, and that James Fletcher, the drawer, had a *bonâ fide* account at the bank, I paid Williams the amount of it. I have since passed the cheque through my bankers, who have returned it marked "no effects."

† Alter according to circumstances.

James Willson on oath saith : I am a Police Sergeant of the E division. I have inquired at the Holborn Branch of the London and County Bank, and find that James Fletcher had an account there at one time, when the cheque-book, including the cheque produced, was issued to him. There is still a balance of a few shillings remaining to his credit at the bank, but he ceased to be a customer there about three months ago. I have inquired at his last-known address, but he has left there, and I can find no trace of him.

APPENDIX C.

FORM OF INDEMNITY ON RE-DELIVERY OF PROPERTY TO FINDER.

I,   of   do hereby acknowledge to have received from   the following article , viz. :—   , found by me and delivered to the care of the Police, and in consideration of the re-delivery to me, I undertake to return it [or them] or the value, in the event of the loser, or lawful owner, hereafter claiming, and proving his right, to the property, subject to any deduction for advertisements or other reasonable payments actually made in endeavouring to find the real owner.

Witness,   Dated the   day of   , 18 .
Stamp (to be paid by finder).   (Signed)

APPENDIX D.

FORM OF INDEMNITY FOR REIMBURSEMENT OF EXPENSES IN AN EXTRADITION OR FUGITIVE OFFENDER'S CASE.

WHEREAS, on an information laid by me, the undersigned, a Warrant has been granted by   a Magistrate of the   of   for the arrest of   on a charge of

AND WHEREAS information has been obtained that the said   is now in or on the way to

AND WHEREAS, at my request, the Secretary of State for the Home Department, on behalf of Her Majesty's Government, has agreed, on the terms and conditions hereinafter stated, to take the necessary steps under   †   with a view to obtain the surrender of the said

† "The Extradition Act, 1870," or "the Fugitive Offenders Act, 1881," or (where the fugitive is in a foreign country with which there is no Extradition Treaty) "such steps as may seem to him to be advisable."

NOW I, the undersigned, do hereby agree and undertake, for myself, my executors, administrators, and assigns, to pay on demand to the said Secretary of State, or to the Secretary of State for the Home Department for the time being, or to any person duly authorised to act on behalf of the said Secretary of State, all expenses incurred by Her Majesty's Government, or any person acting on behalf of Her Majesty's Government, in taking steps to obtain the surrender of the said
and in obtaining and carrying out such surrender, and in conveying the said   to England and otherwise in pursuance of the said Warrant.

AND I further agree and undertake to indemnify the Secretary of State for the Home Department for the time being against any expenses to which he or any person acting on his behalf may be put, and against any compensation or damages paid by or on behalf of the said Secretary of State in his discretion, or in consequence of any legal proceedings in the event of the unlawful arrest of any person erroneously supposed to be the said   if in the opinion of the said Secretary of State such unlawful arrest is caused by imperfect or inaccurate information or description given by me.

     Witness my hand this day of   18 .
     Name
     Address
Signed by the said
in the presence of
   Address

APPENDIX E.

Form of Affidavit for Obtaining Production of a Prisoner or a Witness.

I,   an Inspector in the Police Force make oath and say that the evidence of , a prisoner in H.M. Prison , is necessary to the ends of justice in the case of , to be heard at , on the , at o'clock; and I, the said , accordingly apply that a warrant, or order, may be issued for the production of the said as a witness, at the time and place mentioned, according to the provisions of the Statute 16 & 17 Vict., c. 30, s. 9.

     Sworn, &c.

APPENDIX F.

Form of Recognisance conditioned for Appearance, or for doing some other Thing in, to, or before, or in a proceeding in, a Court of Summary Jurisdiction.

The   day of   18   .
  We the undersigned   of
of   and   of
severally acknowledge ourselves to owe to our Sovereign Lady the Queen the several sums following—namely, the said   as principal, the sum of   and the said
and   as surety the sum of   each, to be levied on our several goods, lands, and tenements if the said   fails in the condition hereon endorsed.
                    Signed (*where not taken orally*)
                              A. B.
                              L. M.
                              N. O.
Taken [orally] before me the   day of   18   .
                    J. P.
            One of Her Majesty's Justices of the Peace
              for the County of
                    or
            Clerk of the Court of Summary Jurisdiction
              for the Petty Sessional Division of
                    or
            Superintendent of the   police, *or as
              the case may be.*

Note.—*Where the recognisance is taken orally, omit the words "the undersigned," and insert the word " orally " after " taken."*

Condition Endorsed.

The condition of the within-written recognisance is such that if the within bounden   appears before the Court of Summary Jurisdiction sitting at   on   day, the   day of   , at the hour of   in the noon, to answer [further] to the charge made against him by   and to be [further] dealt with according to law [*or* appears before the Court of Summary Jurisdiction sitting at   for sentence when called upon, *or as the case may be*] then the said recognisance shall be void, but otherwise shall remain in full force.

APPENDIX G.

LIST of the RAILWAY TERMINI and PRINCIPAL STATIONS in the METROPOLITAN and CITY POLICE DISTRICTS, and the POLICE STATION nearest to each, to the Inspector on Duty at which telegrams asking that a train, which had already started from the Provinces, be met, should be sent by constabulary forces :—

Name of Railway.	London Termini.	Nearest Police Station.	Remarks.
Brighton and South Coast	London Bridge (Gen. Man.) Victoria .. Kensington ..	Stones End (M)+ CottageRoad(B) Kensington (T)	Route to and from France, viâ Newhaven and Dieppe, and viâ Littlehampton and Honfleur.
Chatham and Dover	Victoria (Gen. Man.) Holborn Viaduct	CottageRoad(B) Snow Hill (City)	Route to and from France and Belgium, viâ Dover and Calais, or Ostend.
South-Eastern	London Bridge (Gen. Man.) Cannon Street Charing Cross	Stones End (M) Seething Lane (City) Bow Street (E) or Scotland Yd	Route to Dover for Calais and Ostend, and to Boulogne and Paris, viâ Folkestone (tidal service).
North-Western	Euston Square (Gen. Man.) Willesden Junc.	Albany Street(S) Willesden (X)	Route to and from Scotland, and to and from Ireland viâ Holyhead.
Great Eastern	Liverpool Street Bishopsgate ..	Bishopsgate (City) Hoxton (G)	Route to and from Rotterdam and Antwerp, viâ Harwich.
South-Western	Waterloo (Gen. Man.) Vauxhall	Kennington Road (L)	Route to and from Havre and the Channel Islands, viâ Southampton.
Great Northern	King's Cross (Gen. Man.)	SomersTown(Y)	Route to and from Scotland, and Ireland and America viâ Liverpool.
Midland	St. Pancras (Gen. Man., Derby).	SomersTown(Y)	Route to and from Ireland and America, viâ Liverpool.
Great Western	Paddington (Gen. Man.)	Paddington (X)	Route to and from Ireland viâ Holyhead, Bristol, or Milford, and France viâ Weymouth.

† The letter denotes the Police Division.

N.B.—The Metropolitan Police Office, with all its departments, will be moved from Scotland Yard and Whitehall Place in the course of 1890 to the Thames Embankment, close to the Westminster Bridge District Railway station, and near Charing Cross. Communications with respect to "CRIMINAL" business should be addressed to "The Assistant Commissioner (Robert Anderson, Esq., LL.D.), Criminal Investigation Department, Metropolitan Police Office," and upon all other matters to "The Commissioner of Police of the Metropolis."

The City Police Office (Commissioner—Colonel Sir James Fraser, K.C.B.) is in Old Jewry, E.C.—close to Cannon Street railway station.

Full details concerning the distribution of every force in Great Britain and Ireland are given in the annual Police Almanack.

APPENDIX H.

Form of Declaration to Accompany every Warrant or Summons sent by Post by a Provincial Police Force for Execution by another Police Force, which latter Force can then get it Endorsed by a Magistrate for Execution or Service within the fresh Jurisdiction.

I,   of   , hereby solemnly declare that the signature   to the document now produced and shown to me, and marked A, is in the handwriting of   , of

Declared before me the   day of   18

Justice of the Peace.

APPENDIX I.

Form of Endorsement on a Warrant or Summons for Execution or Service beyond the Jurisdiction of Issue.

Proof on solemn declaration (or oath) having this day been made before me the undersigned that the name of
to the within warrant (or summons) subscribed, is of the handwriting of the Justice of the Peace within mentioned, I authorise
, who brings to me this warrant (or summons), and all other persons by whom it may be lawfully executed (or served), and all constables of the County of   ,
to execute (or serve) the same within the said County.

Dated the   day of   18

Justice of the Peace for the County of

INDEX.†

Abandoning children, 17
Abduction, 17
Abortion, 17
Absconding from duty, 17
—— delinquents, 155
Abusive language, 18
Access to premises, 18
Accessories to crime, 18
—— before the fact, 18
—— after the fact, 18
Accidental death, 19
Accidents, 18
—— in streets, 18
—— in public places, 18
——, Points to be attended to in cases of, 19
Accomplices, 19
Accounts of police, 76
Accounting, False, 82
Accoutrements, 22
Accusations of crime, 79, 178
Accused, Answer of, 24
Acquittal, 19
Actions against police, 19
Activity of police, 20
Acts of Parliament, 20
Administering unlawful oaths, 121
Admission to bail by police, 27
Adulteration of food, 20
Advertising reward for return of stolen property, 20
Affidavits, 20
Affiliation order, 28
Affirmations, 20
Agents, Misappropriation by, 20
Aggravated assault, 25
Aid to the injured, 21
Aiding prisoners to escape, 21
Alarm of fire, 21
Allowances, Compassionate, 46
Alms, Collecting fraudulently, 123
Analysis of medicine for poison, 131
Animals, 22
——, Advertisement of stolen, 133
——, Baiting, 43
——, Bringing, for slaughter, 95
——, Cruelty to, 56
——, Cruelty to, by drovers, 70
——, Exposing, for sale, 76
——, Killing and maiming, 22
—— in possession of prisoners, 90

Animals, Poisoning, 132
——, Stealing, 22
——, —— deer, 60
——, —— dogs, 68
——, —— horses, 96
——, —— sheep, 169
——, Straying, 90
Annoyance, 22
Anonymous letters, 46.
Antecedents of prisoners, 22
Apoplexy, mistaken for drunkenness, 71
Applications by police, 22
—— to join Metropolitan Police, 35
Appointments, 22
Apprehend, Requests to, 159
Apprehension, 22
—— by warrant, 22
—— without warrant, 23
—— of beggars, 29
—— of deserters, 62
Apprentices, Failing to provide for, 23
——, Causing bodily harm to, 23
Aqueducts, Destruction of, 32
Area gates, Open, 24
—— thieves, 24
Argument, 24
Armlets, 24
Arms, Unlawful training in, 184
Arrest, 24
——, Determination to, 65
—— in extradition cases, 79
——, Illegal, 98
—— without warrant, 23
Arson, 25
Assaults, Aggravated, 25
——, Common, 25
——, Indecent, 25, 99
——, ——, on males, 170
——, Marital, 97
—— on police, 25
—— resulting in bodily harm, 25
Assembly, Unlawful, 161, 184
Assistance to police, 25
Assisting justice, Rewards for exertion in, 161
Assizes, 167
Assuming the character of a constable, 26

† Originally compiled by F. J. KIRCHNER, of the Criminal Investigation Department, Metropolitan Police, author of "*Fugitive Offenders:* being the Law and Practice relating to Offenders flying to or from Great Britain." (Stevens and Sons, Chancery Lane, London, W.C.)

Asylums for lunatics, 110
Attempted crime, 26
—— murder, 118
Attention, 26
Attic larcenies, 26
Attorney, Power of, 135
Authorities, Parochial, 125
Authority, Local, 109

Baby-farming, 26
Backing warrants, 26
Bagatelle, 31
Bail, Admission to, 27
——, Justifying, 106
Bailees, 27
Balls, Private, 141
Bank notes, Forgery of, 27
——, Lost or stolen, 27
——, ——, Stopping, 27
——, Tracing of, 28
Bankrupts, 28
Base copper, Coining, 43
Bastardy, 28
Bathing, Indecent, 100
Battery, 28
Bawdy houses, 28
Beats, Constables', 28
Beetle, Colorado, 104
Beggars, 29
Bell-pulling, 29
Bestiality, 29
Betting, 30
—— houses, 30
—— in public places, 30
—— in streets, 30
—— on highways, 30
Bicycles, 30
Bigamy, 30
Bill in criminal cases, 31
Billiards, 31
Bills offering reward, 160
—— of indictment, 101
Birds, Protection of wild, 31
——, Stealing, 31
Births, Concealment of, 48
——, Registration of, 157
Boats conveying explosives, 77
Bodies, Dead, 59
Bonâ fide travellers, Sale of intoxicating liquors to, 149
Bonds, 32
——, Forgery of, 32
——, Uttering of forged, 32
Bonfires, 32
Books, Obscene, 121
Borrowing money by police, 32
Bottle collecting, 166
Boxing matches, 141
Breach of the peace, 32
Breaking into houses by false keys, 83
Breaking doors in pursuit of prisoners, 24

Bribery of police, 32
Bridges, 32; destroying, 32
Brothels, 32
Buoys, Damage to, 58
Burden of proof, 33
Burglars, Efforts to trace, 33
Burglary, 33
Burial, 34
Burns, Treatment of, 86

Cabmen, Offences of, 35
Cab ranks, 35
Cabs, 34
Candidates for Metropolitan Police, 35
Cardsharping, 36
Carriages, 36
—— containing explosives, 77
——, Dog, 68
——, Hackney, 91
——, Larcenies from, 37
——, Royal, 36
Carriage larcenies, 37
Cattle drovers, 73
—— plague, 37
—— Stealing, maiming, killing, 38
——, Straying, 38
Causing death, 38
Cautioning a prisoner, 38
Cells, 38
Central Criminal Court sittings, 167
Certificates of previous conviction, 137
Challenge to fight, 39
Character, Evidence of, 39
——, Obtaining situation by false, 82
—— of a constable, Assuming the, 26
Charge of stations, 39
——, Declining to, 47, 187
Charges, 39
Charitable contributions, Fraudulently obtaining, 123
Chattel, Definition of, 40
Cheating at play, 40
Child abandonment, 17
—— murder, 101
—— stealing, 40
Children, Dangerous performances by, 41
——, Defilement of, 41
——, Destitute, 101
—— found, 40
—— —— dead, 40
——, Illegitimate, 98
——, Incorrigible, 99
——, Neglect of, 41
——, Offences against, 40
——, Offences of, 40
——, Prevention of cruelty to, 41
——, Vaccination of, 184
Chimneys on fire, 42

202   POLICE CODE.

Choking, 42
Churches, Breaking into, 163
———, Indecent behaviour in, 67
Circumstantial evidence, 42
Civil actions against police, 19
Civility, 42
Clipping Coin, 43
Closing of public houses, 147
Clubs, 43
Cock-fighting, 43
Coercion, 43
—— of married women, 113
Coin, Counterfeit, 55
——, Defacing, 55
——, Uttering base copper, 55
——, —— —— or foreign, 43
Coining, 43
—— copper money, 43
—— foreign money, 43
Collars, Numbers on, 121
Colonies, Surrender of criminals to and from, 44
Clorado beetle, 104
Common assault, 25
—— lodging-houses, 45
—— nuisance, 46
—— —— on highways, 93
Communications, Confidential, 46
——, Privileged, 141
—— to Police, 46
Comparison of handwriting, 91
Compassionate allowances, 46
Competency of witnesses, 47
Complaints against police, 47
—— by police, 47
Compounding felonies and misdemeanors, 47
Concealing mistakes, 117
Concealment of birth, 48
Conditions of police service, 48
Conduct, False pretence by, 83
—— money, 48
Confessions, 48
Consent, 49
—— not recognised by law, 49
Conspiracy, 49
—— to defeat justice, 49
Conspirators, 50
Constable, assuming character of, 26
Constables, Detached, 63
—— duties, 50
—— on beat duty, General rules for, 28
——, Special, 171
Constabulary forces, 50
Contagious Diseases (Animals) Act, 37
Contraband goods, 51
Contract of service, Failure to fulfil, 57
Conversion of goods by bailees, 27
Conveyance of Explosives, 77

Convict Supervision Office, 53
Convicts, 52
——, Information by, 52
—— on licence, 52
——, Photographs of, 53
Convictions, Previous, 137
Co-operation of police, 53
Coroners, 53
——, Inquests by, 53
—— juries, 53
Correspondence of police forces, 53
——, Dealing with, 53
Corrosive fluid throwing, 54
Counterfeit coin, 55
—— Arrested for uttering, 55
County Councils, 55
Crime, Accessories to, 18
—— Acts, Prevention of, 135
——, Attempt to commit, 26
——, Conspiracy to commit, 49
——, Detection of, 63
——, Inciting to, 98
——, List of principal, 23
—— not requiring warrant to arrest, 23
—— subject to extradition, 80
Criminal cases, Bill in, 31
—— indictments, 101
—— Investigations, Director of, 65
Criminals, Habitual, 91
Cross-examination, 56
—— on written notes, 120
Crowds, Pickpockets in, 129
Crown Office subpœnas, 174
Cruelty to animals, 56
—— to children, 41
Culpable negligence, 58
Custody of prisoners, 138
——, Rescue from, 159

Damage to buoys, 58
—— to fences, 84
—— to machinery, 58
—— to property, 58
—— to public drinking fountains, 88
—— to rivers, 58
—— to vessels, 58
—— to viaducts, 32, 156
——, Wilful, 187
—— by tenants, 58
Dangerous performances by children, 41
Dead bodies, 59
—— ——, Burial of, 34
—— ——, Disposing unlawfully of, 34
—— ——, Examination of, 59
—— ——, Inquest on, 103
Dead body, Finding child's, 40
Dealers in old metal, 123
Dealing with police correspondence, 53

Death, Accidental, 19
—— by misadventure, 59
—— by violence, 117
——, Causing, 38
——, Registration, 157
Declaration, Dying, 71
——, False, 83
Deer Stealing, 60
Defilement of children, 41
—— of girls under age, 41
—— of women, 60
Demanding property with menaces, 60
Demeanor of police, 60
Demolition of houses, Riotous, 162
Depositions, 60
Description of persons, 61
—— of property stolen, 172
Deserters, 62
——, Concealing, 62
Deserting families, 63
Desertion, 62
Destitute persons, 63
Destroying any aqueduct, 32
—— any bridge, 32
—— any viaduct, 32
Detached constables, 63
Detection of crime, 63
—— ——, Use of telegraph in, 177
Detectives, 63
Determination to arrest, 65
Direct evidence, 74
Director of Criminal Investigations, 65
Discharging firearms, 65
Discipline, 65
Disease, Infectious, 102
Dismissal of police, 65
Disobedience of orders, 66
Disorderly houses, 66
—— ——, Preferring complaint against, 66
Disputed ownership of property, 66
Dissuading witnesses from testifying, 66
Distraint of goods, 66
Districts, Police, 132
Disturbing the public peace, 161
Divine service, 67
Divisions, 67
Divorce proceedings, 67
Documentary Evidence, 68
Dog carriages, 68
—— fighting, 43
—— licences, 68
—— stealing, 68
Dogs, Ferocious, 68
—— found, 68
—— Mad, 68, 111
Domestic larcenies, 166
—— quarrels, 97
Doors and windows open, 69
Dress of police, 69

Drill, 69
Drilling, Unlawful, 184
Drinking, 69
Drivers asleep, or not holding the reins, 69
Driving, Furious, 88
Drovers, 70
Drowning, Treatment of persons rescued from, 181
Drugging, 70
Drunken cabmen, 35
—— persons, 70
—— postmen, 135
Drunkenness, 70
—— and insensibility, 12, 71
Duels, 39
Duties, Import, Evasion of, 170
—— of constables, 50
—— of Inspectors, 104
—— of Sergeants, 166
——, Special, 171
Duty, 71
——, Absconding from, 17
——, Neglect of, 119
——, Parading for, 125
Dwelling-houses, 71
Dying declarations, 71
—— ——, Signing of, 72

Education of police, 72
Elections, 72
Embezzlement, 73
—— by police, 133
Emetics, 131
Empty houses, 73
Endorsement of warrants, 26
Engravings, 73
Erasures, 74
Escape from reformatories, 157
—— of prisoners, 74
Evidence, 74
—— as to handwriting, 91
——, Circumstantial, 42
——, Documentary, 68
——, Hearsay, 92
—— of character, 31
—— of husband and wife, 97
——, Opinions not, 124
——, Queen's, 155
Examination of witnesses, 76
Exercising horses, 76
Exertions in assisting justice, 161
Exhibit, 76
Exhibition, indecent, 100
Expenses of police, 76
Experts in handwriting, 77
Expirees, 77
Explosives, 77
——, Conveyance of, 77
Exposure, Indecent, 100
Extortion, 78
Extradition, 79

Extradition, crimes for which it is granted, 80
—— treaties, 79

Facilitating prisoner's escape, 74
Factors, Misappropriation by, 20
Fairs, 82
False accounting, 82
—— assertion, 82
—— character, 82
—— declaration, 83
—— keys, 83
—— personation, 83
—— pretences, 83
—— ——, Obtaining money by, 83
Families, Desertion of, 63
Fares, Police railway 156
Fastenings to houses, 84
Felonies and misdemeanors, Compounding, 47
Felonious access to premises, 18
Felony, 84
Females, 84
Female prisoners, Searching of, 165
Fences, 84
——, Damage to, 84
——, Stealing, 84
Ferocious dogs, 84
Fight, Challenging to, 39
——, Prize, 141
Finding property, 85
Fines, 85
Fire, Alarm of, 85
——, Chimneys on, 42
Firearms, Discharging, 65
——, Licences for, 90
——, Persons drunk in possession of, 70
Fires, 85
Fireworks, 86
First offenders, 86
Fits, 86
Fixed points, 86
Fixture stealing, 108
Food, Adulteration of, 20
Footmarks, Detection by, 87
——, Wilful obstruction on, 87
Forbearance and moderation, 87
Foreign coin, Uttering, 43
Foreigners, 87
Forgery, 87
Forgery of bank notes, 27
—— of bonds, 32
—— of receipts, 156
Form of indemnity for delivery of property, 101
—— of personal description, 61
—— of proclamation in riots, 161
Fortune-telling, 88
Found, Dogs, 68
Fountains, Damage to, 88
Fowl-stealing, 88

Fraud, 88
Fraudulent bankrupts, 28
Fruit-stealing, 88
Fugitives from the colonies, 44
—— to the colonies, 44
—— to the Continent, 79
—— criminals, 155
Fund, Superannuation, 127
Furious driving, 88
—— riding, 88
Furniture removing to avoid payment of rent, 89

Gambling, 89
—— in refreshment houses, 157
Game licences, 89
——, Taking or destroying, 89
Gaming-houses, 89
Girls under sixteen, Carnal knowledge of, 41
—— under eighteen, Abduction of, 17
——, Defilement of, 60
Goods, Contraband, 51
——, Distraint of, 66
——, Finding of lost, 85
——, Obtaining, by false pretences, 83
Gossiping, 90
Government rewards, 160
Grain, Poisonous, 132
Grand juries, 106
Gratuities to police, 161
Gratuity to constables' widows, 46
Greenyards, 90
Grievances of, and requests by, police, 47
Grievous bodily harm, 90
Guilty knowledge, 90
Gun licences, 90
Gunpowder, Retail dealing with, 77

Habeas corpus, 91
Habitual criminals, 91
——, Registry office of, 91
Hackney carriages, 34, 91
Handbills, 130
——, Obscene, 121
Handcuffs, 91
——, when used, 91
——, when used unnecessarily, 91
Handwriting, 91
——, Experts in, 77
Hanging, Treatment of persons rescued from, 181
Harbouring police, 149
—— prostitutes, 149
—— thieves, 150
Hawkers, 126
Hearsay evidence, 92
Helmets, Numbers on, 121
High treason, 92
Highways, 93
——, Betting on, 30

POLICE CODE.   205

Highways, Gambling on, 89
——, Making bonfires on, 93
——, Performances on, 93
Hints, Sanitary, 164
Home Office, 94
Homicide, 94
—— becoming manslaughter, 95
—— becoming murder, 95
Horseflesh, Sale of, 95
Horse slaughtering, 95
—— stealing, 96
Horses, exhibiting for sale, 76
Hotel larcenies, 96
Housebreaking, 96
—— implements, 96, 175
Houses, Bawdy, 32
——, Betting, 30
——, Common lodging, 45
——, Disorderly, 66
——, Dwelling, 71
——, Empty, 73
——, ——, Marking, 112
——, Fastenings to, 84
——, Gaming, 89
——, Public dancing, 56
——, Public, 144
——, Refreshment, 157
Human being, Definition of, 95
Humane Society, 97
Husband and wife, 97

Identification of prisoners, 98
Ignorance of Law, Plea, 98
Illegal arrest, 19, 22, 98
—— pawning, 98
Illegitimate children, 98
Illness in streets, 18
—— in public places, 18
Improper characters at fires, 85
Incendiarism, 25
Inciting to crime, 98
Incompetency of witnesses, 99
Incorrigible children, 99
—— rogues, 99
Indecent assault, 25, 99
—— exhibitions, 100
—— exposure, 100
—— language, 100
—— prints and songs, 100
Indemnity, 100
—— for property, 100
——, Form of, 101
Indictments, 101
Industrial schools, 101
—— ——, Assisting children to escape from, 101
Infanticide, 101
Infected places and districts, 37
Infectious diseases, 102
—— —— in common lodging-houses, 45
—— ——, Sanitary hints in, 164
Informality, 102

Information, 102
—— preceding the issue of a warrant, 185
—— to police from convicts, 52
Informations, Printed, 138
Informants, 103
Injured, Aid to the, 21
—— persons, 18, 21
Inquests, 53, 103
Inquiries, Mode of making, 111
Insanity, 103
Insects, 104
Insensible persons, 128
Inspectors of police, 104
—— ——, Duties of, 104
Interference, Unnecessary, 104
Interrogation of prisoners, 104
Intimidation, 104
Intoxicating liquors, Law regarding, 144
Inviting suggestions, 24

Jewel larcenies, 105
Judges, Her Majesty's, 106
Judicial separation, 67
Jurisdiction, 106
——, Summary, 174
Juries, 106
Justice, Assisting, 25
——, Obstruction of, 122
Justifying bail, 106

Keeping observation, 106
Keys, False, Larceny by, 83
—— of premises, 107
Kidnapping, 40
Killing, 107
Knowledge, Guilty, 90

Ladders as means of felonious access, 107
Language, Abusive, 18
——, Indecent, 100
Lanterns, 107
Larcenies, Attic, 26
—— from carriages, 37
—— in hotels, 96
——, Jewel, 105
——, Portico, 26
Larceny, 107
—— by inmates, 166
——, Simple, 170
Law, Ignorance of, 98
Lead stripping, 108
Leading questions, 108
Legal aid, 154
Letters, 53
——, post, Stealing, 134
——, threatening, Sending, 179
Libel, 108
Licence holders, 52
Licences of cabs and cab-drivers, 91
—— for dogs, 68

Licences under Explosive Acts, 77
—— for factories of explosives, 77
—— for fairs, 82
——, Game, 89
——, Gun, 90
——, Hawkers' and pedlars', 126
—— for houses for cattle slaughter, 95
—— by local authority, 109
——, Refreshment houses, 157
——, Renewal of, to licensed victuallers, 144
—— for sale of intoxicating liquors, 144
Licensed convicts, 52
—— houses for lunatics, 110
—— victuallers, 144
Limitation of proceedings, 108
Liquors, Intoxicating, Sale of, 144
Lithography, 109
Loan office swindlers, 109
Local authority, 109
Lodging-houses, Common, 45
Long-firm frauds, 109
Lost property, 109
—— ——, Duty in finding, 109
Lotteries, 110
Lunatics, 110

Machinery, Damaging, 111
Mad dogs, 111
Mails, Offences in connection with, 134
Making inquiries, 111
Malice aforethought, 112
——, Definition of, 112
Malicious injury to property, 58
Malingering, 112
Manslaughter, 112
Man-traps, 112
Marine store dealers, 112
Marking places at night, 112
Marriage, Proof of, 113
Married women, Coercion of, 113
—— —— screening husbands, 113
Married women's property, 113
Masters' and Mistresses' duty as regards servants, 166
Medicines, Poisonous, 131
Meetings, 113
Memorials from police, 113
Memory, 114
Menaces, Demanding property with, 60
Metal dealers, 123
Metropolitan Police, 114
—— ——, Assistance by, 53
—— —— candidates, 35
—— —— jurisdiction, 106
—— —— magistrates' warrants, 185
Military and police, 171
Misadventure, Death by, 59

Misapplication of goods by bailees, 27
Misappropriation by agents and factors, 20
Miscarriage, 17
Misconduct of police, 115
Misdemeanants (1st, 2nd, and 3rd class), 117
Misdemeanor, 117
Misdemeanors, Compounding, 47
Mistakes, 117
Money, Borrowing, 32
——, Conduct, 48
—— expended in public service, 76
—— lending, 32
Murder, 117
—— of children, 101
Mutiny, 119

Neatness, 119
Necessaries of life, 144
Necessity as an excuse, 119
Neglect of children, 41
—— of duty, 119
Negligence, Culpable, 58
Newspapers, Correspondence with, 119
Night, Legal definition of, 130
——, Marking places at, 112
Notes, Reference to, in witness-box, 120
Noxious drugs, Administering, 70
Nuisance, Common, 46
—— in streets, 120
Numbers on collars and helmets, 121

Oath, Signification of, 121
——, Unlawful, 121
Obscene letters, Sending, 108
—— publications, 121
Observation, Keeping, 106
Obstruction of footpaths, 122
—— of highways, 93
—— —— by performances, 93
—— —— by prostitutes, 143
—— of justice, 122
—— of police, 122
Obtaining money or goods by false pretences, 83
Occasions, Public, 144
Offences against property, 58
—— children, 40
—— of children, 40
Offenders, Pursuit of, 155
Official correspondence, 53
—— secrets, Betrayal of, 123
Old metal dealers, 123
Open-air preaching, 124
Open doors and windows, 69
Opinions, 124
Orange-peel on pavement, 124
Orders, 124

POLICE CODE.   207

Orders, Disobedience of, 66
Ownership, 125
—— of property, Disputed, 66

Palmistry, 88, 162
Parading for duty, 125
Parliament, Acts of, 20
Parliamentary elections, 72
Parochial authorities, 125
Pauper lunatics, 110
Pawnbrokers, 125
—— lists, 126
Pawning, Illegal, 98
Peace, Breach of, 32
Pedlars, 126
Penal servitude, 52
Pencils and pocket-books, 127
Pensions and gratuities, 127
Performances in the streets, 127
Perjury, 128
Personal violence (husband and wife), 97
Personation, False, 128
Persons, Annoyance of, 22
——, Confessions of, 48
—— conspiring together, 49
——, Destitute, 63
——, Drunken, 70
—— found insensible, 128
—— —— ——, drunk, 70
—— —— —— in fits, 86
—— injured, 18, 21
—— sending obscene letters, 108
—— setting fire to fireworks, 86
——, suspected, Arrest of, 175
——, ——, Identification of, 98
——, ——, Keeping observation on, 106
——, ——, Stopping of, 175
—— under police supervision, 133
—— wanted, 138
—— ——, Request to apprehend, 159
Petitions, 128
Photographs of habitual criminals, 91
—— of persons sentenced to penal servitude, 53
—— of persons sentenced to police supervision, 53
Photography, 129
Pickpockets, 129
Pictures, Obscene, 121
Placard and printed bills, 130
Places of worship, Disturbance in, 67
Plague, Cattle, 37
Plain-clothes police officers, 63
Play, Cheating at, 40
Poaching, 130
Pocket-books, 114, 127

Points, Fixed, 86
Poisoning animals, 132
Poisons and poisoning, 131
Police, Actions against, 19
——, Admission to bail by, 27
——, Applications by, 22
——, Appointments for, 22
——, Assaults on, 25
——, Assistance to, 25
—— at fires, 85
—— avoiding argument, 24
—— becoming accessories, 21
—— borrowing money, 32
——, Bribery of, 32
——, Civility by, 42
——, Communications to, 46
——, —— between, 53
——, Complaints against, 47
——, Complaints by, 47
——, Demeanor of, 60
——, Depositions of, 60
—— detaining animals in infected districts, 37
—— detecting crime, 63
—— districts, 132
—— drinking, 69
—— entering licensed premises, 151
——, Expenses of, 76
—— finding doors and windows open, 69
—— forces, Co-operation between, 53
—— Gazette, 132
—— giving improper evidence, 74
——, Giving refreshments to, 80
——, Harbouring, 80
——, Inspectors, 104
—— inspecting premises for slaughtering, 95
—— lending money, 32
—— losing prisoners, 74
——, Metropolitan, 114
——, Misconduct of, 115
—— noticing open area gates, 24
—— —— removal of goods, 89
—— officers, Dismissal of, 65
—— on fixed points, 87
——, Private employment of, 133
—— promotion, 142
——, Property found by, 109
——, —— in possession of, 125
——, Punishment of, 116
—— putting leading questions, 108
—— quitting without notice, 17
—— receiving bribes, 32
—— regulations, 158
——, Resignation of, 159
——, Resisting, 160
——, Rewards to, 161
—— service, Conditions of, 48
—— standing at attention, 26
—— stealing or embezzling, 133

Police supervision, 133
—— taking charge of keys, 107
—— —— indemnity, 100
—— treatment of foreigners, 87
——, Unnecessary interference by, 104
—— working beats, 28
Political meetings, 113
Portico larcenies, 134
Portraits of delinquents, 73, 91
Post letters, 134
—— office, 134
—— men, &c., 135
Pounds, 90
Power of attorney, 135
Preaching in open air, 124
Premises, Access to, 18
——, Keys of, 107
Pretences, False,
Prevention of Crime Acts, 135
Previous convictions, 137
Principals, 19
Printed bills, 130
—— informations, 138
Prints and songs, Indecent, 100
Prison regulations, 140
—— warders, 185
Prisoners, 138
——, Aiding escape of, 21
——, Antecedents of, 22
—— as witnesses, 142
——, Cautioning, 38
——, Cells occupied by, 38
—— discharged by magistrates, 19
—— giving information, 52
——, Identification of, 98
—— insensible, 128
——, Interrogation of, 104
—— property, 141
——, Searching, 165
——, Statements of, 24, 38, 138
——, Travelling with, 179
Prisons, 140
Private parties, Police at, 141
—— employ, Police in, 143
Privileged communications, 141
Prize fights, 141
Proceedings, Divorce, 67
——, Limitation of, 108
Procurators Fiscal, 142
Procuring abortion, 17
Production of a prisoner as a witness, 142
Promotion of police, 142
——, Education necessary for, 72
Proof, Burden of, 33
Property, Demanding, with menaces, 60
——, Detaining, 141
——, Disputed ownership of, 66
—— found, 85
——, Police giving up, 100
—— lost, 109

Property, Married women's, 113
——, Offences against, 58
——, Pawning another person's, 98
——, Prisoner's, 141
——, Receiving stolen, 156
——, Removal of, in case of fire, 85
——, Stolen, 178
——, ——, Engraving, 73
Prosecutions, Withdrawal from, 187
Prostitutes, 143
—— accosting drunken persons, 143
——, Harbouring, 149
——, Indecent assault upon, 99
Proving handwriting, 91
—— ownership, 125
Provision of necessaries, 144
Provocation excusing homicide 95
Public occasions, 144
—— houses and publicans, 144
—— places, Betting in, 30
—— Prosecutions, Director of, 154
Publications, Obscene, 121
Publicity, 119
Publishing a libel, 108
Punishment of Police, 116
Pursuit of offenders, 155

Queen's evidence, 155
Questioning, 155
—— delinquents, 65
Questions, Leading, 108

Raffles, 110
Railway offences, 156
Rape, 156
Re-apprehension of prisoners, 19
Re-examination, 76
Receipts, Forgery of, 156
Receiving stolen goods, 156
—— suggestions, 24
Recognisances, 157
Reformatory schools, 157
Refreshment of police, 69, 149
—— houses, 157
—— for prisoners, 138
Refusing assistance to police, 25
Registered houses for baby-tending, 26
—— premises for explosives, 77
Registering names of common lodging-house keepers, 45
Registers, 157
——, Tampering with, 157
Registration of births, deaths, 157
Regulating of traffic at parties, 36
—— —— on public occasions, 144
—— —— generally, 158
Regulations, 158
Relieving officers, 63
Remands, 158
Removal of the armlet, 24

Rent, Evading payment of, 89
Reports, 159
——, Erasures in, 74
Request to apprehend, 159
Rescue from custody, 159
Resignation, 159
Resisting police, 160
Retail dealing with gunpowder, 77
Reward bills, 160
—— for return of stolen property, Advertising, 160
Rewards for assisting justice, 161
—— to police, 161
Riding furiously, 88
Riot, 161
—— Act, 161
Riotous behaviour while drunk, 70
—— demolition of houses, &c., 162
Rivers, Damage to, 58
Robbery, 162
Rogues, Incorrigible, 99
—— and vagabonds, 162
Royal carriages, Passage of, 36
—— family, Offences against, 92

Sacrilege, 163
Sale of gunpowder, 77
—— of poisons, 131
Saluting, 163
Sanitary hints, 164
Scalds, Treatment of, 86
Schools, Industrial, 101
——, Reformatory, 157
Search warrants, 165
—— —— for betting houses, 30
——, ——, Prevention of Crimes Act, 135
Searching a prisoner, 165
Secrecy, 165
Securities, valuable, Stealing, 185
Seduction, 165
Seed, Selling poisonous, 132
Sergeants, 166
Servants, Irregularities of, 166
——, Constables accepting gifts from, 166
——, Police gossiping with, 90
—— presenting false character, 82
—— suspected of offences, 166
Service, Divine, 67
Sessions, assizes, &c., 167
Sheep stealing, 169
Ships, Destroying, 169
——, Explosives in, 77
Shooting, 169
Showing horses in streets, 76
Shutters, Insecure, 170
Sickness, Feigning, 112
Simple larceny, 170
Situations, Application by police for other, 22
Sketches of stolen property, 172
Slander, 170

Slang terms, 170
Slaughtering horses, 95
Slides upon ice or snow on footways, 170
Smuggling, 170
Sodomy, 170
Soldiers, 171
——, Desertion of, 62
——, friendship with police, 171
Special constables, 171
—— duties, 171
Spring guns, Setting, 112
Statements of prisoners, 24, 38, 138
Stations, Regulation of, 171
——, Charge of, 39
Statute law, 20
Stealing birds, 31
—— children, 40
—— deer, 60
—— dogs, 68
—— fowls, 88
—— fruit, 88
—— horses, 96
—— sheep, 169
Steps to be taken in accidents, 18
Stolen jewellery, 105
—— property, 172
—— goods, Receiving, 156
—— ——, Pawning, 98
Stone-throwing, 172
Stray animals, 90
—— dogs, 68
Street-crossings, Keeping clear, 158
—— music, 172
—— performances, 127
Stretchers, 173
Subornation of perjury, 128
Subpœnas, 174
Subsistence, Persons without means of, 162
Suffocation, Treatment in cases of persons rescued from, 181
Suicide, 174
Summary jurisdiction, 174
Summonses, 175
Superannuation Fund, 175
Supervision of police, 133
Surrender of persons from foreign countries, 79
—— —— to and from the colonies, 44
Suspected persons about in early morning, 175
—— ——, Detention of, 175
—— ——, Stopping by police on fixed-point duty, 175
—— ——, Footmarks of, 87
—— ——, Keeping observation on, 106
—— ——, Power to arrest, 176
Suspected poisoning cases, 131
Suspension of police, 177
Sworn depositions, 60

N

Telegrams, 177
Telegraphic communication, Interfering with, 177
Temper, Forbearing, 178
—— provoking assaults, 25
Tenants, Damage by, 58
Terms, Slang, 170
Testimonials to police, 178
Testifying, Dissuading witnesses from, 66
Theft, 170
—— by police, 133
Thieves, Domestic, 166
——, Harbouring, 150
—— knowledge of beats, 28
Threatening language, 18, 178
—— letters, 179
—— ——, Handwriting of, 91
Threats, 178
Throwing stones, 172
Ticket-of-leave men, 52
Tolls, Police exemption from, 179
Tools, Damaging, 58
——, Housebreaking, 96, 175
Traffic regulation at parties, 36
—— —— in streets, 158
—— —— on public occasions, 144
Traitors, 92
Tramps, 162
Tramways, 179
Transmitting applications, 22
Travellers, *bonâ fide*, Sale of Intoxicating liquors to, 144
Travelling with prisoners, 179
Treason-felony, 180
Treasure trove, 180
Treaties of extradition, 79
Treatment of burns, 86
—— of persons rescued from drowning, hanging, or suffocation, 181
—— of scalds, 86
Trees, Stealing, 182
——, Setting fire to, 188
Trespass, 159
Trial, Police attending, 167
Truncheons, Use of, 184

Unclaimed property, Police surrendering, 100
Undue violence by police, 19, 24
Uninhabited houses, 73
Unjust detention, 176
Unlawful assembly, 161, 184
—— drilling, 184
Uttering base copper or foreign coin, 55
—— forged documents, 55, 88

Vaccination, 184
Vagabonds, 162

Vagrancy, 185
Valuable securities, Stealing, 185
Vessels, Damage to, 58
——, Wrecked, 189
Viaducts, Damaging, 32, 156
Violence, Intimidating by, 104
——, Undue, by police, 19, 24
Visitors of the sick, 125
Vitriol throwing, 54
Voluntary confessions, 48
Vouchers for disbursements, 76

Warders of prisons, 185
Warrant, Application for, 22
——, Apprehension by, 23
——, Arrest without, 23
Warrants, 185
——, Backing of, 26
——, Bastardy, 28
——, Distress, 66
—— for betting-houses, 30
——, Extradition, 79
—— in cases of embezzlement, 73
—— in cases of fugitive offenders, 44, 79
——, Proving handwriting on, 26
——, Search, 165
Widows' pensions, 46
Wife desertion, 63
Wife's protection order, 187
Wife and husband, 97
Wild birds, Protection of, 31
Wilful damage, 58
Wills, 187
Windows left open, 69
Withdrawal from prosecution, 187
Witnesses, 187
——, Accomplices as, 19
——, Competency of, 47
——, Conduct money to, 48
——, Depositions of, 60
——, Dissuading, 66
——, Evidence of, 74
——, Examination of, 76
——, Expert, 77
——, Husband and wife as, 97
—— in taking a charge, 39
——, Incompetency of, 99
——, Opinions of, 124
——, Prisoners as, 142
Wives of police officers, 48
Women, Abduction of, 17
——, Forcible carnal knowledge of, 60
—— under age, Defilement of, 41
——, Married, 113
——, Miscarriage of, 17
Woods, Setting fire to, 188
Wounding, 188
Wrecking, 189
Writ of habeas corpus, 91

www.ingramcontent.com/pod-product-compliance
Lightning Source LLC
Chambersburg PA
CBHW062155080426
42734CB00010B/1702